First World War
and Army of Occupation
War Diary
France, Belgium and Germany

41 DIVISION
122 Infantry Brigade
Queen's Own (Royal West Kent Regiment)
11th Battalion
3 May 1916 - 31 October 1917

WO95/2634/3

The Naval & Military Press Ltd
www.nmarchive.com
Published in association with The National Archives

Published by

The Naval & Military Press Ltd

Unit 10 Ridgewood Industrial Park,

Uckfield, East Sussex,

TN22 5QE England

Tel: +44 (0) 1825 749494

www.naval-military-press.com

www.nmarchive.com

This diary has been reprinted in facsimile from the original. Any imperfections are inevitably reproduced and the quality may fall short of modern type and cartographic standards.

© Crown Copyright
Images reproduced by permission of The National Archives, London, England, 2015.

Contents

Document type	Place/Title	Date From	Date To
Heading	WO95/2634/4		
Heading	11th Bn Q.O. Roy. West Kents May 1916-1917 Oct.		
Heading	War Diary Of The 11th Battalion "The Queen's Own" Royal West Kent Reg (Lewisham) from 2nd May 1916 to 31st May 1916 Volume 1		
War Diary	Havre	03/05/1916	04/05/1916
War Diary	Godewaersvelde	05/05/1916	05/05/1916
War Diary	Outersteene	05/05/1916	09/05/1916
War Diary	Blanch Maison	09/05/1916	19/05/1916
War Diary	Blanche Maison	19/05/1916	27/05/1916
War Diary	Papot	28/05/1916	28/05/1916
War Diary	Ploegsteert	29/05/1916	31/05/1916
War Diary	Ploegsteert Wood	01/06/1916	03/06/1916
War Diary	Papot	04/06/1916	05/06/1916
War Diary	Ploegsteert Wood	11/06/1916	17/06/1916
War Diary	Papot	18/06/1916	22/06/1916
War Diary	Ploegsteert Wood	24/06/1916	30/06/1916
War Diary	Ploegsteert	01/07/1916	01/07/1916
War Diary	Papot	02/07/1916	04/07/1916
War Diary	Hill 63	05/07/1916	08/07/1916
War Diary	Grande Munque Farm	09/07/1916	14/07/1916
War Diary	Hill 63	15/07/1916	28/07/1916
War Diary	Papot.	29/07/1916	31/07/1916
Miscellaneous	Reference St Yves. Sheet 10 Part of Sheet 28 Operation Order No 6 by Lieut Col: A.F. Townshend Appendix no. 1.		
War Diary	Papot.	01/08/1916	01/08/1916
War Diary	Ploegsteert.	03/08/1916	07/08/1916
War Diary	Papot.	09/08/1916	12/08/1916
War Diary	La Creche.	14/08/1916	14/08/1916
War Diary	Meteren	15/08/1916	15/08/1916
War Diary	Fletre.	16/08/1916	24/08/1916
War Diary	Brucamps.	25/08/1916	06/09/1916
War Diary	Dernancourt	07/09/1916	10/09/1916
War Diary	Fricourt.	11/09/1916	15/09/1916
War Diary	Flers.	15/09/1916	17/09/1916
War Diary	Dernancourt.	18/09/1916	30/09/1916
Miscellaneous	Medical Exercise. 41st Divisional Order No. 998.	02/09/1916	02/09/1916
Miscellaneous	Reference attached.	03/09/1916	03/09/1916
Operation(al) Order(s)	Operation Order No. 22. by Lieut. Col. A.C. Corfe, Commanding 11th Bn. R. West Kent Rgt.	03/10/1916	03/10/1916
Operation(al) Order(s)	Operation Order No. 20 by Lieut. Col. A.F. Townshend. Commanding 11th Royal West Kent Regt.	14/09/1916	14/09/1916
Miscellaneous	Assembly Table to Accompany 122nd Inf. Bde. Order. No. 40.		
Heading	11th R.W. Kent October 1916.		
Miscellaneous	On His Majesty's Service. To The A.G. Office at the Base	04/11/1916	04/11/1916
War Diary	Dernancourt	01/10/1916	01/10/1916
War Diary	Mametz	02/10/1916	03/10/1916

War Diary	Eaucourt L'Abbaye	03/10/1916	10/10/1916
War Diary	Mametz	11/10/1916	11/10/1916
War Diary	Dernancourt	12/10/1916	12/10/1916
War Diary	Ribemont	13/10/1916	17/10/1916
War Diary	Neuville	18/10/1916	20/10/1916
War Diary	Eecke	21/10/1916	23/10/1916
War Diary	Piebrouck	24/10/1916	24/10/1916
War Diary	Reninghelst	25/10/1916	27/10/1916
War Diary	Voormezeele Sector.	28/10/1916	31/10/1916
Operation(al) Order(s)	Operation Orders 21 by Lieut. Col. A.C. Corfe. Commanding 11th Bn. R. West Kent Rgt.	01/10/1916	01/10/1916
Miscellaneous	Jam.	06/10/1916	06/10/1916
Miscellaneous	Barrage Time Table. To Accompany 41st Division Order No. 49 of 5-10-16.	06/10/1916	06/10/1916
Map			
Operation(al) Order(s)	122nd Infantry Brigade Order No. 55		
Miscellaneous	K. R. R. to Occupy		
Miscellaneous		06/10/1916	06/10/1916
Miscellaneous	Jam.	08/10/1916	08/10/1916
Miscellaneous	March Table.		
Operation(al) Order(s)	122nd Infantry Brigade Order No. 56	10/10/1916	10/10/1916
Miscellaneous	Battalion Orders by Lieut. Col. A.C. Corfe, Commanding 11th Bn. R. West Kent Regt.	13/10/1916	13/10/1916
Miscellaneous	Supply Arrangements.	13/10/1916	13/10/1916
Miscellaneous			
Miscellaneous	41st. Division No. 282/S.7.	14/10/1916	14/10/1916
Miscellaneous	41st. Divn. No. 282/S.7.	14/10/1916	14/10/1916
Miscellaneous	Billeting List 41st. Division.	15/10/1916	15/10/1916
Miscellaneous	4th. Army. No. A/253/41. XV Corps A. No. A.C.2315. 41st. Division No. A.81/2. XV Corps.	15/10/1916	15/10/1916
Miscellaneous	122nd. Infantry Brigade. Supply Arrangements During Move.	15/10/1916	15/10/1916
Operation(al) Order(s)	122nd Infantry Brigade Order No. 57	15/10/1916	15/10/1916
Miscellaneous	Movement Table.		
Operation(al) Order(s)	Operation Order No. 29 by Lieut. Col. A.C. Corfe. Commanding Bow Battalion.	15/11/1916	15/11/1916
Operation(al) Order(s)	122nd Infantry Brigade Order No. 59	16/10/1916	16/10/1916
Miscellaneous	March Table to Accompany 122nd Infantry Brigade Order No. 59		
Miscellaneous	Warning Order. 122nd Infantry Brigade Order No. 58	16/10/1916	16/10/1916
Miscellaneous	Headquarters, 41st Division. (G)	17/11/1916	17/11/1916
Miscellaneous	Headquarters, 122nd Infantry Brigade.	12/10/1916	12/10/1916
Operation(al) Order(s)	Operation Order No. 23. by Lieut. Col. A.C. Corfe, Commanding 11th Bn. R. West Kent Regt.	19/10/1916	19/10/1916
Operation(al) Order(s)	Operation Order No. 24. by Lieut. Col. A.C. Corfe, Commanding 11th Bn. R. West Kent Regt.		
Operation(al) Order(s)	Operation Order No. 25, by Lieut. Col. A.C. Corfe. Commanding 11th Bn. R. West Kent Regiment.	24/10/1916	24/10/1916
Operation(al) Order(s)	Operation Order No. 30 by Lieut. Col. A.C. Corfe, Commanding 11th Bn. R. West Kent Regt.	21/11/1916	21/11/1916
Operation(al) Order(s)	Operation Order No. 31. by Lieut. A.W. Puttick, Commanding Bow Battalion.	26/11/1916	26/11/1916
Miscellaneous	Fourth Army No. 335 (G.S.). 41st Division.	27/10/1916	27/10/1916
Operation(al) Order(s)	Operation Order No. 26, by Lieut. Col. A.C. Corfe, Commanding 11th Bn. R. West Kent Rgt.	27/10/1916	27/10/1916
Miscellaneous	41st Div. G. 454.	29/10/1916	29/10/1916

Operation(al) Order(s)	Fourth Australian Division Steloi Group Artillery Order No. 10.	22/10/1916	22/10/1916
Miscellaneous	12th. East Surrey Regt.	29/10/1916	29/10/1916
Operation(al) Order(s)	122nd Infantry Brigade Order No. 65	29/10/1916	29/10/1916
Miscellaneous	C Form (Original). Messages And Signals.		
Miscellaneous	A Form Messages And Signals.	06/10/1916	06/10/1916
War Diary	St. Eloi	01/11/1916	01/11/1916
War Diary	Reninghelst	02/11/1916	07/11/1916
War Diary	St. Eloi.	08/11/1916	14/11/1916
War Diary	Reninghelst	15/11/1916	21/11/1916
War Diary	St. Eloi	22/11/1916	27/11/1916
War Diary	Reninghelst	27/11/1916	30/11/1916
Operation(al) Order(s)	Operation Order No. 27 by Lieut. Col. A.C. Corfe, Commanding Bow Battalion.	02/11/1916	02/11/1916
War Diary	St. Eloi.	01/12/1916	01/12/1916
War Diary	Left.	02/12/1916	07/12/1916
War Diary	Reninghelst.	08/12/1916	13/12/1916
War Diary	St. Eloi Left	14/12/1916	21/12/1916
War Diary	Reninghelst	22/12/1916	27/12/1916
War Diary	St. Eloi Left.	28/12/1916	31/12/1916
Operation(al) Order(s)	Operation Order No. 32. by Lieut. A.W. Puttick, Commanding 11th Bn. Royal West Kent Regt.	01/12/1916	01/12/1916
Operation(al) Order(s)	Operation Order No. 28, by Lieut. Col. A.C. Corfe, Commanding 11th Bn. R. West Kent Regt.	07/11/1916	07/11/1916
Operation(al) Order(s)	Operation Order No. 33. by Lieut. A.W. Puttick, Commanding 11th Bn. R. West Kent Rgt.	07/12/1916	07/12/1916
Operation(al) Order(s)	Operation Order No. 34 by Lieut. Col. A.C. Corfe, Commanding 11th Battn. "The Queen's Own" Royal West Kent Regt. (Lewisham).	13/12/1916	13/12/1916
Operation(al) Order(s)	Operation Order No. 35 by Lieut. Col. A.C. Corfe Commanding 11th Bn. The "Queens Own" Royal West Kent Regt.	20/12/1916	20/12/1916
Miscellaneous	Christmas Oreder.	25/12/1916	25/12/1916
Operation(al) Order(s)	Operation Order No. 36. by Lieut. Col. A.C. Corfe, Commanding 11th Bn. "The Queen's Own Royal West Kent Regiment. (Lewisham).	27/12/1916	27/12/1916
Miscellaneous	Special Order Of The Day by General Sir Douglas Haig, G.C.B., G.C.V.O., K.C.I.E., A.D.C., Commander-in-Chief British Armies in France.		
War Diary			
War Diary	Reninghelst	14/01/1917	20/01/1917
War Diary	St. Eloi	21/01/1917	26/01/1917
War Diary	Reninghelst	27/01/1917	31/01/1917
Operation(al) Order(s)	Operation Order No. 37. by Lieut. Col. A.C. Corfe, Commanding 11th Bn. The Queen's Own (Royal West Kent) Regiment.	01/01/1917	01/01/1917
Miscellaneous	11th Battalion Royal West Kent Regiment. Programme of Work for 5th & 6th Jan. '17.		
Operation(al) Order(s)	Operation Order No. 38, by Lieut. Col. A.C. Corfe, Commanding 11th Bn. The Queen's Own (Royal West Kent) Regt. (Lewisham).	06/01/1917	06/01/1917
Operation(al) Order(s)	Operation Order No. 39 by Lieut. Col. A.C. Corfe, Commanding 11th Bn. "The Queen's Own" Royal West Kent Regiment.	13/01/1917	13/01/1917
Miscellaneous	Headquarters, 122nd Infantry Brigade.	13/01/1917	13/01/1917

Operation(al) Order(s)	Operation Order No. 40, by Captain J.C. Beadle, Commanding 11th Bn. The Queen's Own (Royal West Kent) Regiment. (Lewisham).	20/01/1917	20/01/1917
Operation(al) Order(s)	Operation Order No. 41. by Captain J.C. Beadle, Commanding 11th Bn. The Queen's Own (Royal West Kent) Regiment.	26/01/1917	26/01/1917
Miscellaneous	Special Idea. Order for O.C. of Defending Company.		
Miscellaneous	Special Idea. German Order to O.C. Advanced Guard 3 Companies.		
Miscellaneous	General Idea.		
War Diary	Reninghelst	01/02/1917	01/02/1917
War Diary	St. Eloi.	02/02/1917	08/02/1917
War Diary	Reninghelst	09/02/1917	15/02/1917
War Diary	St. Eloi.	16/02/1917	20/02/1917
War Diary	Reninghelst	21/02/1917	25/02/1917
War Diary	St. Eloi.	26/02/1917	28/02/1917
Operation(al) Order(s)	Operation Order No. 42. by Captain J.C. Beadle, Commanding 11th Bn. The Queen's Own (Royal West Kent) Regt.	01/02/1917	01/02/1917
Operation(al) Order(s)	Operation Order No. 43 by Lieut. Col. A.C. Corfe, Commanding 11th Bn. Royal West Kent Rgt.	07/02/1917	07/02/1917
Operation(al) Order(s)	Operation Order No. 44. by Lieut. Col. A.C. Corfe, Commanding 11th Bn. Royal West Kent Rgt.	08/02/1917	08/02/1917
Operation(al) Order(s)	Operation Order No. 45 by Lt. Col. A.C. Corfe, Commanding 11th Bn. The Queen's Own (Royal West Kent) Regiment.	08/02/1917	08/02/1917
Operation(al) Order(s)	Operation Order No. 46. by Lieut. Col. A.C. Corfe, Commanding 11th Bn. The Queen's Own (Royal West Kent) Regt.	15/02/1917	15/02/1917
Operation(al) Order(s)	Operation Order No. 48. by Major J.C. Beadle, Commanding 11th Bn. The Queen's Own (Royal West Kent) Regt.	20/02/1917	20/02/1917
Operation(al) Order(s)	Operation Order No. 47 by Major J.C. Beadle, Commanding 11th Bn. The Queen's Own (Royal West Kent) Regiment.	20/02/1917	20/02/1917
Operation(al) Order(s)	Operation Order No. 49. by Lieut. Col. A.C. Corfe, Commanding 11th Bn. The Queen's Own (Royal West Kent) Regt. (Lewisham).	25/02/1917	25/02/1917
Miscellaneous	C.O. & Second in Command.	08/02/1917	08/02/1917
Miscellaneous	C.O. & Second in Command.	09/02/1917	09/02/1917
Miscellaneous		09/02/1917	09/02/1917
Miscellaneous	Appendix B.	08/02/1917	08/02/1917
Miscellaneous	11th Bn. The Queen's Own (Royal West Kent) Regiment.	10/02/1917	10/02/1917
War Diary	Appendix A. Statement By 2/Lieut. French Night of 8/9th February. 1917.		
War Diary	St. Eloi.	01/03/1917	03/03/1917
War Diary	Reninghelst.	04/03/1917	09/03/1917
War Diary	St. Eloi	10/03/1917	15/03/1917
War Diary	Reninghelst.	16/03/1917	21/03/1917
War Diary	St. Eloi.	22/03/1917	28/03/1917
War Diary	Reninghelst.	29/03/1917	31/03/1917
War Diary	Reninghelst. M.5.a. Sheet 28.	01/04/1917	03/04/1917
War Diary	St. Eloi. Sheet 28. S.W. O.2.	04/04/1917	09/04/1917
War Diary	Reninghelst. M.5. Sheet 28.	10/04/1917	16/04/1917
War Diary	St. Eloi. Sheet 28. S.W. O.2.	18/04/1917	20/04/1917

War Diary	St. Eloi.	20/04/1917	22/04/1917
War Diary	Reninghelst	23/04/1917	23/04/1917
War Diary	Steenvoorde (Ref. Hazebrouck 5a.)	25/04/1917	25/04/1917
War Diary	Broxeele	27/04/1917	27/04/1917
War Diary	Zouafques.	28/04/1917	30/04/1917
Operation(al) Order(s)	Operation Order No. 50. by Lieut. Col. A.C. Corfe, Commanding 11th Bn. The Queen's Own (Royal West Kent) Regt. (Lewisham).	03/03/1917	03/03/1917
Operation(al) Order(s)	Operation Order No. 51. by Lieut. Col. A.C. Corfe, Commanding 11th Bn. "The Queen's Own" Royal West Kent Regiment. (Lewisham).		
Operation(al) Order(s)	Operation Order No. 57. by Lieut. Col. A.C. Corfe, Commanding 11th Bn. "The Queen's Own" Royal West Kent Regiment. (Lewisham).	08/04/1917	08/04/1917
Operation(al) Order(s)	Operation Order No. 55. by Lieut. Col. A.C. Corfe, Commanding 11th Bn. The Queen's Own (Royal West Kent) Rgt.	03/04/1917	03/04/1917
Operation(al) Order(s)	Operation Order No. 51. by Lt. Col. A.C. Corfe, Commanding 11th Bn. The Queen's Own (Royal West Kent) Rt. (Lewisham).	09/03/1917	09/03/1917
Operation(al) Order(s)	Operation Order No. 58 by Lieut. Col. A.C. Corfe, Commanding 11th Bn. "The Queen's Own" Royal West Kent Regt. (Lewisham).	11/04/1917	11/04/1917
Operation(al) Order(s)	Operation Order No. 60 by Lieut. Col. A.C. Corfe, Commanding 11th Bn. "The Queen's Own" Royal West Kent Regiment. (Lewisham).		
Operation(al) Order(s)	Operation Order No. 52. by Lt. Col. A.C. Corfe, Commanding 11th Bn. The Queen's Own (Royal West Kent) Rt. (Lewisham).	15/03/1917	15/03/1917
Operation(al) Order(s)	Operation Order No. 59 by Lieut. Col. A.C. Corfe, Commanding 11th Bn "The Queen's Own" Royal West Kent Regiment. (Lewisham).	17/04/1917	17/04/1917
Operation(al) Order(s)	Operation Order No. 53. by Lieut. Col. A.C. Corfe, Commanding 11th Bn. The Queen's Own (Royal West Kent) Rt. (Lewisham).	21/03/1917	21/03/1917
Operation(al) Order(s)	Operation Order No. 61 by Lieut. Col. A.C. Corfe, Commanding 11th Bn. "The Queen's Own" Royal West Kent Regt. (Lewisham).	24/04/1917	24/04/1917
Operation(al) Order(s)	Operation Order No. 62. by Lieut. Col. A.C. Corfe, Commanding 11th Bn. "The Queen's Own" Royal West Kent Regt. (Lewisham).	26/04/1917	26/04/1917
Operation(al) Order(s)	Operation Orders No. 63 by Lieut. Col. A.C. Corfe Comdg. 11th R.W.K. Regt.	27/04/1917	27/04/1917
Operation(al) Order(s)	Operation Order No. 54. by Lieut. Col. A.C. Corfe, Commanding 11th Bn. The Queen's Own (Royal West Kent) Rt. (Lewisham).	28/03/1917	28/03/1917
Miscellaneous	Code Of Signals For Offensive Operations Only		
Miscellaneous	Signal Communications		
Miscellaneous	Carrying Parties and Material		
Miscellaneous	Gas And Smoke		
Miscellaneous	Appendix "D" Marking Of Graves And Effects.		
Miscellaneous	Routes and Communication Trenches		
Map			
Miscellaneous	Artillery		
Miscellaneous	Machine Gun And Trench Mortar Arrangements.		

Miscellaneous	Administrative Instructions in Connection With Forthcoming Operations.		
Miscellaneous	Table "A"		
Miscellaneous	Appendix "B".		
War Diary	Zouafques. Ref. Hazebrouck 5a. & Sheet 27 N.E.	01/05/1917	12/05/1917
War Diary	Broxeele Ref. Hazebrouck S.A.	15/05/1917	15/05/1917
War Diary	Steenvoorde	16/05/1917	16/05/1917
War Diary	Reninghelst Ref. M.5.a. Sheet 28.	17/05/1917	17/05/1917
War Diary	Dickebush. H.28. Sheet 28.	20/05/1917	20/05/1917
War Diary	St. Eloi. Sheet 28. S.W. O.2.	31/05/1917	31/05/1917
Operation(al) Order(s)	Operation Order No. 67. by Lieut. Col. A.C. Corfe, Commanding 11th Bn. Royal West Kent Rgt. (Lewisham).	19/05/1917	19/05/1917
Operation(al) Order(s)	Operation Order No. 64. by Lieut. Col. A.C. Corfe, Commanding 11th Bn. "The Queen's Own" Royal West Kent Regiment. (Lewisham)	14/05/1917	14/05/1917
Operation(al) Order(s)	Operation Order No 65 by Lieut Col. A.C. Corfe Commdg 11th Battn Royal West Kent Regt	15/05/1917	15/05/1917
Operation(al) Order(s)	Operation Order No 66 by Lt Col. A.C. Corfe Commdg 11th Battn R. West Kent Regt	16/05/1917	16/05/1917
Operation(al) Order(s)	Operation Order No. 68. by Lieut. Col. A.C. Corfe, Commanding 11th Bn. "The Queen's Own" (Royal West Kent) Regt. (Lewisham).	30/05/1917	30/05/1917
Heading	On His Majesty's Service. 11th R.W. Kent War Diaries June 1917		
Miscellaneous	XI R.W. Kent. Rgt. Vol 14		
Miscellaneous	War Diary May 1917 (to the attached)	01/06/1917	01/06/1917
War Diary	St. Eloi.	01/06/1917	05/06/1917
War Diary	Micmac North	05/06/1917	05/06/1917
War Diary	St. Eloi.	06/06/1917	18/06/1917
War Diary	Elzenwalle	19/06/1917	27/06/1917
War Diary	Roukloshille	28/06/1917	30/06/1917
Operation(al) Order(s)	Operation Order No. 69. by Lieut. Col. A.C. Corfe, Commanding 11th Bn. "The Queen's Own" (Royal West Kent) Regt. (Lewisham).	04/06/1917	04/06/1917
Operation(al) Order(s)	Operation Orders No. 70. by Lieut. Col. A.C. Corfe, Commanding 11th Bn. "The Queen's Own" (Royal West Kent) Regt. (Lewisham).	05/06/1917	05/06/1917
Operation(al) Order(s)	Operation Orders No. 71. by Lieut. Col. A.C. Corfe, D.S.O., Commanding 11th Bn. "The Queen's Own" (Royal West Kent) Regt. (Lewisham).	06/06/1917	06/06/1917
Miscellaneous	Report On Attack 7th June, 1917.	11/06/1917	11/06/1917
Operation(al) Order(s)	Operation Orders No. 72 by Lieut. Col. A.C. Corfe, D.S.O., Commanding 11th Bn. "The Queen's Own" (Royal West Kent) Regt. (Lewisham).		
Miscellaneous	Operation Orders by Lt. Col. A.C. Corfe, D.S.O. Commanding 11th (S) Battn. "The Queen's Own" (Royal West Kent) Regt. (Lewisham).	13/06/1917	13/06/1917
Miscellaneous	O.C., A.B.C. & D.	14/06/1917	14/06/1917
Miscellaneous	Headquarters, 122nd Infantry Brigade.	15/06/1917	15/06/1917
Operation(al) Order(s)	Operation Order No. 74 By Lt. Col. Corfe, Commanding 11th R.W. Kent Regt.	15/06/1917	15/06/1917
Operation(al) Order(s)	Operation Order. No. 75 By Lt. Col. A.C. Corfe, D.S.O. Commanding 11th. Bn. Royal West Kent Regt.	16/06/1917	16/06/1917
Miscellaneous	Headquarters, 122nd Infantry Brigade.	16/06/1917	16/06/1917

Operation(al) Order(s)	Operation Orders No. 76. by Lieut. Col. A.C. Corfe, D.S.O. Commanding 11th Bn. "The Queen's Own" (Royal West Kent) Regt. (Lewisham).	19/06/1917	19/06/1917
Operation(al) Order(s)	Operation Orders No. 77. by Major J.G. Beadle, Commanding 11th Bn. "The Queen's Own" (Royal West Kent) Regt. (Lewisham).	27/06/1917	27/06/1917
Miscellaneous	March Table To Accompany Operation Order No. 70. 11th Royal West Kent Regiment.		
War Diary	Roukloshille.	01/07/1917	22/07/1917
War Diary	Westoutre.	23/07/1917	23/07/1917
War Diary	Spoil Bank	24/07/1917	31/07/1917
Operation(al) Order(s)	Operation Order No. 78, by Lieut. Col. A.C. Corfe, D.S.O., Commanding 11th Bn. "The Queen's Own" (Royal West Kent) Regt. (Lewisham).	19/07/1917	19/07/1917
Miscellaneous	Barrage Time Table for Practice Only. Ref:- O.O. 78 of 19.7.17.		
Miscellaneous	Administrative Arrangements for Forthcoming Operations, ref:- Operation Order No. 78 dated 19th July, 1917.	19/07/1917	19/07/1917
Miscellaneous	Exercise-Attack-20th July, 1917.	20/07/1917	20/07/1917
Operation(al) Order(s)	Operation Order No. 79, by Lieut. Col. A.C. Corfe, D.S.O. Commanding 11th Bn. "The Queen's Own" (Royal West Kent) Regt. (Lewisham).	22/07/1917	22/07/1917
Operation(al) Order(s)	Operation Order No. 80 by Lieut. Col. A.C. Corfe, D.S.O., Commanding 11th Bn. "The Queen's Own" (Royal West Kent) Regt. (Lewisham).	24/07/1917	24/07/1917
Miscellaneous	Report On Attack Dated 31st July, 1917.	31/07/1917	31/07/1917
War Diary	Hollebeke.	01/08/1917	04/08/1917
War Diary	Reninghelst.	05/08/1917	09/08/1917
War Diary	Hollebeke.	10/08/1917	13/08/1917
War Diary	Elzenwalle	13/08/1917	13/08/1917
War Diary	Roukloshille	14/08/1917	19/08/1917
War Diary	Staple	20/08/1917	31/08/1917
Operation(al) Order(s)	Operation Order No. 81, by Lieut. Col. A.C. Corfe, D.S.O., Commanding 11th Bn. "The Queen's Own" Royal West Kent Regt. (Lewisham).	10/08/1917	10/08/1917
Operation(al) Order(s)	Operation Order No. 82 by Lieut. Col. A.C. Corfe, D.S.O. Commanding Bow Battalion.	12/08/1917	12/08/1917
Operation(al) Order(s)	Operation Order No. 83 by Lieut. Col. A.C. Corfe, D.S.O., Commanding 11th Bn. "The Queen's Own" Royal West Kent Regt. (Lewisham).	19/08/1917	19/08/1917
Operation(al) Order(s)	Operation Order No. 84. by Lieut. Col. A.C. Corfe, D.S.O., Commanding 11th Bn. "The Queen's Own" Royal West Kent Regt. (Lewisham).	20/08/1917	20/08/1917
Miscellaneous	Instruction No. II.		
Miscellaneous	Tanks		
Miscellaneous	Table Shewing Distribution Of Barrage In Depth		
War Diary	Boisdinghem.	01/09/1917	13/09/1917
War Diary	Wallen Cappell.	14/09/1917	15/09/1917
War Diary	Le. Roukloushille	16/09/1917	16/09/1917
War Diary	Ridge Wood.	17/09/1917	22/09/1917
War Diary	Caestre.	23/09/1917	26/09/1917
War Diary	Teteghem	27/09/1917	27/09/1917
War Diary	La Panne.	28/09/1917	30/09/1917
Miscellaneous	Report on Operations Sept. 20th-Sept. 23rd, 1917.-Attack on Tower Hamlets.		

War Diary	La Panne.	01/10/1917	14/10/1917
War Diary	Coxyde Bains	15/10/1917	28/10/1917
War Diary	Petite Synthe.	29/10/1917	31/10/1917
Operation(al) Order(s)	Operation Order No. 91, by Lt. Col. J.C. Beadle, M.C. Commanding 11th Bn. "The Queen's Own" Royal West Kent Regt. (Lewisham).	14/10/1917	14/10/1917
Operation(al) Order(s)	Operation Orders No. 91a. by Lieut. Col. J.C. Beadle, M.C. Commanding 11th Bn. "The Queen's Own" Royal West Kent Regt. (Lewisham).	29/10/1917	29/10/1917
Miscellaneous	11th Bn. "The Queen's Own" Royal West Kent Regt. (Lewisham).		
Miscellaneous	Appendix "A".		
Miscellaneous	Headquarters, 122nd Infantry Brigade.	01/10/1917	01/10/1917
Miscellaneous	Musketry Course.	02/10/1917	02/10/1917
Miscellaneous	11th Battalion "The Queen's Own" Royal West Kent Regiment. Lewisham.	02/10/1917	02/10/1917

W095/26342(4)

W095/26342(4)

41ST DIVISION
122ND INFY BDE

11TH BN Q.O. ROY. WEST KENTS

MAY 1916 - MAR 1918

1917 OCT

TO ITALY 1917 NOV
BN DISBANDED 1918 MAR

1st W Surrey
Vol 1 41
122/41

CONFIDENTIAL

WAR DIARY

OF THE

11ᵀᴴ Battalion "The Queen's Own" Royal West Kent Regᵗ (Lewisham)

from 2ⁿᵈ May 1916 TO 31ˢᵗ May 1916

VOLUME 1

May '16

WAR DIARY or INTELLIGENCE SUMMARY

Army Form C. 2118

Instructions regarding War Diaries and Intelligence Summaries are contained in F. S. Regs., Part II. and the Staff Manual respectively. Title Pages will be prepared in manuscript.

(Erase heading not required.)

Place	Date	Hour	Summary of Events and Information	Remarks and references to Appendices
HAVRE	3/5/16	7.30 p.m.	Arrived from SOUTHAMPTON & proceeded to Rest Camp. no. 5 - Strength 31 Officers & 974.	GH
	4/5/16	5 p.m.	Entrained HAVRE for HAZEBROUCK & continued our journey to GODEWAERSVELDE. One C. was killed on journey by jumping out of train in a tunnel.	GH
HAZEBROUCK	5/5/16	6.30 a.m.	Detrained at 6.30 a.m. & marched to OUTERSTEENE (in billets)	GH
OUTERSTEENE	5/5/16	3 p.m.	Arrived & billeted in farm houses. Strength officers 31, O/R 941	GH
	7/5/16	12 p.m.	Capt. G. M. G. Caithey joined from 9th Scottish Rifles. Demonstration with wet gas.	GH
	8/5/16	3.15 p.m.	Inspected by III Army Corps Commander - (General Sir H.C.O. PLUMER O.M.G.K.CB)	GH
			25 Signallers attached to 9th Scottish Rifles for instruction in the trenches.	GH
	9/5/16	7 a.m.	Left OUTERSTEENE for BLANCHE MAISON	GH
BLANCHE MAISON	"	3 p.m.	Arrived & billeted in farm houses. Some difficulty in billeting - heavy rain. Strength 32 officers 943 O/R.	GH
			Was out & one billeted the battalion arrived	
	10/5/16	7 a.m.	Half the officers & 40 N.C.O's attached to 9th Scottish Rifles for instruction for 2 days in the trenches at PLOEGSTEERT WOOD.	GH
	11/5/16	12 p.m.	Captain R. LAKIE, RICHARD DICK M. LAWRENCE took command	GH
	12/5/16	7 a.m.	Remainder of officers & 40 N.C.O's attached to 9th Scottish Rifles for instruction in trenches at PLOEGSTEERT WOOD.	GH
	"	12 p.m.	1st Party returned from trenches after instruction - no casualties.	GH
	13/5/16	12 p.m.	2nd party returned from trenches after instruction - no casualties -	GH
	14/5/16	11 a.m.	Lecture R.O.G. West -	GH
	15/5/16	10 a.m.	Brigade Tact. Alarm - Battalion including Transport out by 10.50 a.m.	GH
	16/5/16	3 a.m.	Brigade manager staff lecture gas report Ord. S.'s K AMMATIONS- all ranks notified - 2 men shown A.B.	GH

1875 Wt. W593/826 1,000,000 4/15 J.B.C.&A. A.D.S.S./Forms/C. 2118.

WAR DIARY or INTELLIGENCE SUMMARY

Army Form C. 2118

(Erase heading not required.)

Place	Date	Hour	Summary of Events and Information	Remarks and references to Appendices
BLANCHE MAISON	19/5/16	7am	4 officers & 80 O/R. attached 9th Scottish Rifles for instruction in trenches for 2 days. Party consists of 1 officer & 10 O/R from each numbered Platoons per company.	att
"	21/5/16	7am	4 officers & 80 O/R attached to 9th Scottish Rifles for instruction in trenches for 2 days. Party consists of 1 officer + 10 O/R from even numbered Platoons per company	att
"	"	12.30pm	Party of 19/5/16 returned from trenches	att
	23/5/16	1pm	Party of consists of 1 O/R.	att
			Party of 21/5/16 returned from trenches	att
	27/5/16	11.40pm	Gas "alert" ordered by 24th Division	att
PAPOT	28/5/16	4am	Leave BLANCHE MAISON for PAPOT at B8c91 sheet 36.	att
PLOEGSTEERT	29/5/16	4.15am	Take over trenches 121, 122, 123, PLOEGSTEERT. Enemy very quiet.	att
	30/5/16	—	Situation Normal - Enemy quiet.	att
	31/5/16	—	Situation normal - Enemy quiet - Visit from Divisional Commander.	att

A.D. Gilmour Capt adj
11/R.W. Kent Regt

Army Form C. 2118

11/R West Kent
Vol 2
122/41.

WAR DIARY
or
INTELLIGENCE SUMMARY
(Erase heading not required.)

Instructions regarding War Diaries and Intelligence Summaries are contained in F.S. Regs., Part II. and the Staff Manual respectively. Title Pages will be prepared in manuscript.

Place	Date	Hour	Summary of Events and Information	Remarks and references to Appendices
PLOEGSTEERT WOOD	1/6/16	6pm	Trench Mortar Battery (Stokes) starts registering. Enemy reply with Rifle grenades – Casualties – 4 killed, 8 wounded – Strength 32 officers 928 O/R.	
		8.30pm	British Observation Balloon broke loose & passed overhead, being shelled heavily by both sides – Two observers landed in our lines with safety –	
			Position in line. We occupy Trenches 121/123 – 15th HANTS on our right – 18th K.R.R.C. on our left –	
	2/6/16		Very quiet –	a/t
	3/6/16		Very quiet.	
PAPOT	4/6/16	5am	Relieved by 32 R.Fusiliers & proceed to rest billets at PAPOT (B3c8b sheet 36). Casualties for week in trenches – 6 killed 8 wounded	o/t
	5/6/16		Provide 540 men daily for working parties for R.E. work in PLOEGSTEERT – Normal –	c/t
PLOEGSTEERT WOOD	11/6/16	5am	Take over Trenches 121,122,123 from 32 R.Fusiliers. Position in Line – 15th HANTS on our right – 18th K.R.R.C. on our left –	c/t
	12/6/16 to 15/6/16		Casualties during rest period – 1 killed 4 wounded NILL – Situation – very quiet – Normal, very quiet –	o/t

WAR DIARY
or
INTELLIGENCE SUMMARY
(Erase heading not required.)

Army Form C. 2118

Place	Date	Hour	Summary of Events and Information	Remarks and references to Appendices
PLOEGSTEERT WOOD	16/6/16	11.25 am	WIND- N.E. "GAS ALERT" ordered by G.O.C.	CA
		10 am	Draft 39 o/Ranks - arrived at our rest billets PAPOT 2/Lts R.G. ROGERS, 2/Lt P.T. COOKSEY, 2/Lt HEATH. J.O.- 34 o/Rs & 8 bombers leave trenches to proceed to CASSEL to prepare for a bombing raid to take place at a future date - 1 officer + 50 o/Rs accompany them as working party.	
	17/6/16	12.30 am	gas alarm - gas cloud from N.E. passed Bn. H.Q. - no gas from our front - S.O.S. signal sent by Rocket + phone - Enemy's trenches tested with intense bombardment by our evening artillery -	CA
	"	2.30 am	All quiet - no casualties from gas	
PLOEGSTEERT WOOD	"	5 am	Relieved by 32 R. Fusiliers & proceed to rest billets at PAPOT Casualties for period in trenches. 1 killed 1 wounded - Strength - 37 officers (including M.O.) O/Rs. 955 -	a X
PAPOT	18/6/16	11.45 pm	gas alarm - no gas near us - normal conditions 1.45 am -	
	21/6/16		1 killed 1 wounded employed with tunnelling Company	
	22/6/16	11.30 pm	gas alarm - no gas near us - Resume normal conditions 12.15 am	CA
PLOEGSTEERT WOOD	24/6/16	5 am	Take over trenches 121, 122, 123 - 15th HANTS on our right - 16th K.R.R.C. on our left - Casualties for period in rest billets) or working parties - NILL	CA
		11.30 am	Battalion H.Q. shifted - 3 casualties - moved to new Battle Head Quarter dug-outs.	
	25/6/16 to 29/6/16		Very quiet -	GA

Army Form C. 2118

WAR DIARY
or
INTELLIGENCE SUMMARY
(Erase heading not required.)

Place	Date	Hour	Summary of Events and Information	Remarks and references to Appendices
PLOEGSTEERT WOOD	30/1/16	7.30 am	Our artillery cut German wire from U.15.d.9½.0 to U.15.d.8.10 (S.F. Ives sheet 10 part sheet 28) —	Off
		9.15 pm	Minor enterprise starts. We attacked operation Order no. 6. marked (appendix no 1)	Off
			Result of Raid.— Party found German wire uncut, so were forced to return according to their orders.— Casualties in raiding party 1 wounded — Enemy retaliate killing 6 & wounding 7 — 12 — Total casualties this period 7 killed 16 wounded — 1 Officer 1 wounded	Off
			[2/Lt C.B. SMITH.] Strength 39 officers (including M.O.) 912 O/Rs —	Off

A.J. Grineaus Capt/adj
11/R.W. Kent Reg

WAR DIARY or INTELLIGENCE SUMMARY

Army Form C. 2118

(Erase heading not required.)

Place	Date	Hour	Summary of Events and Information	Remarks and references to Appendices
PLOEG-STEERT.	1/7/16.	5 a.m.	Relieved by 32nd Royal Fusiliers, and proceeded to rest billets at PAPOT, (B3.c.8.3. Sheet 36). Casualties for week ending 1/7/16 = 1 Officer (Lieut.C.B.Smith) wounded. Other Ranks = 7 Killed, 13 Wounded.	S.D.A.
PAPOT.	2/7/16.	-	Strength:- 39 Officers (including M.O.), 912 Other Ranks. Normal.	S.D.A.
	3/7/16.	-	Orders received to proceed to relieve 7th & 8th Australian Inf.Battalions, at trenches 130 - 133,(Our left to rest on River Douve, our right on a point 200 yards N.of Anton's Farm), U.8.a.4.2. to U.14.b.5.9. sheet 28.	S.D.A.
	4/7/16.	5 a.m.	Proceeded to new rest billets at GRAND MUNQUE FARM (T.24.d.3.8.) sheet 28, and took over from 5th Australian Infantry.Battalion.	
HILL 63.		8.30 p.m.	Took over trenches 130, 131, 132, & 133, and part of WINTER TRENCH (U.8.a.4.2. to U.14.b.5.9. sheet 28) from 8th & 7th Australian Infantry Battalions. On our right 18th K.R.R.Corps. On our left 6th Australian Infantry Battn.	C.J.
	5/7/16	-	Very quiet, situation normal.	C.J.
	8/7/16.	9.30 p.m.	Relieved by 12th East Surrey Regt., and proceeded to rest billets at GRAND MUNQUE FARM (T.24.d.3.8. sheet 28). Casualties for week ending 8/7/16 = 1 Killed, 6 Wounded.	S.D.A.
GRANDE MUNQUE FARM.	9/7/16.	3.30 p.m.	Headquarters and buildings in vicinity shelled by shrapnel and H.E. (5.9). Buildings damaged slightly - no casualties.	S.D.A.
	14/7/16.	8.30 p.m.	Reinforcement of 4 Officers = Lieut. F.G. Fraser, 2/Lt. H.D.P.Hall, 2/Lt. A.R. Morgan, and 2/Lt. D.J.V.Knott., from 12th Battn. R.West Kent Regt.	S.D.A.
HILL 63.	15/7/16.	10 p.m.	Took over trenches (U.8.a.4.2. to U.14.b.5.9.) T.130 - 133 & part of WINTER TRENCH from 12th Bn. East Surrey Regt. Casualties for week ending 15/7/16 = Other ranks 2 wounded.	
	17/7/16.	8 a.m.	Wind N.E. General Gas Alert ordered. 2/Lieut.A.D.Bateman, proceeded to England, for transfer to R.F.C.	S.D.A.
	19/7/16.-22/7/16.		Very quiet and situation normal.	S.D.A.
	22/7/16.	3 p.m.	WINTER TRENCH and C.T. THE ONLY WAY, shelled rather heavily with T.M's., and H.E. Slight damage done to trenches, - 2 casualties. 2 Front line companies relieved by the support and reserve companies.	C.J.
	23/7/16.		Casualties for week ending 22/7/16 = 1 Killed, 3 wounded.	C.J.

Army Form C. 2118

WAR DIARY
or
INTELLIGENCE SUMMARY

(Erase heading not required.)

Instructions regarding War Diaries and Intelligence Summaries are contained in F.S. Regs., Part II. and the Staff Manual respectively. Title Pages will be prepared in manuscript.

Place	Date	Hour	Summary of Events and Information	Remarks and references to Appendices
HILL 63.	25/7/16.	—	Enemy shell trenches 131,132 & 133, with Trench Mortars, and fired about 150 bombs. Slight damage to front line parapet. No casualties.	c.27
	26/7/16.	11.50 p.m.	Gas Alarm sounded – no gas on our front, and resumed "Gas Alert" conditions at 12.35 a.m.	c.27
	28/7/16.	12.55 a.m.	Gas Alarm sounded – no gas on our front, and resumed "Gas Alert" conditions at 1.40 a.m.	c.27
	28/7/16.	10 p.m.	Relieved by 109th Brigade as follows:- Trenches 130 & 131 relieved by 1 Coy. 14th Royal Irish Rifles; Trenches 132 & 133 by 11th Royal Inniskilling Fusiliers; Reserve Company and Headquarters by 11th Royal Inniskilling Fusiliers; Subsidiary Line from Locality 1 to DEAD COW FARM by 14th Royal Irish Rifles; from DEAD COW FARM to LE ROSSIGNOL by 9th Royal Inniskilling Fusiliers. Casualties from 23rd to 28th = 2 Killed, 4 Wounded.	c.27
PAPOT.	29/7/16. 30/7/16. 31/7/16.	2 a.m.	Took over rest billets at PAPOT (B.9.b.3.7. sheet 36). Working parties of 300 men, working in PLOEGSTEERT WOOD. Strength = Officers 43, Other Ranks 875.	c.27

A.F. Townshend L'.Col.
Cmd. 11th Royal West Kent Reg

Appendix No. 1.

SECRET

Copy No 2.

REFERENCE: ST YVES, SHEET 10, PART OF SHEET 28

OPERATION ORDER. No 6
by Lieut Col. A.F. Townshend

1. It is intended to carry out minor enterprises to capture prisoners and do as much damage as possible to the enemy in co-operation with the Divisional Artillery.
The date and hour of Zero will be notified later.

2. The 11th Battalion Royal West Kent Regiment will carry out one of these raids, others being executed simultaneously by each of the two Battalions of the 122nd Brigade on our right.

3. The raiding parties will consist of:-
   (a) 2/Lieut Cooksey and 11 men of "A" Coy and 4 Battalion Bombers
   (b) 2/Lieut Rogers and 11 men of "B" Coy and 4 Battalion Bombers
   (c) Covering parties of 8 men under 2/Lieut Heath.
   (d) One N.C.O and 3 men R.E., as Demolition party.
   2/Lieut Rogers will be in command.

4. At - 45 minutes Artillery open fire for 30 minutes on the hostile trenches along the Battalion front as far NORTH as U.15.b.1½.5½., the bombardment being intense and wire cutting from U.15.d.9½.0. to U.15.d.8.10.

   At - 15 minutes Artillery ceases fire for 15 minutes.

   (At ZERO, Gas is discharged for 15 minutes).

   At ZERO plus ½ minute, Artillery recommences bombardment. (If no Gas is used the Artillery bombardment will recommence at ZERO)

   (At ZERO plus 15 Gas turned off).

   At ZERO plus 20 All Trench Mortars cease fire
   "   "   " 23 Raiding parties start
   "   "   " 28 Artillery lifts
   "   "   " 28 Raiding parties advance to enemy's trenches
   "   "   " 43 Raiding parties vacate enemy's trenches
   "   "   " 53 Artillery ceases fire

5. When the Raiding party advances it will enter the hostile trenches at U.15.d.8½.4½., and the two parties (a) and (b) will work outwards, bomb dug-outs, capture prisoners, and do as much damage as possible, especially to the Machine Gun and Trench Mortar Emplacements. They will remain in hostile trenches till plus 43 minutes.

6. The covering party will remain in a fold of ground about half way across NO MAN'S LAND, to assist the withdrawal of the party, cover it with fire if necessary and pass back prisoners and wounded. Two men will accompany the raiding party up to the foot of the enemy's parapet to pass on messages etc.

P.T.O

7. The signal for recall will be Buglers sounding a succession of "G"s in our front line trenches. Strombus Horns will also be sounded and whistles blown. O.C. "A" and "B" Coy's will order these signals to commence at the right moment.

8. The Battalion Bombers will be armed with 18 bombs each and with Knob-kerries; The raiding party with 10 bombs each and with Knob-kerries and the covering party with rifles. Officers will take Revolvers.

9. The raiding party will carry wire cutters, electric torches, white tape (to guide them on their homeward journey) and four ladders 6 feet long. Bomb Aprons and White Sleeves worn.

10. All Identity Discs and other marks of identification on clothing, equipment etc will be removed and no papers taken.
Anyone captured should give no information but his name and rank.

11. Watches will be synchronized at 5 a.m. and 5 p.m. at a date to be named later.

12. Should the enemy's wire be found to be uncut, the parties will return at once.

13. While raiding parties are in the enemy's trenches, Infantry and Lewis Machine Guns in our trenches on the flanks of the point of attack will maintain a brisk fire on the trenches opposite. Stops must be arranged.

14. All Troops will take Gas Alert precautions when the bombardment starts; men are not to show their heads over the Parapet. The bays containing the Cylinders will be cleared of troops.

15. The raiding party are not to enter Dug-outs in enemy's trenches. They should take sharp knives for cutting off shoulder straps and marks of identification from dead or wounded Germans, and should search pockets for any documents and papers. (German soldiers usually carry their papers in the tail pockets of their tunics)

16. Result to be reported "PRIORITY" at once to Battalion Headquarters, and a full report to be sent as soon as possible afterwards.

(Sd) A.F. Townshend Lieut Colonel
Commd^g 11th R.W. Kent Regt.

Copies to:

1. Office copy
2. War Diary
3. C.O.
4. O/c "A" Coy
5. O/c "B" Coy
6. 2/Lt Rogers
7.
8.
9. O/c "D" Coy
10.
11.
12.

Army Form C. 2118

Vol 4
11. R W Kent

11 R W Kent

WAR DIARY or INTELLIGENCE SUMMARY

(Erase heading not required.)

Place	Date 1916.	Hour	Summary of Events and Information	Remarks and references to Appendices
PAPOT.	Aug.1st.		Strength :- Officers 42, Other Ranks 875.	
PLOEGST-EERT.	3rd.	5 a.m.	Took over Trenches 121/3 from 32nd Royal Fusiliers. On our right 15th Hants; on our left, 18th King's Royal Rifle Corps.	
	4th.	10 p.m.	Gas Alert ordered - Wind N.E.	
	5th.		Strength :- Officers 42, Other Ranks 866.	
	5th.	11.55 p.m.	Patrol sent out consisting of Lieut.M.H.Allen, 2/Lt.P.T.Cooksey, 1 Sgt., 1 Cpl. 2 Men - Lieut.R.G.Rogers, joined patrol in no man's land. Patrol was sighted by enemy and was fired on by machine guns. Lieuts. Allen & Rogers, and 1 Cpl. wounded.	
	6th.	11 a.m.	Enemy test wind with Smoke bombs. Smoke came straight across to our trenches. 2nd Lieut.F.F.E.Hernett, attached 122nd Infantry Brigade Trench Mortar Batty.	
	7th.	7.50 p.m.	Our Stokes guns bombard enemy machine gun emplacements. No enemy retaliation. 2nd Lieut.C.W.Habrow, transferred to Royal Flying Corps.	
PAPOT.	9th.	5 a.m.	Relieved by 32nd Royal Fusiliers, and proceeded to rest billets in Rue de Sac, PAPOT. B.3.c.8.6. sheet 36, in Divisional Reserve. Casualties for period in trenches, Killed - Nil. Wounded, 2 Officers, 7 Other Ranks.	
	12th.		Strength :- Officers 39, Other Ranks 858.	
LA CRECHE.	14th.	7 a.m.	The Battalion is relieved by 8th Bn. King's Own Yorkshire Light Infantry, 23rd Division, and proceeded to billets in the La CRECHE Area; A.4,Sheet 36. The Battalion is in V Corps Reserve.	
METEREN.	15th.	6 a.m.	The Battalion moved to billets in the METEREN Area. X.22, Sheet 27.	
FLETRE.	16th.	6 a.m.	The Battalion moved to billets in the FLETRE Area. W.5, Sheet 27, for rest & training.	
	19th.		2nd Lieut. H.C.Fry, transferred to Royal Flying Corps.	
	21st.		Lieut. W.E.Roberts, transferred to Machine Gun Corps.	
FLETRE.	24th.		The Battalion entrained at BAILLEUL 7 a.m. for LONGPRE, (Abbeville Area). Arrived LONGPRE 5 p.m., and marched to BRUCAMPS, (Abbeville Area).	
BRUCAMPS.	25th.		The Battalion Started training for the offensive.	
	31st.		Strength :- Officers 37, Other Ranks 830.	

A.J.Townshend
LT. COLONEL
Commanding 11th Battn. "THE QUEEN'S OWN" Royal West Kent Regt. (Lewisham)

Army Form C. 2118

11th R.W.Kent.
12/41

11th Royal West WAR DIARY or INTELLIGENCE SUMMARY

Sep 16

(Erase heading not required.)

Instructions regarding War Diaries and Intelligence Summaries are contained in F.S. Regs., Part II. and the Staff Manual respectively. Title Pages will be prepared in manuscript.

Place	Date	Hour	Summary of Events and Information	Remarks and references to Appendices
BRUCAMPS.	1/9/16.		Battalion Training.	
	2/9/16.		do. continued.	
			Strength :- Officers 58, Other Ranks 827.	
	3/9/16.		Rest Day (Sunday).	
	4/9/16.		Battalion took part in Tactical Exercise (Medical) - Copy of scheme attached. 2nd Lieuts. Lindsay, Kerr, and Cookson, arrived.	
	5/9/16		Battalion Training. Also packing up preparatory for moving.	
	6/9/16		Marched off from BRUCAMPS at 3.30 a.m. to entrain at LONGPRE. Entrained at LONGPRE at 8.30 a.m., and detrained at MERICOURT at 12.15 p.m. Proceeded by route march at 1.30 p.m. to E.9 a & c (ALBERT) via DERNANCOURT. Battalion camped in Bivouacs at E 9.a & c (ALBERT) south west of ALBERT.	
DERNANCOURT.	7/9/16.		Battalion Training.	
	8/9/16.		do.	
	9/9/16.		do.	
			Strength :- Officers 41, Other Ranks 829. Draft of 19 N.C.O's & men arrived.	
	10/9/16.		Rest Day (Sunday). 2Lieuts. Yorke & Edmunds, arrived. 2nd Lieuts. Morgan & Lindsay, proceeded to IV Army School.	
FRICOURT.	11/9/16.		Battalion proceeded by route march to F 14.a. south west of FRICOURT, and camped in bivouacs.	
	12/9/16.		Battalion Training.	
	13/9/16.		do.	
	14/9/16.		Battalion, less transport, Drafts etc, who were left behind in Transport Lines outside FRICOURT, proceeded by route march to road junction F.8.a.4.0. Draft of 50 N.C.O's & Men arrived during this day. On the march to the rendezvous, 2/Lieut. Argent was missed from his Company, his absence was reported to C.O. & Adjutant.	
	15/9/16.	6.20 a.m.	The Battalion took part in the attack on FLERS, being supporting Battalion to the 15th Hampshire Regt. (Operation Orders No.20, and Report on Action by 2/Lieut.G.D.HENDERSON, attached herewith.) The following Officers went into action :- Lt. Col. A.F.TOWNSHEND., Capt & Adjt.A.J.JIMENEZ., 2/Lt.G.D. HENDERSON, 2/Lt.H.R.SMITH., Major G.A.HERON., Lieut.S.J.JONES., Lt.J.O.HEATH., 2/Lt.H.R.SMITH., 2/Lt.P.T.COOKSEY., Capt.G.M.G.CULLEY., 2/Lt.T.G.PLATT., Capt.S.L.SIMMONDS., 2/Lt.N.C.BARRS., 2/Lt.F.J.ARGENT., Capt.A.E.DICKINSON., 2/Lt.G.T.MANSFIELD., & 2/Lt.G.SMITH.; with Lt.R.PUTTOCK, Medical Officer.	

Army Form C. 2118

WAR DIARY
or
INTELLIGENCE SUMMARY

Sheet 2.

(Erase heading not required.)

Instructions regarding War Diaries and Intelligence Summaries are contained in F.S. Regs., Part II. and the Staff Manual respectively. Title Pages will be prepared in manuscript.

Place	Date	Hour	Summary of Events and Information	Remarks and references to Appendices
FLERS.	15/9/16.	cont.	In this action for the first time TANKS were used in the attack. During the action Lt.Col.A.F.TOWNSHEND, was mortally wounded, Capt.CULLEY, Lieut. Jones, & 2nd Lt.G.Smith, killed, 2nd Lt.Mansfield, wounded & missing., Major Heron, Capt Dickinson, Lt. Puttock, 2/Lt.Barrs, 2/Lt.H.R.Smith, 2/Lt.C.F.Hall, 2/Lt.Phatt, & 2/Lt.Cooksey, wounded and evacuated. 2/Lt. Henderson, wounded At Duty. Brigade re-organised at GREEN DUMP, and Battalion occupied CARLTON TRENCH Capt.S.L.Simmonds, returned to Transport Lines with a party of men, under the impression that the Battalion had been relieved. 2/Lieut.Morley, called to the trenches with Reserve Lewis Gunners, and later Major Corfe, to assume Command of Battalion.	
	16/9/16.		Battalion in Reserve in CARLTON TRENCH. Reinforcements of all available fighting strength, except draft, together with remaining Officers, i.e. Capts. Stone & Richardson, Lieuts. Puttick, Fraser, & Purver, 2/Lieuts. Prior, Knott, Yorke, Russell, Edmunds, Kerr & Cookson, were called up to the Battalion. 2/Lieuts. Knott, Yorke, Russell & Edmunds, were attached temporarily to the K.R.R.C. (18th), while Lt.Fraser, 2nd Lieuts. Morley, Cookson, & Kerr, were returned to Transport Lines. At 6.30.p.m. 2/Lieut.Hall,H.D.P., arrived from Transport Lines with a party of stragglers; he returned at 9 p.m. Capt. Jimenez, Adjutant, was evacuated. Lieut. Puttick took over duties as Acting Adjutant.	
	17/9/16		Burying Party under Lieut. Purver, sent out during afternoon, was unable to do very much owing to hostile shell fire. Lieut. Prior, sent to MONTAUBON, but was sent back, as A Working Party under 2/Lt. Prior, sent to MONTAUBON, but was sent back, as it was not required.	
DERNAN- COURT.	18/9/16.	8.30 a.m.	Weather very wet. Battalion was relieved by the 2/5th.Lancs.Fusiliers, at 8.30. a.m., and marched to bivouacs at E.15,a. Draft of 75 N.C.O's & Men arrived.	
	19/9/16.	1 p.m. 4 p.m.	Strength:- Amended to 19/9/16 = Officers 30, Other Ranks 639. Brigade Inspected and congratulated by G.O.C. &Divisional General. Camp moved on to drier ground about 300 yards N.W.	
	20/9/16. 21/9/16.		Reorganisation of Battalion commenced. Reorganisation and Training. 2/Lt.Kerr, Appointed understudy to Adjutant.	

1875 Wt. W593/826 1,000,000 4/15 J.B.C. & A. A.D.S.S./Forms/C.2118.

WAR DIARY
or
INTELLIGENCE SUMMARY

(Erase heading not required.)

Army Form C. 2118

Place	Date	Hour	Summary of Events and Information	Remarks and references to Appendices
DERNAN-COURT.	22.9.16. 23.9.16.		Reorganisation and Training. Lieut. B.A.Purver,Appointed Company Commander of "A" Coy from 16/9/16. Capt. L.V.Stone. " " " "B" " " 16/9/16. 2/Lieut.H.G.Redmond-Prior, " " " "C" " " 23/9/16. Capt. P.Clarke-Richardson, " " " "D" " " 16/9/16. Battalion and Company Training. Draft of 31 N.C.O's & men arrived.	[sgd]
	24/9/16.		Battalion and Company Training. Strength :- Officers 30, Other Ranks. 713.	
	25/9/16. 26/9/16.		Battalion and Company Training. 2/Lieuts. S.A.Wheeler and R.J.Gibbons, attached to Battn. from East Surrey Regt. Battalion and Company Training continued.	
	27/9/16. 28/9/16. 29/9/16.		Battalion and Company Training. " " " " 2/Lieut. W.N.Hall, joined Battalion for duty. Training Continued.	
	30/9/16.		2/Lieuts. Bothamley,H.W.H., Croneen, A., Ashton, J.H., Squire,F., Ashworth,B.W., Watson, R. and Radclyffe,G., joined Battalion for duty. Strength :- 30 Officers, 749 Other Ranks.	

                         [signature] Lieut.Colonel.
              Commanding 11th Bn.R.West Kent Regt.

MEDICAL EXERCISE.   Copy. No. 15

41st Divisional Order No.298.

                                                8/9/16.

1. On Sept. 4th the X Corps will attack and take the hostile
   system of trenches on the line, BRUCAMPS - ERGNIES and extending
   in depth to the CHAUSEE BRUNE HAUT.

2. The objectives for the 41st Div. will be :-
   1st Objective.
        The enemy's front trench on the line of the road ERGNIES -
   BRUCAMPS (both villages exclusive).
   2nd Objective.
        Enemy's support trench 100 yards N.E. of and parallel to
   above road.
   3rd Objective.
        Enemy's third line along CHAUSEE BRUNE HAUT between cross
   roads at C of CHAUSEE to cross roads at A of BRUNE HAUT.

3. Brigades will be formed up for assault by 9 a.m. 4-9-16, as
   follows :-
        122nd Infantry Brigade on Right) Represented by 11th Bn.
        123rd   "   "   " Left) Royal West Kent Regt.
   In rectangle contained by British front trench 250 yards S.W. of
   and parallel to ERGNIES - BRUCAMPS road and the roads from
   ERGNIES & BRUCAMPS to FAMECHON and WINDMILL (1 mile N. of AILLY).
        The Dividing line between Brigades will be a line
   drawn from WINDMILL to the first N of BRUNE HAUT.
        Each Brigade will be disposed as follows :-
   2 Battalions in front line (represented by 2 Coys. 11th R.W.K.)
   1 Battalion in support) (imaginary)
   1   "   in reserve)
        124th Inf. Bde. will be in Divl. Reserve in area between
   the WINDMILL - FAMECHON Road and AILLY.

4. The assault will be delivered at 0.00 hour, in accordance
   with following Artillery Table :-
   - 0.45 mins. - Bombardment of enemy system of trenches.
   - 0.15   "   - Hurricane bombardment.
     0.00   "   - Barrage lifts to behind front line trench.
   ⅓ 0.03   "   - Barrage lifts to behind support trench.
   ⅓ 1.30   "   - Intensive bombardment of third line.
   ⅓ 2.00   "   - Barrage lifts to behind third line.
   ⅓ 2.00   "   )
         to   ) - Final barrage behind third line.
   ⅓ 3.00   "   )

5. Zero (0.00) hour will be at 9.30 a.m.

6. Strong Points will be established at -
            In Front Line......................
            In Support Line....................
            In Third Line......................

7. Dumps of S.A.A., Grenades, Water etc. will be as per Appendix.

8. 123rd and 124th Brigade Report Centres will be at WINDMILL.
   Battalion Report Centres for leading Battns will be in front
   line trench.

9. Medical arrangements. - Orders as to the situation of Main
   Dressing Stations etc. will be issued by A.D.M.S. 41st Div.
        Clearing Station will be at ABBEVILLE.

10. Reports to AILLY LE HAUT CLOCHER.

11. Acknowledge.

                                                Major G.S.

References attached.
Ref. Maps LENS 6.

1. Training Programme for tomorrow is cancelled, and the Battalion will take part in a Medical Exercise.

2. 122nd Infantry Brigade will be represented by C & D Coys., under Major A.C. Corfe. 123rd Infantry Brigade by A & B Coys., under Captain G.M.C. Culley. Each Company will represent 1 Battalion in front line.

3. Tallies will be issued this evening to Company Commanders. Half will be issued before and at the taking of 1st objective, and the remainder at the taking of the second objective. They will be placed in the right hand breast pocket of the soldier's tunic.

4. The Medical Officer will have 16 Regimental Stretcher Bearers and Maltese Cart with him. He will be attached to "A" Company. Another Medical Officer and 16 Stretcher Bearers will be attached to each of the other Companies.
Men labelled as Sitting and lying cases are not to walk.

5. The 122nd and 123rd Infantry Brigade Headquarters report Centres will be at WINDMILL.

6. The bearer divisions 138th & 139th Field Ambulances, will report to G.O'S C., 122nd and 123rd Infantry Brigades (Major Corfe, and Capt. Culley) at WINDMILL at 8.30 a.m.

7. The Battalion will parade at 8 a.m.
Haversack rations will be carried.

8. The Commanding Officer will see the undermentioned Officers at Headquarters at 9 p.m. today:-
2nd in Command.
Coy. Commanders.
2nd in Command of "A" & "B" Coys.

9. Snipers, Headquarter Lewis Gunners, and Signallers, will not take part in the operations. Companies will take their Lewis Gunners but not the guns.

10. Orderly Room - on return to Billets.

11. Sick Parade at 6.30 a.m.

12. Breakfasts at 7 a.m.

(Sgd) A. J. Jimenez. Capt. & Adjt.
11th Royal West Kent Regiment.

3/9/16.

S E C R E T.   OPERATION ORDER No. 22.   Copy No. 4
by Lieut. Col. A.C.Corfe,
Commanding 11th Bn. R. West Kent Rgt.

3rd October, 1916.

1. The 122nd Infantry Brigade will relieve the 3rd New Zealand Rifle Brigade, in the line today. The Battalion will take over from the 1st Battalion New Zealand Rifles.

2. Guides will be at THISTLE DUMP S.10.c.4.1. at 3.15 p.m. today, to meet this Battalion.
   All movements to THISTLE DUMP will be by Companies at 200 yards distance. After passing this point, by Platoons or smaller parties.

3. Dress - Fighting Order with Greatcoats.

4. Companies will report to Battalion Headquarters on completion of relief, using the following code word - WET.

5. Battalion Headquarters will be at --------- (to be notified hereafter).

6. Brigade Headquarters will be at S.6.a.6.6.

7. All packs will be stacked at large shelter by Battalion Orderly Room by 12 noon.

8. 2/Lieut. Kerr, will be in Command of Battalion Details. He will see that all bivouacs and tents are struck this afternoon and neatly packed. After which he will march his details to the 12th East Surrey Lines, S.19.d., and then report to Major FURLEY., Commander of the 122nd Brigade Details.

9. All Units going into Firing Line will carry the unexpired portion of today's rations, tomorrow's, and their Iron Rations.

10. Lewis Gun Teams and Company Signallers will proceed with the first platoon of their company to THISTLE DUMP.

(Sgd) A. C. Corfe, Lieut. Col.
Commanding 11th Bn. R. West Kent Regt.

Copy No. 1 C.O.   9 M.O.
       2 Adjutant.   10. Transport Offr.
       3 War Diary.   11. Signalling Offr.
       4 Office Copy.   12. Lewis Gun Offr.
       5 O.C. "A" Coy.   13. Quartermaster.
       6 O.C. "B" "   14. R.S.M.
       7 O.C. "C" "
       8 O.C. "D" "

OPERATION ORDER

By Lieut. Col. A. N. _____
Commanding 12th Royal West Kent Regt.

Ref.Map sheet 57 c SW.
In the Field.
Sept. 14th 1916.

SITUATION 1.   The 122nd Infantry Brigade has been ordered to attack enemy on Sept. 15th 1916.
The role of the Brigade is to capture the enemy's defences as follows:-
1st Objective (GREEN LINE) enemy's trenches 800 yds. South of FLERS SWITCH TRENCH from junction of road 3.d.7.9. to junction of COFFEE LANE S.6.c.2.7. (exclusive)
No halt will be made in TEA SUPPORT, but if necessary men must be left to deal with dug-outs.
2nd Objective (BROWN LINE), enemy's trenches running S.E. i.e. FLERS TRENCH from T.1.a.1.6. to N.36.d.3.6.
3rd Objective (BLUE LINE). The village of FLERS to road junction N.31.a.2.5. The 122nd Infantry Brigade will capture FLERS.
4th Objective (RED LINE). To establish line N.30.c.7.8. to N.30.c.3.6. to road junction N.26.b.0.6. (exclusive).

INTENTION 2.   The 122nd Infantry Brigade will attack in 4 stages. 15th Hampshire Regt. on right, 18th K.R.R.C. on left; 11th Royal West Kent Regt. supporting the right Battalion, and 12th East Surrey Regt. supporting the left Battalion.
The attack will be carried out as per attached time table.

ASSEMBLY 3.   The Battalion will assemble by 2 a.m. in accordance with attached Assembly table.

FORMATION 4.   The Battalion will attack in 4 lines, each Company on a platoon front in the following order from Right to left A Coy., B Coy., C Coy., D Coy. except for platoons detailed for special purposes.
The leading lines will follow the 15th Hampshire Regt. at 70 yards distance, the same distance being maintained between each line. Should Lewis or Artillery formation be found the most suitable according to the nature of the enemy's fire.

ARTILLERY 5.   The artillery will bombard as per attached table and will form a creeping barrage.

FLANKS 6.   The 12Oth Infantry Brigade will be on the right of our Brigade, and the New Zealand Infantry Division on the left.

DIVIDING LINES 7.   Between 122nd & 121st Infantry Brigades: LONGUEVAL FLERS ROAD inclusive to 121st Infantry Brigade.
Between 122nd Infantry Brigade & New Zealand Division: the ___ Boundary ___

2.

continued: 11. as long as the Hampshire Regt., is in front.
Vigilant Mirrors are to be attached to the back of every 10th man.
Panels and lamps will also be frequently used to report the situation.

BATTALION H.Q. 12. Battalion Headquarters will move up the left of the
& VISUAL SIGNAL LONGUEVAL FLERS ROAD, and the Signalling Officer will
STATIONS. establish visual stations where possible.
Visual Stations will be established at S.18.c.1.2.,
S.18.b.0.2., S.15.d.0.1., S.27.b.3.0., POMMIER REDOUBT.

RUNNERS. 13. These will be organised into relays - Each relay at intervals of about 300 yards.

CARRYING 14. O.C. A. & C. Coys. will each leave 1 platoon at
PARTIES. GREEN DUMP as carrying parties. The Senior Officer will report at Brigade Headquarters at 8 p.m. 14.9.16.

MEDICAL. 15. Advanced Dressing Station - THE QUARRY S.22.c.2.5.
Regt. Aid Post - Assembly Trench and will move after Battalion.
Main Dressing Station 138th Field Ambulance, on main MAMETZ - MONTAUBAN ROAD.

DUMPS. 16. GREEN DUMP is B.O.C. for R.A.A. BOMBS, WATER, FLARES,
P. GRENADES, ROCKETS.

BATTLE STOPS 17. The Provost Sergeant will remain at P.C. a.5.0. (Sheet
62 d) near 138th Field Ambulance, to march stragglers to Brigade H.Q. as required. Regimental Police will be established in the trenches to take names and units of stragglers and to send back those fit to return to their units, a special mark being put against those without arms.

PRISONERS 18. Companies will send Prisoners of War with an escort of
OF WAR. 10% to Battalion Headquarters.

WATCHES. 19. Watches will be synchronised at 12 midnight on 14/15-
9-16, at Brigade Headquarters.
The Sniping Officer will report there with 2 watches.
Companies will each send 1 Officer to Battalion H.Q. at 12.30 a.m. 15/9/16., to synchronise watches.

APPROACH 20. MILK LANE is the only approach avenue allotted to
AVENUE. 122nd Infantry Brigade.

COMMUNICATION 21. O.C. "D" Coy., will tell off a platoon to dig forward
TRENCHES. a communication trench to join up with our 1st wave in the 1st objective. This will be dug in conjunction with the 12th East Surrey Regt., from the point where the two regiments touch one another.

STRONG POINTS 22. O.C. "B" Coy will arrange to construct a Strong Point
North of FLERS to defend perimeter of village with flanking fire. The garrison found by "B" Coy. will be 1 platoon with a Lewis gun.
Other Strong Points are being constructed by other units in the Brigade, and when they are garrisoned the troops occupying the 1st. & Second trenches and other troops will be reorganised ready to advance when ordered.

LEWIS GUNS. 23. Headcarts will not be required further than POMMIER REDOUBT.
Companies must carry their guns and magazines from that point. Special Lewis Gun parties will be detailed to push beyond each objective gained and sieze tactical points not occupied by enemy.

TOOLS.	24.	Every 6th man will carry a tool, proportion 1 pick to 6 shovels.
EQUIPMENT	25.	Fighting Order.
RATIONS.	26.	All troops will carry when going into the attack :- (a) Rations for 18th. (b) One Iron Ration. (c) Extra Soup Ration. Waterbottles must be filled and used most sparingly.
GAS HELMETS.	27.	2 to be carried, 1 in "alert" position.
REPORTS.	28.	The situation will be reported to Battalion H.Q. as frequently as circumstances permit, especially on any important event such as the capture of an objective.

                                      (Sgd) A. F. Townshend,   Lt. Colonel.
                                               Commanding 11th R. West Kent Regt.

TABLES ATTACHED.

Appendix, Tanks.
Assembly Table.
Time Table of Attack.

Copy No. 1. C.O.
         2. Adjutant.
         3. War Diary.
         4. Office Copy.
         5. O.C. "A" Coy.
         6. O.C. "B" "
         7. O.C. "C" "
         8. O.C. "D" "
         9. Signalling Offr.
        10. Sniping Officer.
        11. 122nd Inf. Brigade.
        12. R. S. M.

ASSEMBLY TIME TO ACCOMPANY 122nd INF. Bde ORDER, No. 40.

Unit	Starting Point	Time	Route to avenue of Approach	Up Avenue of Approach to be used	Unit now in trenches	Trenches to be occupied	Hour by which Assembly to be completed	Remarks
"B" Hants Regt	"	10.0 pm	-	-	-	Assembly Group A.	1 am	
"	"	10 pm	-	MILK LANE PEACH TRENCH	15th Hants	Assembly Group B.	1.30 am	
Surrey Regt	Road Junction F5.a.4.0.	5.15 pm	Via Horse track just North of FRICOURT – MONTAUBAN Road	MILK LANE.	-	Assembly Group D.	11. p.m.	To be rear of area south of us trench by 5 pm
1/4 R.W.Kent Regt	-do-	5.30 pm	-do-	-do-	-	Assembly Group C	2 am	-do-

An officer and 8 guides 1/9th K.R.R.C. will meet 12th E. Surrey Regt and 1/4 E. Kent Regt at FORMIER'S REDOUBT at 5.53 pm on 14-9-16 to direct these units to their assembly trenches. A Staff Officer will meet them.

Vol 6
11th R.W. Kent
October 1916

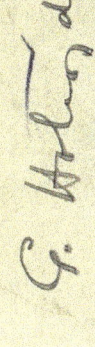

On His Majesty's Service.

For M/R A.G.'s Office

On the River

G. Hely dr.

WAR DIARY or INTELLIGENCE SUMMARY

(Erase heading not required.)

Army Form C. 2118

1/7th Bn. R.W. KENT REGT.
OCTOBER 5th 1916.

Place	Date	Hour	Summary of Events and Information	Remarks and references to Appendices
DERNANCOURT. MAMETZ.	1/10/16.		Rest Day, Sunday. Strength :- Officers 32, Other Ranks 749.	
	2/10/16.		Battalion moved by Route March to bivouacs at S.19 d, south of MAMETZ WOOD; via DERNANCOURT, MEAULTE, FRICOURT, road. (Op.Order 21 attached).	
EAUCOURT L'ABBAYE	3/10/16.		Battalion, less Transport & Details, relieved the 1st New Zealand Rifle Brigade, in the Line; Transport & Details moved to lines at S.19,d, and bivouaced with the remaining Brigade Details. (Op.Order 22 attached). The following officers went into action :- Lt.Col. A.C.Corfe, Capts. L.V. Stone, P.Clarke-Richardson, & S.L.Simmonds., Lieuts. A.W.Puttick, (Adjt), B.A.Purver, J.O.Heath, F.G.Fraser, & W.S.Lacey, (M.O.), 2nd Lieuts. H.G. Redmond-Prior, G.D.Henderson, A.V.D.Morley, R. Watson, R.J.Gibbons, R.G. Cookson, S.A.Wheeler, H.C.Edmunds, G.Radclyffe, & F.J.Argent.	
	4/10/16.		Battalion in Trenches. 2nd Lieuts. Wright, Dean, and Thompson-Smith, arrived at Transport Lines from the G.H.Q. Cadet School. Draft of 29 Other Ranks arrived from Base.	
	5/10/16.		Battalion in trenches. do. Draft of 9 Other Ranks arrived from Base at Transport Lines.	
	6/10/16.			
	7/10/16.		Battalion Strength :- Officers 41, Other Ranks 737. Battalion attacked the German trenches, on the right the 15th Hampshire Regt. on the left the 1.40th Infantry Brigade, on a two Company front. (Inf.Bde. Order No.55 attached). The Battalion was only able to advance 100/150 yards from our front line, being held up by intense machine gun fire, coming both from flanks and direct front. Heavy casualties were incurred in this advance. The following Officers became Casualties. Killed :- Lieuts. Purver, 2nd Lieut. Prior, Gibbons, & Watson. Died of Wounds - Lieut. Lacey; (M.O.), Wounded :- Capts. Clarke-Richardson, Stone, Simmonds. - Lieuts Fraser, 2nd Lieuts. Cookson, Edmunds, Argent, Morley & Radclyffe, Missing - Lt.Heath. Casualties in Other Ranks 323. The supporting Battalion having lost direction, failed to arrive, support was asked for, and 2 Coys. 12th E.Surrey Regt came up about 6 p.m. The Battalion had in the meantime dug in During the night with the assistance of the 12th E.Surrey Regt, the position held was consolidated and a communication trench dug back to the original front line.	
	8/10/16.		Battalion relieved in front line by 23rd Middlesex Regt, and 10th R.W.Kents,	

Army Form C. 2118

WAR DIARY
INTELLIGENCE SUMMARY

(Erase heading not required.)

Instructions regarding War Diaries and Intelligence Summaries are contained in F.S. Regs., Part II. and the Staff Manual respectively. Title Pages will be prepared in manuscript.

Place	Date Oct. 1916.	Hour	Summary of Events and Information	Remarks and references to Appendices
EAUCOURT L'ABBAYE.	8th.		and proceeded to occupy SWITCH TRENCH (order attached). 2/Lt. Cartmell. Joined from Base, and 2/Lt.Donnet, from Lewis Gun Course at Le Touquet, arrived at Transport Lines. Capt. McCricrick, R.A.M.C. attached to Battalion, vice Lt. Lacey, (Died of Wounds). Battalion in SWITCH TRENCH.	
	9th.	5.45 a.m.	2nd Lieuts. Donnet, Thompson-Smith, Wright, Dean, & Cartmell, with 20 O.R. left Transport Lines to reinforce Battalion in Switch Trench.	
		2.30 p.m.	2nd Lieuts. Kerr, Bothanley, Squire, Hall, W.N., Hall, H.D.P., Ashworth, and Ashton, with 35 O.R. proceeded to Carlton Trench. Transport Personnel, Q.M. Stores and burial party of 8 O.R. under 2/Lt. Croneen, only left in transport lines. 2/Lt. Radclyffe, returned to transport lines from Field Ambulance. Battalion in Switch Trench.	
	10th.		2/Lt.Kerr, with the 6 above mentioned officers and 35 O.R. arrived at Switch trench from Carlton trench as reinforcements. Battalion left Switch Trench, and proceeded by route march to bivouacs at S.20	
MAMETZ.	11th.	6 a.m.	a. east of MAMETZ WOOD. (Inf.Bde Order 56 attached).	
DERNAN-COURT.	12th.	9 a.m.	Battalion proceeded by rail from X.29.b. to MEAULTE Junction, and from there by route march to old bivouacs at E.15.a.	
RIBEMONT.	13th.	11 p.m.	Battalion proceeded by route march to billets at RIBEMONT. Company reorganization and refitting. 2/Lt. Lindsay, rejoined from Course at FLIXECOURT : 2nd Lt. Radclyffe, evacuated to Field Ambulance, and 2/Lt. Ashton, promoted to be 1st Lieut. The following officers placed temporarily in Command of Coys. 2nd Lt. Henderson, "A" Coy; 2/Lt. Wright, "B" Coy ; 2/Lt.Wheeler, "C" Coy ; & 2/Lt. Donnet, "D" Coy. Draft of 157 O.R. arrived from Base.	
	14th.		Company reorganisation and refitting. Strength :- Officers 30, Other Ranks 669.	
	15th.		Sunday, Day of Rest.	
	16th.		Battalion paraded for presentation of Medals Ribbons by G.O.C. Lieut. Fraser, (wounded in action 7/10/16) arrived from ROUEN, and placed temporarily in Command of "D" Coy. vice 2/Lt.Donnet, given temporary Command of the Lewis Gunners. Company reorganisation and training. Draft of 70 O.R. arrived from Base. Transport moved by road to NEUVILLE. (Inf.Bde order 57 attached).	

WAR DIARY
or
INTELLIGENCE SUMMARY

(Erase heading not required.)

Army Form C. 2118

11th Bn R.W. Kent Regt.

October 1916

Instructions regarding War Diaries and Intelligence Summaries are contained in F.S. Regs., Part II. and the Staff Manual respectively. Title Pages will be prepared in manuscript.

Place	Date	Hour	Summary of Events and Information	Remarks and references to Appendices
RIBEMONT.	Oct.1916. 17th.		2/Lt. Cartmell, evacuated to Field Ambulance. Draft of 34 O.R. arrived from Base. Battalion proceeded by rail from MERICOURT to OISEMONT (Inf. Bde Order 58 attached).	
	"	9 p.m.	Transport arrived at NEUVILLE.	
NEUVILLE.	18th.	9.30 a.m.	Battalion detrained at OISEMONT and proceeded by route march to billets at NEUVILLE & FORCEVILLE.	
	19th.		2/Lt. T.C.Wright, proceeded on leave to England. Company Training.	
	20th.	7 a.m.	Battalion proceeded by route march to LONGPRE.	
		2.15 p.m.	Battalion entrained with Transport at LONGPRE, and proceeded by rail to CAESTRE.	
EECKE.	21st.	12.15 a.m.	Battalion detrained at CAESTRE and proceeded by route march to billets at EECKE, (Op.Order 25 attached)	
			Company Training. 2/Lieut. Morgan returned from Hospital at AMIENS, (illness contracted during Trench Warfare Course at FLIXECOURT). Strength, Officers 30, Other Ranks 774.	
	22nd.		Sunday, Day of Rest.	
	23rd.		Company Training. Capt. Beadle from 2/1st Royal East Kent Mounted Rifles arrived from Base.	
PIEBROUCK.	24th.	9.45 a.m.	Battalion proceeded by route march via GODEWAERSVELDE to billets at PIEBROUCK in the MONT DES CATS area, (Op.Order 24 attached).	
RENINGHELST.	25th.	8.10 a.m.	Battalion proceeded by route march to ALBERTA Camp at RENINGHELST, (Op. Order 25 attached). 2/Lt. G.C.Cooke, of 2/1st R.E.K.M.R. arrived from Base	
	26th.		Battalion Training & reorganisation. The C.O.; Lieut.Henderson, & 2/Lts. Squire, & Kerr, proceeded to VOORMEZEELE SECTOR, for the purpose of visiting the trenches. 2/Lt.Henderson, promoted to 1st Lieut.	
	27th.		Battalion Training & organisation. Inspection of Battalion by Army, Corps, and Divisional Commanders. Lieut. Fraser, 2/Lieuts Donnet & Wheeler, visited trenches in VOORMEZEELE Sector.	
VOORMEZ-EELE SECTOR.	28th.		Battalion moved into trenches in VOORMEZEELE SECTOR and relieved 11th Bn. Queen's Royal West Surrey Regt. (Op.Order 26 attached). 2/Lieut. Bloodworth, reported for duty at Transport Lines from 2/1st R.E.K.M.R.	

Army Form C. 2118

WAR DIARY
INTELLIGENCE SUMMARY

(Erase heading not required.)

Instructions regarding War Diaries and Intelligence Summaries are contained in F.S. Regs., Part II. and the Staff Manual respectively. Title Pages will be prepared in manuscript.

Place	Date	Hour	Summary of Events and Information	Remarks and references to Appendices
VOORMEZ- EELE SECTOR.	Oct. 1916 29th		2/Lieut. Bloodworth, joined Battalion in the trenches. 2/Lieuts. Knight, Freeman, Bell, Rooney, & Sewell, reported for duty at Transport Lines from Base. Capt. Simmonds, reported at Transport Lines, and Capt. Beadle, proceeded from Trenches to take charge of him.	
	30th.		2/Lieuts. Knight, Freeman, Bell, Rooney, & Sewell, joined Battalion in trenches.	
	31st.		Our own Artillery bombarded enemy trenches. (Inf.Bde.Order 65, & St.ELOI Group Artillery Order 10, attached) Strength:- Officers 37. Other Ranks 786. Battalion in Trenches.	

Lieut.Colonel.
Commanding 11th Battn.Royal West Kent Regt.

SECRET.   OPERATION ORDERS 21   Copy No. 3
            by Lieut.Col. A.C.Corfe.
            Commanding 11th Bn. R.West Kent Rgt.

            1st October, 1916.

Reference Maps :- 62D,N.E., 57D S.E., 57C S.W.

1.   The 41st Division will relieve the New Zealand Division in the left Sector XVth Corps Front on October 3/4th.

2.   As a preparatory move, the 122nd Infantry Brigade will march from its present bivouac to bivouac in S.19d, south of MAMETZ WOOD on the 2nd October.

3.   Starting point will be level crossing E.18.b.9.3.

4.   Route will be "Fairweather track" North of the DERNANCOURT - MEAULTE-FRICOURT Road - FRICOURT. As far as FRICOURT there will be an interval of 500 yards between battalions. After this movement will be by Companies at 300 yards distance, and troops will keep to track as far as possible.

5.   Time of passing starting point 10.17 a.m.

6.   First Line Transport, baggage and Supply Wagons will march with Units

7.   Dress - Full Marching Order.

8.   Rations: The unconsumed portion of the day's rations will be carried on the man.

9.   Reveille 6 a.m.   Breakfast - 6 a.m.
     Battalion Parade 9.30 a.m., on Battalion Parade Ground, column of route facing South. Order - Signallers, Snipers, A, Band, B", C", D.

10. Officers Kits must be packed on the road South West of the Camp by 8.30 a.m. Mess boxes must be packed on the road South West of the Camp by 8.30 a.m.

11. The following Advance Party will be ready to move early in the morning, aat an hour to be notified later:-
     Lieut. Fraser, and 4 other ranks to be detailed from each Coy.,
     L/Cpl. Bradley, 1 Headquarter Pioneer, and 2 Battalion Runners.
     The above advance party will report to Major R.G.FURLEY, of the 15th Hampshire Regt.   On arrival at the new Camping ground they will report to the Staff Captain, 122nd Infantry Brigade.

12. All tents and bivouacs will be struck under Company arrangements. They will be neatly stacked with poles etc. on the side of the road running South West of the Camp, by 7.45 a.m.
     Each Company will each detail six men to strike and stack Headquarter shelters.
     This Party will be under Sergt. Fraiser.

13. A Rear Party will be left behind to clear up the Camp. O.C. "A" Coy will detail 1 Senior N.C.O. and 10 men to form this party. This party will be under the Command of an Officer to be detailed by the 12th East Surrey Regt., and will reprt on arrival in the New Camp to the Staff Captain 122nd Infantry Brigade.

14. Company Commanders will each detail 1 Runner to proceed with the Advance Party together with 4 Headquarter Runners. This party will report to Sergt. Woodhall at 8.30 a.m., outside Orderly Room and will carry rations of the 2nd and rations for the 3rd instant.

15. "B" & "C" Companies will draw 1 Lewis Gun Handcart from Q.M. and will be responsible for same. Lewis Gun Handcarts will be drawn by Pack Ponies and will march in rear of their Companies.

                                                          P.T.O.

2.

16. 2nd Lieut. Edmunds, with 2 N.C.O's to be detailed by O.C. "D" Coy. will march in rear of Battalion to collect all stragglers.

17. The Transport under the Transport Officer, will arrange to join up with the Battalion as it passes.

                        (Sgd) A. C. Corfe. Lieut. Col.
                           Commanding 11th Bn. R. West Kent Regt.

Copy No. 1   C.O.   9. Signalling Offr.
         2   Adjutant.   10. Snipers.
         3.   War Diary.   11. Quartermaster.
         4.   Office Copy.   12. Transport Offr.
         5.   O.C. "A" Coy.   13. Medical Offr.
         6.   O.C. "B" "   14. Lewis Gun Officer.
         7.   O.C. "C" "   15. R.S.M.
         8.   O.C. "D" "

SECRET.   B.M.494

~~JACKAL.~~
JACKDAW.
JAM.
~~JAR.~~
~~JOIST.~~

The following Units will endeavour to construct
Strong Points at the following places:-

JACKDAW.   No.1 Strong Point at M 18.d.6.9.

JAM.   No.4 Strong Point at M 18.c.45.70.

JAR.   { No. 2 Strong Point at M 18.d.5.4.
           { No. 3 Strong Point at M 18.c.6.2.

Numbers 1, 2 and 3 will each be provided with a Lewis Gun.

JOIST will arrange that one of his guns detailed for SUNKEN
ROAD will occupy No.4 Strong Point.

Please acknowledge.

                                              A/Hudson Thurmm
                                              Captain.
                                              Brigade Major.
6-10-16.   J A Y.

S E C R E T.   B.M.495

~~JACOB.~~
~~JEROME.~~
JAM.
~~JAR.~~
~~JOIST.~~
~~SPARROW.~~

    XV Corps Code correction for Code "A" from midnight
6th/7th October will be :-

        H = + 2.

                                              Captain.
                                        Brigade Major.
6-10-16.   J A Y.

B.M.493
Please acknowledge.

<u>SECRET.</u>   <u>BARRAGE TIME TABLE.</u>

To accompany 41st Division Order No. 49 of 5-10-16.

<u>TIME.</u>
00.00 (ZERO)   Barrage will open on a line about 150 yards in front of our line.
    Leading Infantry will advance and get close up under the Barrage.

00.02 - plus
(ZERO ~~+~~ 2 mins.)   The Barrage will creep forward at the rate of 50 yards per minute until it reaches a line 200 yards beyond the first objective (GREEN LINE).
    The Barrage will remain on this line till 00.X (ZERO plus X mins.)
    The GREEN LINE will be altered in front of the 41st Division Sector so as to include the new Trench running E. and W. through N 13 c 4½.5. and conform with the advance of the 47th Division, and will run as follows :-
    N 13 d 5.5. - N 13 c 45.50 - M 18 d 5.6. - M 18 d 6.3. - M 18 c 0.3. - thence to XIII Corps Area about M 17 d Central. 122nd Infantry Brigade will, however, arrange to follow up the Creeping Barrage along the GIRD Trench and GIRD SUPPORT and establish blocks as close as possible to the Barrage which will be on German trenches 200 yards beyond the GREEN LINE.

00.Y
(ZERO plus Y mins)   The Infantry will again advance from the GREEN LINE and place itself close under the Barrage.

00.Z
(ZERO plus Z mins)   The Barrage will creep forward at the rate of 50 yards per minute until it reaches a line 200 yards in advance of the BROWN LINE and will remain on this line until the position of our Infantry on the BROWN LINE has been consolidated.

    From ZERO Hour Stationary Barrages have been arranged on certain objectives but will lift off them in front of the Creeping Barrages, the movements of which only concern the attacking Infantry.

6-10-16.   X, Y and Z minutes will be communicated later.

Trenches Corrected
to 6.10.16
6   A-A New Trenches
Scale 1:10,000

Ligny Thilloy

le Barque

Luzenhof Farm Bn HQ

Gird Support

Gird Trench

Secret

Copy No..6...

122nd INFANTRY BRIGADE ORDER NO.55

Reference Map 57C S.W. 1/20,000
and Map "D" GUEDECOURT to BAPAUME (attached).

----

1. SITUATION. At Zero hour on 7th October the offensive will be continued by the Fourth Army on the Left, and the Sixth French Army on the Right.
The 124th Infantry Brigade will be on the right, and the 140th Infantry Brigade on the left of the 122nd Infantry Brigade.

The Divisional Reserve to the 41st Division is going to consist of 123rd Infantry Brigade,
3 Field Coys.R.E. (less 2 Sections).
19th Middlesex Regt. (?)
Troop South Irish Horse.

INTENTION. The 122nd Infantry Brigade will carry out the attack with the 15th Hampshire Regt., and the 11th Royal West Kent Regt in the front line, and the 18th Kings Royal Rifle Corps in close support.
The 12th East Surrey Regiment will be in Brigade Reserve.

One Section 228th Field Company R.E. will be accommodated in FLERS Trench, by O.C. 12th East Surrey Regt. from 3 p.m. on 6th October.
They will be ready to go forward to assist in consolidation, with a carrying party found by 12th East Surrey Regt.

3. ASSEMBLY AREAS. The Assembly Areas of the 122nd and 124th Infantry Brigades are shown in the attached Map "B".
The 122nd Infantry Brigade will be assembled in their present positions.

4. ARTILLERY & OBJECTIVES The attack will be preceded by a bombardment commencing at 3.15 p.m. 6th October till Zero hour. There will be no intense fire before Zero hour.
The attack will be carried out in two stages as shown on Map "D".
Details of the Time Table of the creeping and stationary Barrages will be issued later.
Heavy Artillery is dealing with hostile defences, approaches, villages etc.

5. DIVIDING LINES. The Dividing Lines are shown on attached map.

6. LENGTH OF FRONT. The length of Front covered by 122nd Infantry Brigade is approximately 1000 yards.

7. FORMATION. The 15th Hampshire Regt., and 11th Royal West Kent Regt., will be disposed in their front line trenches and will each advance in two waves on a two company front.
The 18th Kings Royal Rifle Corps will advance from their present line in the same formation in rear of the right centre.

7. CLEARING UP and BLOCKS - BOMBS O.C., 15th Hampshire Regiment will detail a party of bombers for mopping up and if necessary blocking GIRD TRENCHES.
Every Officer, N.C.O., and man will carry two Mills bombs in his pockets.

Consolidation/-

K.R.R. to occupy
Strong point at
Mid-day tomorrow

Heart to go to D
Coy at 9. AM
tomorrow

Wilcox to A Coy at
9. AM

Write OC 6th London

Hampshire Bombing
Party — not to go
too far up 2nd Trench
or will we leave all
of them — to —

-2-

8.	CONSOLIDATION.	The objectives will be consolidated as soon as possible and made secure against counter attack.
9.	LEWIS GUNS AND PATROLS.	Lewis Guns and Patrols will be pushed forward beyond the final objective as soon as possible. O.C. 122nd Machine Gun Company will arrange for indirect covering M.G. fire to cover the advance of the infantry during the attack. Vickers Guns will be pushed forward with the attack, with especial reference to the left flank.
10.	STOKES GUNS.	122nd Trench Mortar Battery will bombard in conjunction with the 124th Trench Mortar Battery that portion of GIRD TRENCH and GIRD SUPPORT in front of our present line with Stokes Guns two minutes before Zero Hour (00-2). Stokes Guns will be pushed forward with a view to enfilading any portions of GIRD TRENCHES not taken. The O.C. Special Section R.E. is going to co-operate in clearing those portions of the hostile trenches.
11.	S.O.S. ROCKETS	Arrangements will be made to take forward S.O.S. rockets.
12.	COMMUNICATION with AEROPLANES.	Every Officer and N.C.O., and 50 men per company, will carry two yellow flares. These are to be lighted in front line only on reaching each objective, and at 4 p.m. and 5 p.m. 7th October, and at 7 a.m. 8th October. Panels, lamps and ground sheets will also be used to communicate with the contact aeroplanes.
13.	RUNNER RELAY POSTS.	Battalions will arrange to drop Runner relay Posts at intervals during the advance.
14.	PIGEONS.	Each battalion in the front line will be provided with four pigeons for use if other means of communication fails.
15.	MEDICAL.	Advanced Dressing Stations will be established at THISTLE and GREEN DUMPS and a Divisional Collecting Station at FLAT IRON COPSE.
16.	WATCHES.	Watches will be synchronised by O.C. Signal Company at 9 a.m. and 1 p.m. on 7th October.
17.	ZERO HOUR.	The hour of ZERO will be communicated later.
18.	REPORTS.	Reports of the situation will be transmitted to Bde.H.Q. at the end of every hour after ZERO. Important events, e.g. the capture of an Objective, at once. If the situation is unknown it will be so stated.

Captain.
Brigade Major.
122nd Infantry Brigade.

6th October 1916.
Issued at.. 7/30 a.m.

Copy No. 1 Filed. No.2 War Diary. No.3 41st Division. No.4 12th E.Surrey Regt. No.5 15th Hants Regt. No.6 11th R.W.Kent Regt. No.7 18th K.R.R.C.	Copy No. 8 122nd M.G.Coy. No. 9 122nd T.M.Batty. No.10 123rd Inf.Bde. No.11 124th Inf.Bde. No.12 140th Inf.Bde. No.13 Staff Captain. No.14 Bde.Transport Officer.	No.15 297th Coy. No.16 228th Fd. Coy.R.E. No.17 139th Fd. Ambulance. No.18 122nd Bde. Signals.

SECRET.

~~JACKAL.~~
~~JACKDAW~~
JAM.
~~JAR.~~
~~JOIST~~
~~SPARROW.~~
~~QUAD~~
QUIET.
JEWEL.

B.M.541.

JAY will be relieved by QUAIL tonight.

1. QUIET will assemble in original Front Line Trenches from Junction of GIRD TRENCH to Divisional Left Boundary by 4 p.m.

2. QUILL is going to take over new Front Line from junction of GIRD SUPPORT inclusive to Divisional Left Boundary. JACKAL and JAM will each supply 5 Guides and JAR 6 Guides to meet QUILL at Junction of ABBEY ROAD and GOOSE ALLEY at 5.30 p.m. runners will be at Junction SWITCH TRENCH & FISH ALLEY at 4.30 p.m. The latter supplied by Bde.Sigs

3. QUAD is going to take over new Trench dug and original front line from Brigade Right boundary to GIRD SUPPORT exclusive, with 4 platoons. JACKDAW will supply 4 Guides to meet QUAD at Junction of TURK LANE and North Road at 6.30 p.m. runners supplied by Bde.Sigs. will be as in para 2 at 5.30 p.m.

4. Above mentioned Guides will act as guides to platoons of relieving Battalions.

5. On relief JACKDAW and JAR will move into FLERS TRENCH East and West of junction with TURK LANE respectively.

JACKAL and JAM on relief will proceed to SWITCH TRENCH via FISH ALLEY.

Guides from QUAIL are going to meet JACKAL and JAM at junction of SWITCH with FISH ALLEY to guide them into their trenches on arrival.

JACKAL will be in Trench just in Front of old SWITCH LINE and JAM in Trench just behind.

6. JOIST and SPARROW will arrange details of relief with QUART and BLOT.

On relief JOIST will proceed to CARLTON TR. and xxxx, SPARROW to THISTLE DUMP.

-2-

7. Communications ... will have to include ... where Report Centre is already open. In addition to arrange Report Centre at ......

8. ...... is going to take over present headquarters of ..., and ..... the present headquarters of ....

9. Completion of Relief will be reported to ....

10. Command will pass at ..... reporting that their battalions are in position in front line and support trenches.

11. Rations and water will be dumped for ...... and ... in ...... Road, and for ...... and ..., xxxxxxxxxxxxxxxx on ..... Road opposite ...... Church.

12. Units concerned will be responsible to stop their transport opposite ...... after being notified of probable time of arrival.

13. Acknowledge.

Captain,
Brigade Major.

MARCH TABLE.

UNIT.	STARTING POINT.	TIME.	ROUTE.	REMARKS.
Headquarters, 122 Infantry Brigade, 122nd M.G.Company.	From Cavalry Track crosses to GAZA - LAZARUS ROAD.	To pass starting point at 8 a.m.	Via LAZARUS CROSS.	Distance 3½ miles
13th A.Surrey Regt.	-do-	9 a.m.	-do-	-do-
11th R.W.Kent Regt.	-do-	9.15 a.m.	-do-	-do-
104th R.A.F.Corps.	-do-	10. a.m.	-do-	-do-
14th Hampshire Regt.	-do-	10.30 a.m.	-do-	-do-
13th R.F.A.Battery.	Will move independently.			

Secret

Copy No. 6

122nd INFANTRY BRIGADE ORDER NO.56

Reference Map Sheet 57C.S.W. 1/20,000
----

1. The 30th Division is going to relieve the 41st Division in the Left Sector of the XVth Corps Front.

2. The 21st Infantry Brigade is going to relieve 122nd Infantry in the Divisional Reserve Area on 11th inst.

3. The relief will be completed by 12 noon.

4. The 122nd Infantry Brigade will, on relief, proceed to Camp S 20 a East of MAMETZ WOOD in accordance with the attached March Table.

5. The 12th East Surrey Regiment and 11th Royal West Kent Regiment will be clear of the SWITCH LINE by 8 a.m. and will move by FISH ALLEY. (On no account will TURK LANE be used).

6. The 122nd Trench Mortar Battery will arrange to hand over his guns to the 21st Trench Mortar Battery and to take over the guns belonging to the latter. * Details to be arranged between Battery Commanders.

7. Units on relief will march by Companies at intervals of 300 yards between each.

8. Command of Divisional Reserve Area will pass to Brigadier General Commanding 21st Infantry Brigade at 10 a.m. 11th October.

9. 122nd Infantry Brigade Report Centre will close at CARLTON TRENCH at 10 a.m. on 11th inst., and will open at S 20 a at the same hour.

10. The 41st Division Report Centre is going to close at FRICOURT CHATEAU at 10 a.m. on 11th inst, and open at BUIRE CAMP at the same hour, at which hour the Command of Front held by 41st Division will pass to G.O.C. 30th Division.

11. The Camp to which 122nd Infantry Brigade is proceeding is situated at S20.a.9.5. and it will be vacated by 10 a.m. on 11th/12th by 124th Infantry Brigade, who proceed there tonight.

The necessary orders as to sending advance parties have been issued to the Officers Commanding details of respective Brigades.

A.Y. Julian Thomas
Captain,
Brigade Major,
122nd Infantry Brigade.

10-10-16.
Issued at 7.p.m.

Copy No. 1 Filed.
  No. 2 War Diary.
  No. 3 41st Division.
  No. 4 12th E.Surrey Regt.
  No. 5 15th Hants.Regt.
  No. 6 11th R.W.Kent Regt.
  No. 7 18th K.R.R.Corps.

No. 8 122nd M.G.Coy.
No. 9 122nd T.M.Battery.
No.10 21st Infantry Brigade.
No.11 123rd Infantry Brigade.
No.12 124th Infantry Brigade.
No.13 Staff Captain.
No.14 Bde.Transport Officer.

* 122 T.M. B. will also hand over handcarts but will not take over guns & handcarts in exchange until arrival in Fayencourt at a later date.

BATTALION ORDERS
by Lieut. Col. A.C.Corfe,
Commanding 11th Bn.R.West Kent Regt.

13th October, 1916.

1. SICK PARADE   7.30 a.m.

2. ORDERLY ROOM   9 a.m.

3. TOMORROW'S WORK.
   7 - 7.30 a.m. Physical Training.
   9 a.m. - 12.30 p.m.) Company Training
   2 - 4.30 p.m.   ) and organisation.

4. COMPANY COMMANDERS.
The following officers are placed temporarily in Command of the Companies as stated :-

   2nd Lieut. Henderson, G.D.   "A" Coy.
   "   Wright, T.C.   "B" "
   "   Wheeler, S.A.   "C" "
   "   Bonnot, W.   "D" "

5. TEMPORARY TRANSFERS.
The following N.C.O's are temporarily transferred for instructional purposes :-
   G/21002. Sgt. Toomer, W.E. "A" Coy to "C" Coy.
   G/8074. "   Pragnell, F.   " " " "B" "

6. TRANSFER.
G/6457. Pte. Hoogh, D.W. "D" Coy., is transferred to "A" Coy. from this date.

7. REVERSION.
G/10545. Cpl. Waters, A.H. "D" Coy. reverted to private dated 13/10/16.

8. STRENGTH. INCREASE.
The undermentioned N.C.C's and men having joined the Battalion from No.40 Infantry Base Depot, are taken on Strength and posted to "A" Company :-

G/11135 Pte.	Bonnett, F.	G/11463. Pte.	Easthope, H.
G/14944. "	Prieth, A.	G/15093. "	Jarman, W.
G/15020. "	Parish, J.	G/15834. "	Awcock, F.
G/17451. L/C.	Truscott, F.H.	G/17454. "	Clark, C.
G/17455. Pte.	Vine, W.	G/17456. "	Poulter, H.
G/17457. "	Barnes, C.	G/17548. "	Richardson, T.
G/17459. "	Lewis, T.	G/17460. "	Somerville, T.
G/17462. "	Atkins, C.	G/17432. A/S.	Dorman, W.
G/17475. L/S.	Taylor, J.	G/17477. Cpl.	Wilson, R.
G/17473. A/C.	Fothergill, J.	G/17484.	Haydon, F.
G/17466. Pte.	Bardon, J.	G/17485. L/C.	Brand, W.
G/17482. "	Corder, F.	G/17476. "	Gage, C.
G/17474. L/C.	Gibbs, D.	G/17468. Pte.	Guy, A.
G/17480. Pte.	Jennings, F.	G/17467. "	Maynard, H.
G/17470. "	Rash, E.	G/17487. "	Rogers, J.
G/17479. L/C.	Salmons, A.	G/17478. L/C.	Simpson, E.
G/17469. "	Sinden, E.	G/17471. Pte.	Staines, C.
G/17483. "	Trundle, A.	G/17481. L/C.	Tweed, R.
G/17488. Pte.	Ward, D.	G/17486. Pte.	Woollard, B.

(Sgd) A. W. Puttick. Lieut. & A/Adjt.
11th Bn. Royal West Kent Regiment.

SUPPLY ARRANGEMENTS.

41st.Division
No. Q.104.

Supply Arrangements during the impending move of the Division from the XV Corps to the X Corps area will be as follows:-

		16th.	17th.	18th.
1.	124th.Brig.Group. less Transport.	Carried on man for entrainment.	Issued by Supply Column on 16th. on arrival in billets.	Issued by Supply Column on morning of 17th.
2.	Transport of Divn. (less Artly)	Carried on man and horse. (for march)	Dumped by Supply Col. and drawn at place of halting for night 16/17th.	Issued in new area on morning of 18th.
3.	Remainder of Divn. (less Artillery)	Issue as usual.	Carried on man for entrainment. Issued by Supply Column.	Issued in new area on morning of 18th.

E.S.White

October 13th.1916.

Captain,
D.A.Q.M.G.
41st.Division.

To:- ALL UNITS.
(LESS ARTLY).

UNIT.	DATE.	STATION OF ENTRAINMENT.

122nd. Infantry Brigade Group.

Brigade Headquarters.
18th. K.R.R.C.
12th. E.Surreys.
11th. R.W.Kents.
15th. Hants.
228th. Field Coy.R.E. } 17th. Oct.   MERICOURT.
138th. Field Amblce.
H.Qs,Divl. R.E.
Section-Signal Coy.
19th. Middlesex.
122nd. M.G.Coy.
122nd. T.M.Battery.

123rd. Infantry Brigade Group.

Brigade Headquarters.
11th. R.W.Surreys.
10th. R.W.Kents.
23rd. Middlesex.
20th. Durham Light Inf.
233rd. Field Coy. R.E. } 17th. Oct.   EDGEHILL.
139th. Field Amblce.
Section-Signal Coy.
Divl. Salvage Coy.
123rd. M.G.Coy.
123rd. T.M.Battery.

124th. Infantry Brigade Group.

Brigade Headquarters.
10th. R.W.Surreys.
26th. Royal Fusiliers.
237th. Field Coy. R.E. } 16th. Oct.   EDGEHILL.
124th. M.G.Coy.
Section-Signal Coy.
Railhead Postal Details.

32nd. Royal Fusiliers.
21st. K.R.R.C.
140th. Field Amblce.
124th. T.M.Battery.   } 16th. Oct.   MERICOURT.
Divisional Headquarters.
Divl. Sanitary Section.

41st. Division No.282/S.7.

Reference my No. 282/S.7. dated 14th. October 1916, Detraining Stations will now be as follows and not as therein stated.

122nd. Infantry Brigade Group, ...OISEMENT.
123rd. Infantry Brigade Group, ... ditto.
124th. Infantry Brigade Group, ...AIRAINES.

Captain,
D.A.Q.M.G.
41st. Division.

14th. October 1916.

41st. Divn. No. 282/S.7.

1. The 41st. Division, less Divisional Artillery and all Transport, will entrain by Tactical Trains according to the attached table.

2. Detraining station will be LONGPRE LES CORPS SAINTS.

3. Actual times of entrainment and detail of trains will be issued later.

4. It must be clearly understood that in a Tactical Train <u>only</u> Personnel, Packs and Lewis Gun Handcarts may be entrained.
During the last move this <u>order was very generally</u> unobserved.
The Divisional Commander will take a serious view of any attempt to infringe this order and any kit in excess of that authorised brought to the station of entrainment will be left behind entirely at the units risk.

5. Units should arrive at the entraining station one and a half hours before advertised time of departure.

6. Care should be taken in loading Lewis Gun Handcarts as accommodation will be limited and unnecessary occupation of space is to be avoided.

7. The Motor Ambulances will move by road under orders of the A.D.M.S. who will arrange for two motor ambulances to meet each Regiment of infantry at the detraining station to pick up any sick.

8. Supply arrangements are issued separately.

9. Lorries will meet trains at detraining station to convey packs to billets.

E.S. White.

Captain,
D.A.Q.M.G.
41st. Division.

14th. October.

SECRET.

BILLETING LIST 41st. DIVISION.

D.H.Q.	HALLENCOURT.
H.Q.TRAIN.	-do-
19th. MIDDLESEX.	-do-
H.Q.122nd.INFANTRY BRIG.	CAUMONT.
12th. EAST SURREY.	HUPPY.
15th. HAMPSHIRE.	HUPPY.
11th. R.WEST KENTS.	NEUVILLE & FORIEVILLE.
18th. K.R.R.C.	DOUDELAINVILLE.
122.M.Gun CO.	ERONDELLE.
122 TRENCH MORTAR BATTERY.	-do-
228th.FIELD CO R.E.	FRESNE'-TILLOLOY.
138th. FIELD AMBULANCE.	-do-
No.2.COY.DIV.TRAIN.	HUCHENNEVILLE.
123rd.INFANTRY BRIG H.Q.	HOCQUINCOURT.
11th. QUEENS.	LIMEUX.
10th. R.W.KENTS.	CITERNE.
23rd.MIDDLESEX.	MERELESSART.
20th. D.L.I.	CITERNE.
123rd.M.G.CO.	FRUCOURT.
123rd.T.M.BATTERY.	-do-
233rd.FIELD CO R.E.	BELIEFONTAINE.
139th. FIELD AMBULANCE.	WANEL.
NO.3.CO.DIV.TRAIN.	GRANDSART.
124th. INF.BRIGADE H.Q.	AIRAINES.
10th. QUEENS.	-do-
26th. R.FUSILIERS.	-do-
32nd.R.FUSILIERS.	LONGPRE.
21st. K.R.R.C.	SOREL.
124th. M.G.Co.	AIRAINES.
124th. T.M.BATTERY.	-do-
237th. FIELD CO.R.E.	ALLERY.
140th. FIELD AMBULANCE.	BETTANCOURT.
No.4.CO.DIV.TRAIN.	AIRAINES.
DIVISIONAL SUPPLY COLMN.	LONGPRE.
MOBILE VET SECTION.	LONGPRE.
SANITARY SECTION.	HALLENCOURT.

Major,
D.A.A.&Q.M.G.
41st.Division.

Oct. 15th. 1916.

4th. Army. No. A/253/41.
XV Corps A. No. A.C.2315.
41st. Division No. A.81/2.

XV Corps.

The following suggestions in relation to Chilled Feet and Frostbite are forwarded for your information:-

(a) A special gum boot store, with a changing room or shed with facilities for cleaning and drying the foot and putting on dry socks and boots, should be provided for each unit within a reasonable distance of the front line of trenches.
Arrangements should be made for heating, and seats provided for the men to sit on when changing socks and boots.

(b) Gum boots, to dry properly, should be in the correct position, standing or hung up with the top kept well open. They should be well dried inside with a cloth before being stood or hung up.

(c) Shelves should be provided to store the ankle boots, care being taken that pairs of boots are tied together when taken off, chalk for marking them should be provided.

General Routine Order No. 1275 of 29/11/15 is printed in pamphlet form, and can be obtained from the Stationery Services.

Headquarters,					(Signed) J. WHITEHEAD, Lt. Col.
Fourth Army.						A.A.G., Fourth Army.
11th. Oct.1916.

For information. This matter will be taken up by the Division immediately on arrival in our new Area.
All Units should provide themselves with the necessary number of copies of G.R.O. No. 1275.

Major,
D.A.A. & Q.M.G.,
41st. Division.

15th. October 1916.

4th. Army. No. A/253/41.
XV Corps A. No. A.C.2315.
41st. Division No. A.81/2.

XV Corps.
==========

The following suggestions in relation to Chilled Feet and Frostbite are forwarded for your information:-

(a)   A special gum boot store, with a changing room or shed with facilities for cleaning and drying the feet and putting on dry socks and boots, should be provided for each unit within a reasonable distance of the front line of trenches.
   Arrangements should be made for heating, and seats provided for the men to sit on when changing socks and boots.

(b)   Gum boots, to dry properly, should be in the correct position, standing or hung up with the top kept well open. They should be well dried inside with a cloth before being stood or hung up.

(c)   Shelves should be provided to store the ankle boots, care being taken that pairs of boots are tied together when taken off, chalk for marking them should be provided.

General Routine Order No. 1275 of 29/11/15 is printed in pamphlet form, and can be obtained from the Stationery Services.

Headquarters,   (Signed) J.WHITEHEAD, Lt. Col.
Fourth Army.   A.A.G., Fourth Army.
11th. Oct.1916.

==========

            For information. This matter will be taken up by the Division immediately on arrival in our new Area.
            All Units should provide themselves with the necessary number of copies of G.R.O. No. 1275.

                                            Major,
                                            D.A.A. & Q.M.G.,
15th. October 1916.   41st. Division.

122nd. INFANTRY BRIGADE.
SUPPLY ARRANGEMENTS DURING MOVE.

Rations for 122nd. Infantry Brigade Train parties for consumption on 17th. will be delivered by motor lorry on 16th.

Units in Camp at E.14.b. will take over rations from motor lorries which will halt at the level crossing at E.15.Central.

Rations for Units at RIBEMONT will be delivered as near as possible to their Headquarters. The two units there should have relays of guides by the church to guide lorries to Headquarters.

Battalions will detail ration parties of 1 N.C.O. and 40 men to man-handle their rations from lorries to their Headquarters. (Brigade H.Q. 1 N.C.O. and 10 men),(M.G.Coy and T.M.B. 1 N.C.O. and 20 men).

Rations for consumption of 18th. will be delivered by motor lorry on the morning of the 18th. All units will detail 1 man to report at 8.0a.m. on the 18th. at Brigade H.Q. at CAUMONT to guide lorries to their units.

Units will reserve sufficient rations from the previous day to provide breakfast for men on the morning of the 18th.

Arrangements have been made to ration Transport details en route

15-10-1916.

             Captain.
             Staff Captain.
           122nd. Infantry Brigade.

Copy No. 6

122ND INFANTRY BRIGADE ORDER No. 57

Reference Maps, 1/40,000 Sheet 62ᵈ N.E.
1/100000 AMIENS.
1/100,000 ABBEVILLE.

....

1. The Transport of 41st Division and 3 Infantry Brigades and Mobile Veterinary Section is going to march on 16th October to AREA 5.

2. The whole column is going to be under command of Lt.-Col. Molony. A.S.C.

3. The First Line and Train Transport, bicycles, and all horses of units, 122nd Infantry Brigade, 228th Field Company R.E. and 138th Field Ambulance will form the 122nd Infantry Brigade Group.

4. The head of the 122nd Infantry Brigade Group will pass the cross roads at RIBEMONT D27.b.1.1. at 10.30 a.m. October 16th and march in rear of 123rd Brigade Group.

5. Units of the 122nd Infantry Brigade Group will march in accordance with attached table of movement.

6. The 122nd Infantry Brigade Group will be under the Command of Major H.de C. Blakeney, 12th East Surrey Regt.

7. The following distances will be maintained:-
   (a) 100 yards between Transport of each unit (e.g. battalions, Field Company, Field Ambulance.)
   (b) 800 yards between Transport of each Group.

8. Acknowledge.

Issued at ....

15th October 1916.

[signature]
Captain.
Brigade Major.
122nd Infantry Brigade.

Copy No. 1 File.
No. 2 War Diary.
No. 3 41st Division.
No. 4 12th E. Surrey Regt.
No. 5 15th Hampshire Regt.
No. 6 11th R.W. Kent Regt.
No. 7 18th K.R.R. Corps.
No. 8 228th Field Coy. R.E.
No. 9 138th Field Ambulance.
No.10 Major Blakeney.
No.11 Bde. Transport Officer.
No.12 123rd Infantry Brigade.
No.13 124th Infantry Brigade.
No.14 122nd Machine Gun Company.
No.15 122nd Trench Mortar Battery.
No.16 122nd Bde. Signal Section.
No.17 Staff Captain.

MOVEMENT TABLE.

UNITS IN ORDER OF MARCH.	STARTING POINT.	TIME TO PASS.	TO	ROUTE	REMARKS.
Brigade Headquarters) 122nd Machine Gun Co.)	Brigade Transport Lines E.14.d.	9.10 a.m.	ST. SAUVEUR & ARGOEUVES.	Cross Roads D.27.b.1.1.- D.20.b.6.3.- QUERRIEU - AMIENS RD - thence N. of R.SOMME.	Water at QUERRIEU.
15th Hampshire Regt.	-do-	9.13 a.m.	-do-		-do-
18th K.R.R.Corps.	-do-	9.17 a.m.	-do-		-do-
12th East Surrey Regt.	Cross Roads RIBEMONT D.27.b.1.1	10.38 a.m.	-do-	-do-	-do-
11th R.W.Kent Regt.	-do-	10.42 a.m.	-do-	-do-	-do-
138th Field Ambulance.	-do-	10.46 a.m.	-do-	-do-	-do-
228th Field Coy.R.E.	-do-	10.50 a.m.	-do-	-do-	-do-

S E C R E T.   OPERATION ORDER No.29   Copy No. 4
by Lieut.Col. A.C.Corfe,
Commanding BCW Battalion.

15th November, 1916.

1. The Battalion will be relieved by the 11th "Queen's" today, relief starting at 4 p.m.

2. Opposite numbers will take over in the order in which they relieve, and Platoons will march off independently with the guides already detailed leading. Company Commanders will report to Battalion Headquarters as soon as relief is complete. Code word "O.O.29 complied with."

3. All movement will be by platoons at not less than 100 yards distance.

4. Maps, Aeroplane Photographs and Trench Stores, are to be handed over to incoming Unit, and a copy of receipts for Trench Stores handed in to Battalion Headqrs., after relief.
Periscopes & Sniperscopes, may be handed over to opposite number at the discretion of Company Commanders, a separate receipt in duplicate for these being obtained. (These must NOT be confounded with Trench Store Returns.)

5. Officers Trench Bundles, Mess Boxes, Blankets, etc. will be sent to Battalion Headqrs. by 2 p.m. - each Company being responsible for a fatigue party for this, and 4 men per Company to accompany Transport back to Camp in charge of their own Company property.

6. O.C. "C" Coy., will detail a fatigue party of 1 Officer and 20 men to report at Battalion Headqrs., at 3 p.m., and will receive instructions there. These men must report with full equipment ready for moving off.

7. Company Cookers and Transport, under Coy.Quartermaster Sergeants, will meet the Battalion on the road behind DICKEBUSCH about H.27.c.9.5 where men will rest and have tea.

8. Companies will occupy exactly the same accommodation as they left at ALBERTA CAMP.

9. Trenches must be left clean and in good order. A certificate signed by the Officer Commanding opposite number to be obtained and handed in to the Orderly Room with the Trench Stores Returns on arrival at Rest Billet.
Fires will be left in the Cook-houses, and tins of Water etc left.

10. Company Commanders are responsible that all Gum Boots are handed over in as dry a condition as possible (in the manner in which they would like to receive them). On no account are any Gum Boots to be taken out of the trenches.

(Sgd) A. C. Corfe.   Lieut. Colonel.
Commanding BCW Battn.

Copy No.1 C.O.   No.9. Lewis Gun Offr.
      2 Adjutant.   10. Signalling Offr.
      3 Office Copy   11. Sniping N.C.O.
      4 War Diary.   12. Asst. Adjutant.
      5 O.C. "A" Coy.   13. Quartermaster.
      6 O.C. "B" "   14. Transport Sergt.
      7 O.C. "C" "
      8 O.C. "D" "

122nd INFANTRY BRIGADE ORDER NO.59

Copy No........

16-10-16.

Ref.Maps 62D 1/40,000, DIEPPE, ABBEVILLE.

1. Dismounted personnel of the 122nd Infantry Brigade Group will proceed on 17th October to "Area 5" by tactical trains as follows.

UNIT.	Station of Entrainment.	Time of Departure on October 17th.
1st Train.		
122nd Bde. H.Q.)		
Signal Section.)		
12th E.Surrey Regt.)	MERICOURT.	12.00
½ 19th Middlesex Regt)		
138th Fd.Ambulance.)		
2nd Train.		
H.Q. Div. R.E.)		
15th Hants.Regt.)		
½ 19th Middlesex Regt)	MERICOURT.	14.00
228th Field Company)		
122nd M.G.Company.)		
3rd Train.		
11th R.W.Kent Regt.)		
18th K.R.R.Corps.)	MERICOURT.	16.00
122nd T.M.Battery.)		

2. Units of the 122nd Infantry Brigade Group will march to the entraining point in accordance with the attached march table. Officers in command of 19th Middlesex Regt., H.Q. Divisional R.E., 138th Field Ambulance and 228th Field Company R.E., will make their own march arrangements, in order to be at entraining point at least 1 hour before departure of train.

3. Distances of 200 yards between units and 100 yards between companies will be maintained on the march.

4. Units will prepare a marching out state in triplicate. One copy will be sent to Brigade Headquarters by 9.15 a.m., one copy will be handed to the R.T.O., and one copy will be retained.

5. Units must arrive at the entraining point at least 1 hour before departure of train.

6. On arrival at entraining point Officers commanding units will report to the R.T.O.
No unit will enter the station without the permission of the R.T.O.

7. The senior Officer in each train will be O.C. Train.

8. Only personnel, packs and Lewis Gun handcarts will be taken on the tactical trains. All unauthorized baggage brought to the station will be left there.

9. Upon detrainment at OISEMONT units will march to their billeting areas as already detailed in Bde.Order No.58. Upon arrival at their billeting areas they will report to the Brigade Headquarters at the CHATEAU, CAUMONT, giving coordinates or exact description of the position of their H.Q.

10. Report Centre will close at present H.Q. at 9.30 a.m. and open at CAUMONT after arrival of 1st train.

11. Acknowledge.

Lieut.
for Brigade Major.
122nd Infantry Brigade.

Copy No. 1 Filed.
No. 2 War Diary.
No. 3 41st Division.
No. 4 12th E.Surrey Regt.
No. 5 15th Hants.Regt.
No. 6 11th R.W.Kent Regt.
No. 7 18th K.R.R.C.
No. 8 122nd M.G.Coy.
No. 9 122nd T.M.Battery.
No.10 H.Q.Div.R.E.
No.11 19th Middlesex Regt.
No.12 138th Field Ambulance.
No.13 228th Field Company.
No.14 Staff Captain.
No.15 Bde.Signal Section.

MARCH TABLE to accompany 122ND INFANTRY BRIGADE ORDER NO.59

UNIT	STARTING POINT	TIME	TO	ROUTE
Brigade Headquarters.) Bde.Signal Section.)	Bde.H.Q. Transport Lines evacuated 15-10-16.	9.40 a.m.	MERICOURT STATION.	Fair weather track to cross roads N.of RIBEMONT D.27.b.1.1.
12th E.Surrey Regt.	Cross Roads in RIBEMONT T.33.b.9.9.	10.45 a.m.	"	Direct Route.
15th Hampshire Regt.	Bde.H.Q.Transport Lines evacuated 16-10-16.	11.40 a.m.	"	Fair weather track to cross roads N.of RIBEMONT D.27.b.1.1.
11th R.W.Kent Regt.	Cross roads in RIBEMONT T.33.b.9.9.	2.45 p.m.	"	Direct Route.
18th K.R.R.Corps.	Bde.H.Q.Transport Lines evacuated 16-10-16.	1.40 p.m.	"	Fair weather track to cross roads N.of RIBEMONT D.27.b.1.1.
122nd M.G.Company.	-do-	11.40 a.m.	"	-do-
122nd T.M.Battery.	-do-	1.48 p.m.	"	-do-
138th Fd.Ambulance.	Cross-roads N.of RIBEMONT D.27.b.1.1.	10.40 a.m.	"	-do-

Copy No. 5

WARNING ORDER.

122ND INFANTRY BRIGADE ORDER NO.58

Reference Map ABBEVILLE 1/100,000
            82D, N.E. 1/40,000

1. 122nd Infantry Brigade Group will entrain at MERICOURT tomorrow under orders to be issued later.

2. Detrainment Station will be OISEMONT (on DIEPPE Map Longtitude 46, Latitude 52.5).

3. On Detrainment units will march to billetting areas as under:-

UNIT.	Billetting Area.	Distance from OISEMONT
122nd Bde.Headquarters.	GAUMONT.	7 miles.
12th E.Surrey Regt.	HUPPY.	5½ "
15th Hampshire Regt.	HUPPY.	5½ "
11th R.W.Kent Regt.	NEUVILLE & FORSEVILLE.	1½ "
18th K.R.R.Corps.	DOUDELAINVILLE.	3 "
122nd Machine Gun Coy.	ERONDELLE.	10 "
122nd T.Mortar Battery.	ERONDELLE.	10 "
226th Field Coy.R.E.	FRESNE-TILLOLOY.	2 "
138th Field Ambulance.	FRESNE-TILLOLOY.	2 "
No.2 Coy.Div.Train.	HUCHENNEVILLE.	8 "

4. Billetting Officers were given a map showing whole of new area, before their departure.

Captain.
Brigade Major.
122nd Infantry Brigade.

16-10-16.

Copy No. 1 Filed.
No. 2 War Diary.
No. 3 12th E.Surrey Regt.
No. 4 15th Hants.Regt.
No. 5 11th R.W.Kent Regt.
No. 6 18th K.R.R.C.
No. 7 122nd M.G.Coy.
No. 8 122nd T.M.Battery.
No. 9 226th Field Coy.R.E.
No.10 138th Field Ambulance.
No.11 No.2 Coy. Div.Train.

Headquarters,
   41st Division. (G)

B.M. 169

    Herewith Appendices to War Diary of 11th Royal West Kent Regiment for month of October 1916, which it is regretted were not forwarded with Diary.

                                               Brigadier General,
                          Commanding 122nd Infantry Brigade.

17-11-16.

To:-
    Headquarters,

        122nd Infantry Brigade.

I have the honour to submit the following report.

1. **Advance Generally.**

Our advance was carried out in two waves of Company lines C A .
        D B

A & C Coys., got over the top about ten (10) minutes before zero, advanced about 60 yards and laid down. The rear Companies then got out.

The Machine Guns did not open on them at once, nor was there any effective enemy barrage, but there was a lot of enemy sniping.

Just before zero the companies advanced again so as to get close under our barrage. They were then mowed down by Machine Gun fire which came from right and left flanks and from direct front (i.e. the enemy's new trench).

When the barrage lifted they again attempted to advance but were again mowed down. By this time they had lost 75% of their men, all their Officers except one, and most of their N.C.O's. I was in the front line trenches and could see what was taking place. The remnants had started to dig in. I collected about 15 details - Signallers, Runners, Servants etc, and sent them out under 2nd Lieut. Henderson, to make another effort to get forward. By this time I was anxious as we had absolutely no supports.

The 16th K.R.R.C., who were to have been behind us, evidently went to our right - they never appeared in our line.

2nd Lieut. Henderson was ordered by me to consolidate the ground won, if he saw that the casualties would be very heavy by a further advance.

The consolidation was well carried out, and by the morning, with the help of the 12th East Surrey Regiment, a good trench had been dug about 150 yards in advance of our old line.

2. **Artillery of both sides.**

Our artillery does not appear to have done much damage to the enemy's new line at M.17.d.5.3. to M.18.c.6.2.

I saw no Artillery Observation Officers in our front line and am of opinion that the enemy's trenches in this vicinity require a more thorough searching than they got.

Enemy's Artillery. Enemy put heavy barrage on their old trenches, but were evidently not certain of the position of our line. Number of Dud enemy shells was few.

ABBEY ROAD, EAUCOURT ABBEY, GOOSE ALLEY & NORTH ROAD, were continually shelled by H.E.Shrapnel.

3. **Machine Guns.**

Enemy line was I think held chiefly with Machine Guns. This was told me by prisoners.

Our men came under heavy Machine Gun fire on right flank from GIRD TRENCH. They had got the range of the crest and simply ploughed up the ground.

Our Machine Guns pushed up the SUNKEN ROAD, and I did not see the work done by them.

4. **Trench Mortars.**

In my Sector - Nil.

5. **Medical arrangements.**

I had arranged a series of Advanced Dressing Stations from my front line back to M.30.c.2.2., where R.A.M.C. were, but owing to bearers becoming casualties and lack of stretchers, these posts brokedown, and I was compelled to rely entirely on my few remaining bearers.

I sent several urgent messages to try and get up R.A.M.C. Bearers, but saw none in front line until we were being relieved.

Our Medical Officer and Medical Corporal were wounded early in the action, and if a Lance Corporal had not risen to the occasion, our plight might have been a great deal worse.

The front Trenches were very narrow, and were entirely blocked and full of dying and wounded men. This had a bad effect on the morale of the Troops.

I cannot speak too highly of the work done by our few surviving Stretcher Bearers.

R.A.M.C. posts must be closer to front line.

6. Quartermaster's Stores & Transport.

Unfortunately our Dump was situated in an extremely hot spot. There seems to have been great difficulty in getting Stores there. The Regimental Quartermasters did get their Stores up, but unless Water carts are brought up, some other adequate provision should be made for supplying water - Petrol tins were scarce.

It was rather too much to ask troops who were under an incessant bombardment and who were severely shaken, to go down to bring up rations and stores.

The front line was badly supplied with Bombs, Ammunition and tools, on our taking over. I would suggest that supporting troops supply this fatigue parties for bringing up stores.

Supply wagons are not very satisfactory.

They depend too much on the Regimental Transport, and very often send to us to say they want our horses to bring the supplies to our Transport Lines. I think they forget that thethe Regimental Transport have all the worst of the forward roads. They do not make the same effort as the regimental Transport.

Pack animals and especially Mules did excellent work.

7. Reorganising in trenches.

When men cannot get out of their trenches - the trenches are narrow - it is extremely difficult to do any real reorganising.

8. Suggestions contained in above.

Lieut. Colonel,
Commanding 11th Bn. Royal West Kent Regiment.

12/10/16.

C.O.

S E C R E T.   OPERATION ORDER NO. 23.   Copy No.
by Lieut.Col. A.C.Corfe,
Commanding 11th Bn.R.West Kent Regt.

19th October, 1916.

1. The Battalion will move by rail on 20/10/16 from the Fourth Army Area to the Second Army Area.

2. Entraining station will be LONGPRE.
Detraining station will be GODEWAERSUELDE or CAESTRE.

3. Reveille - 4.30 a.m.
Breakfast - 5 a.m.
"A" & "B" Coys., and Headquarters will parade in column of route outside Battalion Headquarters on the road facing South at 7 a.m.
"C" & "D" Coys., will parade in column of route on the FORCEVILLE-WIRY Road facing West, at 7.15 a.m.

4. The unconsumed portion of the day's rations will be carried on the man and waterbottles filled. Rations for the following day on the supply wagons.

5. The Transport Officer will make the necessary arrangements for moving the Cookers and Watercarts. These will be ready to move by 5.30 a.m.

6. The Lewis Gun, Signalling, Snipers, and spare handcarts will be under the charge of 2nd Lieut. Donnet, and will move with the Transport.

7. Officers valises must be at the Transport Lines by 6 p.m. this evening.

8. Mens packs will be stacked at the Transport Lines as per instructions already issued.

9. Order of March - Signallers, Snipers, "A" Coy. Band, "B", "C", and "D" Coys.

10. The M.O's cart will move with Battalion.
"A" & "B" Coys., will send their Mess Boxes to the Transport Lines at 5 a.m. tomorrow morning.
The Mess Cart will call at "D" Coys., Headquarters at 5.30 a.m. for the boxes of "C" & "D" Coys.
The Hand Mess carts will be sent over to the Transport Lines at 6 p.m. this evening.

(Sgd) A. C. Corfe, Lieut.Colonel.
Commanding 11th Bn. R.West Kent Regt.

Copy No.1	C.O.	No.9.	Lewis Gun Offr.
2	Adjutant.	10.	Sgt. i/c Signallers.
3	War Diary.	11.	N.C.O. i/c Snipers.
4	Office Copy.	12.	Transport Officer.
5	O.C. "A" Coy.	13.	Medical Officer.
6	O.C. "B" "	14.	Quartermaster.
7	O.C. "C" "	15.	R.S.M.
8	O.C. "D" "		

SECRET.

OPERATION ORDER No. 24.   Copy No.
by Lieut. Col. A. C. Corfe,
Commanding 11th Bn. R. West Kent Regt.

1. The Battalion will move into billets in MONT DES CATS area tomorrow, 24th October, 1916.

2. Reveille 6.30 a.m.   Breakfasts 8 a.m.
   Sick Parade 7.30 a.m.
   Orderly Room will be held on arrival at the new billets. Time to be notified later.

3. The Battalion & Transport will be formed up in Column of route by 9.50 a.m., Head of column 400 yards East of "A" Coys billets, facing Railway line.

4. Order of March :- Headquarters Company, B, A, Band, C & D, Coys.

5. Officers Kits & Mess Boxes must be at Quartermaster's Stores by 8.30 a.m.

6. Blankets of "B", "C" & "D" Coys, must be stacked in bundles of 10 outside the Quartermaster's Stores by 8.45 a.m.
   "A" Company will stack their blankets in bundles of 10 outside their billets by 9 a.m.
   Company Quartermaster Sergeants will be responsible for the blankets issued to them, and will superintend their loading on the lorry provided for the purpose.
   Company Commanders will please detail loading parties of 4 men per company.
   Headquarters Company will stack their blankets outside Orderly Room by 8.30 a.m.

7. Company Commanders are responsible that their billets are left clean, and the usual certificates must be rendered to the Adjutant to the effect that no damage has been done.

8. The Lewis Gunners will march in rear of Companies. The Lewis Gun Officer will make arrangements with the Transport Officer for the use of as many pack ponies as available.

9. The Transport Officer will make necessary arrangements to have Company Cookers brought to Transport lines.

(Sgd) A. C. Corfe,   Lieut. Colonel.
Commanding 11th Bn. Royal West Kent Regt.

Copy No. 1 C.C.   No. 9. Lewis Gun Offr.
      2 Adjutant.   10. Signalling Sergt.
      3 War Diary.   11. N.C.O. i/c Snipers.
      4 Office Copy.   12. Transport Offr.
      5 C.C. "A" Coy.   13. Quartermaster.
      6 C.C. "B" "   14. Medical Offr.
      7 C.C. "C" "   15. R.S.M.
      8 C.C. "D" "

Adj

SECRET.

OPERATION ORDER NO.25,
by Lieut.Col. A.O.Corfe,
Commanding 11th Bn.R.West Kent Regiment.

Copy No. No 2

24th October, 1916. 30/43

1. The Battalion will march tomorrow to ONTARIO CAMP near RENINGHELST.

2. Reveille 5.30 a.m.
Breakfasts 6 a.m.
Sick Parade and C.O's Orderly Room will be held on arrival at the new camp. Time will be notified later.

3. Order of March :- Headquarter Coy, & Band, B, A, & D. Coys, and will be formed up by 8.40 a.m., head of column 200 yards east "A" Coys. Headquarters, facing East.

4. B, C, & D Coys., will stack their blankets in bundles of 10, outside C Coys., Headquarters by 7 a.m.
O.C. C Coy. will detail a loading party of 3 men.
A Coy. and Headquarters will stack their blankets in bundles of 10 outside Headquarters Coy, billets by 7.15 a.m.
O.C. A Coy. will detail a loading party of 3 men.
Company Quartermaster Sergeants will be responsible that the blankets are correctly labelled and packed on the lorry. In the event of the Battalion moving off before arrival of the lorry, the loading parties will remain behind, and O.C. A Coy. will detail 1 officer to remain to superintend the loading.

5. Officers Mess Boxes and Kits will be brought to Headquarters by 7.15 a.m.

6. 2/Lieut. T.N.Hall, is detailed as advanced officer, and will meet the Staff Captain at R.16.d.7.5. at 6.30 a.m., for the purpose of proceeding to ONTARIO CAMP to take over.
The Transport Officer will arrange for a horse to be at C" Coys. Headquarters at 7.45 a.m.

(Sgd) A.O.Corfe, Lieut. Colonel.
Commanding 11th Bn.Royal West Kent Regt.

Copy No. 1.	O.C.	No. 9.	Transport Offr.
2.	Adjutant,	10.	Medical Officer,
3.	War Diary,	11.	Lewis Gun Offr.
4.	Office Copy.	12.	Quartermaster,
5.	O.C. "A" Coy.	13.	Sniping Cpl.
6.	O.C. "B" Coy.	14.	Signalling Sgt,
7.	O.C. "C" Coy.	15.	R.B.M.
8.	O.C. "D" Coy.	16.	Asst. Adjutant,
		17.	Billeting Offr.

SECRET.

OPERATION ORDER No.30   Copy No. 4
by Lieut.Col. A.C.Corfe,
Commanding 11th Bn.R.West Kent Regt.

21st November, 1916.

1. The Battalion will relieve the 11th Queen's Royal West Surrey Regt. tomorrow, and will take over trenches as hereunder, namely :-
    Right Front Coy.   "C" Coy.
    Left Front Coy.   "D" Coy.
    Right Support Coy.   "A" Coy.
    Left Support Coy.   "B" Coy.

2. Reveille 7.15 a.m.
3. Breakfasts 7.45 a.m.

4. Order and time of March :-
    Lewis Gunners will move off at ..... 9 a.m.
    Signallers (Hd.Qrs.) " " " ..... 9.5 a.m.
    "D" Coy.   will " " " ..... 9.10 a.m.
    "C" "   " " " ..... 9.20 a.m.
    "B" "   " " " ..... 9.35 a.m.
    Headquarters.   " " " ..... 9.45 a.m.
    "A" Coy.   " " " ..... 9.55 a.m.

    Company Signallers will report t' the O.C. Companies to which they are attached and will march with their companies.
    Snipers will move as a Platoon of "C" Company.
    Platoons to march at 100 yards distance.
    Platoon Commanders must not, on any pretext, halt their men in DICKEBUSCH.
    Company Commanders will insist that this interval is kept. They are reminded that this is a Divisional Order.

5. The Battalion will halt and rest at H.27.d.4.1. The Cookers will be sent on earlier, and will have a hot meal ready for the men.

6. The Companies will move off from here as follows :-
    Lewis Gunners.......... at 12 noon (under Lieut.G.Gordon-Smith)
    Signallers (Headquarters). 12.15 p.m.
    "D" Company. .... 12.30 p.m.
    "C" "   .... 12.40 p.m.
    "B" "   .... 12.55 p.m.
    Headquarters............... 1.5 p.m.
    "A" Company................ 1.15 p.m.

7. The Lewis Guns will be taken up by Transport this afternoon, with 2 men per gun. L/Sgt. Hayden, will be in charge of this party.
    He will arrange to change over the "Queen's" Guns for our own, during the course of tomorrow morning.

8. Officers Mess Boxes and Trench Bundles, will be stacked in "A" Coys Officers' Hut. Officers Servants will remain behind with these and come up with the Transport in the evening, and they will also act as a loading party.

9. Blankets in bundles of 10, and mens' packs properly labelled, will be stacked before moving off, as previously.
    O.C. Coys., will see that Officers Valises are given over to their C.Q.M.S's, and stacked in "D" Coys stores, before moving off.

10. A List of Trench Stores taken over will be forwarded to the Adjutant immediately after the relief is completed.

11. The relief will be carried out as quietly and carefully as possible, and completion reported to Battalion H.Q. by phone Code Word "WETTEST"

12. All waterbottles will be filled before moving off.

13. Company Commanders will be held responsible for the cleanliness of their Huts, Lines, Latrines, Wash-houses, etc.

P. T. O.

- 2 -

14. Company Commanders should hand their Company Conduct Sheets into the Orderly Room this evening, and obtain a receipt for same.

15. O.C. "A" Company will please detail a fatigue party of 30 men under an Officer, to report to the Assistant Adjutant at Battalion Headquarters at 5 p.m. tomorrow.

16. O.C. "C", "B" & "D" Coys., will arrange each for a guide to report to the Asst. Adjutant, at 6 p.m. tomorrow, at Battalion Headquarters to guide ration party to Companies.

(Sgd) A. C. Corfe.   Lt. Colonel.
Commanding 11th Bn. R.West Kent Regt.
(Lewisham).

Copy No. 1. C.O.
2. Adjutant.
3. Office Copy.
4. War Diary.
5. C.C. "A" Coy.
6. C.C. "B" "
7. C.C. "C" "
8. C.C. "D" "

No. 9. Lewis Gun Offr.
10. Medical Offr.
11. Quartermaster.
12. Transport Offr.
13. Sniping Sgt.
14. Signalling Offr.
15. Asst. Adjutant.
16. R. S. M.

N.B. O.C. "C" & "D" Coys., will please arrange to have a "TEST S.O.S" during the first night in the trenches.
A full report should be forwarded to Battalion Headquarters, stating the time taken - from handing in the telephone message until the shell passes over the trench.

S E C R E T.   OPERATION ORDER No. 31.   Copy No. 4
by Lieut. A. W. Puttick,
Commanding BCW Battalion.

26th November, 1916.

1. The Battalion will be relieved by the 11th "Queen's" tomorrow, relief starting at 4 p.m.

2. Opposite numbers will take over in the order in which they relieve, and Platoons will march off independently. Company Commanders will report to Battalion Headquarters as soon as relief is complete. Code words "O. O. 31 complied with."

3. All movement will be by Platoons at not less than 100 yards distance.

4. Maps, Aeroplane Photographs and Trench Stores, are to be handed over to incoming Unit, and a copy of receipts for Trench Stores handed in to Battalion Headquarters, after relief.
Periscopes and Sniperscopes, may be handed over to opposite number at the discretion of Company Commanders, a separate receipt in duplicate for these being obtained. (These must NOT be confounded with Trench Store Returns.)

5. Officers Trench Bundles, Mess Boxes, Blankets, etc, will be sent to Battalion Headquarters by 2 p.m. - each Company being responsible for a fatigue party for this, and 4 men per Company to accompany Transport back to Camp in charge of their own Company property.

6. O. C. "A" Company will detail a fatigue party of 1 Officer & 20 men to report at Battalion Headquarters at 3 p.m., and will receive instructions there. These men must report with full equipment ready for moving off.

7. Company Cookers and Transport, under Coy. Quartermaster Sergeants will meet the Battalion on the road behind DICKEBUSCH about H.27.c.9.5 where men will rest and have tea.

8. Two cooks per Company under Sgt. Finch will report to Battalion Headquarters at 2 p.m. and will proceed to H.27.c.9.5.

9. Companies will occupy exactly the same accommodation as they left at ALBERTA CAMP.

10. Trenches must be left clean and in good order. A certificate signed by the Officer Commanding opposite number to be obtained and handed in to the Orderly Room with the Trench Stores Returns on arrival at Rest Billet.
Fires will be left in the Cook-houses, and tins of water etc, left.

11. Company Commanders are responsible that all Gum Boots are handed over in as dry a condition as possible (in the manner in which they would like to receive them). On no account are any Gum Boots to be taken out of the trenches.

(Sgd). A. W. Puttick. Lieut.
Commanding BCW Battalion.

Copy No. 1. C. O.
2. Asst. Adjutant.
3. Office Copy
4. War Diary
5. O.C. "A" Coy.
6. O.C. "B" "
7. O.C. "C" "
8. O.C. "D" "

No. 9. Lewis Gun Offr.
10. Signalling Offr.
11. Sniping N.C.O.
12. Quartermaster.
13. Transport Offr.
14. R.S.M.

C O P Y.

Fourth Army No.335 (G.S.).

41st Division.

I desire to place on record my appreciation of the work done by the 41st Division during the Battle of the Somme and to congratulate all ranks on the brilliant manner in which they captured the village of FLERS on September 15th. To assault three lines of strongly defended trench systems, and to capture the village of FLERS as well, in one rush was a feat of arms of which every officer, non-commissioned officer and man may feel proud.

It was a very fine performance and I offer my best thanks for the gallantry and endurance displayed by all ranks.

The work of the Divisional Artillery in supporting the infantry attacks and in establishing the barrages deserves high praise, and I trust that at some future time it may be my good fortune to have this fine Division again in the Fourth Army.

H. Rawlinson.
General.
Commanding Fourth Army.

H.Q., Fourth Army,
27th October, 1916.

S E C R E T.   OPERATION ORDER No.26,   Copy No.
by Lieut. Col. A.C. Corfe,
Commanding 11th Bn. R. West Kent Rgt.

27th October, 1916.

1. The Battalion will move into Trenches tomorrow, and take over from the 11th Battn. Royal West Surrey Regt.
   Companies will take over as follows:-
   A Coy.   from   A Coy.
   B "   "   B "
   C "   "   D "
   D "   "   C "

   Right Company   A.
   Left   "   D.
   Left Support   B.
   Right   "   C.

2. Order and time of March.
   A Coy. will move off at 10.30 a.m.
   D "   "   "   "   " 10.45 a.m.
   B "   "   "   "   " 11 a.m.
   C "   "   "   "   " 11.15 a.m.
   Headquarters "   "   " 11.30 a.m.
   Signallers will move off with their companies. Snipers will move as a Platoon of A Coy.
   Platoons to march at 200 yards distance. Company Commanders will insist that this interval is kept. This is a <u>Divisional Orde</u>

3. Lewis Gunners will march off at 9.30 a.m. so as to meet guides at road junction at H.34.a.8.6. by 11 a.m.
   2 Limbers will be outside Orderly Room at 9.15 a.m. to carry the Guns and ammunition.
   Officers Mess Boxes and Trench bundles which will be required for trenches, will be stacked at the Quartermaster's Stores by Companies before moving off.

4. O.C. C Coy. will leave a fatigue party of 1 N.C.O. & 10 men as a loading party.
   The Transport Officer will arrange for 1 limber per Company to bring these up after dusk. The loading party will accompany this limber.
   The Transport Officer will arrange for the Officers Mess Cart and M.O's Cart to move off with Headquarters at 11.30 a.m.

5. O.C. Companies and Headquarters will see that Officers Valises are given over to their C.Q.M.S!s, and stacked in Quartermaster's Stores before moving off.

6. Blankets will be stacked in bundles of 10 properly labelled at the Quartermaster's Stores by 8.30 a.m.

7. A List of Trench Stores taken over will be forwarded to the Adjutant immediately after relief is completed.

8. The relief will be carried out as quietly and carefully as possible, and its completion reported to Battalion Headquarters by phone, Code word "WET".

9. All waterbottles will be filled before proceeding to the trenches.

10. Company Commanders will be held responsible for the cleanliness of their Huts, Lines, Latrines, Wash-houses etc.

11. The Commanding Officer looks to all Officers to supervise the care of their mens' feet and will hold them directly responsible that no case of Trench Foot occurs. Careful study of the pamphlet with reference to this is advised.

(Sgd) A. C. Corfe.   Lieut. Colonel.
11th Bn. Royal West Kent Regiment.

C O P Y.

<u>41st Div.</u>
G. 454.

    The Divisional Commander has great pleasure in forwarding the attached.

    Such praise can only make all ranks proud of what they have done, and stimulate them to maintain in the future the name won by the 41st Division.

29/10/16.
                              B.L.Anley.
                          Lt.Colonel, G.S.

SECRET

FOURTH AUSTRALIAN DIVISION.

Copy No. 7.

ST.ELOI GROUP ARTILLERY ORDER NO.10.

In the Field,
Oct. 29th, 1916.

The following operation will take place to-morrow, 30th.inst:-

Bombardment of the Enemy's Trenches in the BLUFF Sector and trenches for 300 yards South of the Canal on the ST.ELOI Sector in simulation of an attack.

TASKS. The ST.ELOI Group will co-operate with Batteries as per margin.

18-PRS.

38th.Bty.
F.L.T. O.4 a.6½.6
to
O.4 a.1.4

Zero to Zero plus 2 hours — Front Line O.4 a.6½.6 to O.4 a.1½.2

2 hours to 2 hours plus 2 minutes. — Quickened Fire as above.

43rd.Bty.
F.L.T. O.4 a.1.4
to
O.4 a.1½.2

2 Hours plus 2 minutes — Barrage lifts at 75 yards per min. till on line B.4 c.8.6 O.4 b.2.4

2 hours plus 8 minutes — Barrage jumps back to front line and remains till 2 hours plus 12 mins. when fire is stopped.

2 hours plus 12 minutes to)
2 hours plus 48 minutes   ) Pause

2 hours plus 48 minutes to)
2 hours plus 50 minutes   ) Front line as before.

2 hours plus 50 minutes — Barrage again moves back as before.

2 hours plus 56 minutes — Barrage jumps back to front line and remains there to Zero plus 3 hours when fire stops.

HOWITZERS.

111th.Bty.
Zero to zero plus 2 hrs. — On Communication Trenches
1 Section on O.4 a.9.4
O.4 a.3½.4

1 Section on O.4 a.9½.4
O.4 a.7½.4½
and thence to O.4 A.5½.5
and O.4 a.7.6

Zero plus 2 hours to   )
2 hours plus 12 minutes)
and   ) Battery on Trench junctions
from zero plus 2 hours 48-mins. from O.4 d.2.2 to O.4 d.1.6
to zero plus 3 hours.   )

Zero plus 2 hours and 12 minutes
to 2 hours plus 48 minutes   Pause.

OPERATION ORDER NO.10 -contd.

TRENCH MORTARS.

X. 4A	Zero to zero plus 2 hours	Bombardment of F.L.T. as for 18-prs., special attention being paid to junction at O.4 a.3½.4
	2 hours to 2 hours plus 8 minutes	Cease fire.
	2 hours plus 8 to 2 hours plus 12 minutes.	Resume fire.
	2 hours plus 12 minutes	Cease fire.

RATES OF FIRE.

18-prs. -

Zero to zero plus 2 hours	- 45 rounds per gun.
2 hours to 2 hours plus 2 minutes.	- 6 " " "
2 hours 2 minutes to 2 hours 8 minutes	- 12 " " "
2 hours 8 minutes to 2 hours 12 minutes	- 12 " " "
2 hours 48 minutes to 2 hours 50 minutes	- 6 " " "
2 hours 50 minutes to 3 hours.	- 24 " " "

Howitzers. -

Zero to zero plus 2 hours   - B.Y.F. 40-seconds

Zero plus 2 hours to 2 hours plus 12 minutes   - B.Y.F. 15-seconds

Zero plus 2 hours and 12-mins. to 2 hours plus 48 minutes - Pause.

Zero plus 2 hours 48 minutes to zero plus 3 hours   - B.Y.F. 15-seconds.

Arrangements for synchronisation of watches will be notified later.

Zero time will be notified later in the following message - "SUBMIT INDENTS DEFICIENCIES AT.......TODAY."

REGISTRATION. At earliest possible moment tomorrow, 30th. inst.

PHOTOGRAPHS. May be seen at Group Headquarters if desired.

ACKNOWLEDGE.

..................Lt.-Col.

```
Copy No. 1 to 38th. Bty.
 "   "  2  "  43rd "
 "   "  3  "  111th."
 "   "  4  "  193rd. Inf. Bde.
 "   "  5  "  4th. A.D.A.
 "   "  6  "  X 4A T.M. Bty.
 "   "  7  "  Left Btn.
 "   "  8  "  War Diary.
 "   "  9  "  File.
```

S E C R E T.   B.M. 773

12th. East Surrey Regt.
15th. Hampshire Regt.
11th. R.W. Kent Regt.
18th. K.R.R.C.
122nd. M.G. Coy.
122nd. T.M. Battery.
233rd. Field Coy R.E.

    Reference O.O. 65 of 29.10.16 "Indent will be submitted at 2 p.m."

    On no account will any reference to the subject be communicated by telephone or buzzer.

    acknowledge by wire.

                                        Captain.
                                      Brigade Major.
                                122nd. Infantry Brigade.

29.10.16.

S E C R E T

Copy No...... 6

122nd INFANTRY BRIGADE ORDER NO.35

Reference Sheets 1/10,000, No.28 N.W. 4 and No.28 S.W. 2.

----

1. A bombardment of the hostile trench system in front of the BLUFF will be carried out by the Corps and Divisional Artilleries at a time to be notified later.

2. The Heavy Artillery bombardment will be carried out in accordance with the attached table.

3. The 4.5" Howitzer batteries of the 47th Division Artillery Group will shell all the communication trenches from the trench running S.E. and N.W. from I 35 c 40.30. to I 34 b 80.20. inclusive, to the canal exclusive.

4. The 4th Australian Divisional Artillery will bombard the following trenches South of the canal -
    O 4 c 20.58 to 90.35.
    and O 4 a 35.40. to O 4 a 90.10.

5. The trenches in O 4 a for about 300 yards South of the canal will be shelled by 18-pdrs.

6. The following lifts and barrages will be carried out in order to simulate an attack:-

    (a). At 2 hours after Zero the fire of the 4.5" and Heavy Howitzers will stop, except fire on objectives behind the enemy's support line.
    (b). At the same time 18-pdrs. will open an intense barrage as in covering an attack.
    (c). At 2 hours 2 minutes after Zero the 18-pdr. barrage will move back at 50 yards a minute until it is 100 yards behind the enemy's support line where it will remain until 2 hours 8 minutes after Zero. It will then be brought back quickly to the front and support lines (as far as safe) and the field and heavy howitzers will open fire simultaneously at their normal rate.
    The 18-pdrs. will cease firing or return to their normal tasks at 2 hours 12 minutes after Zero.
    The same procedure will then be repeated at 2 hours 48 minutes after Zero, ceasing at 3 hours after Zero.

7. Counter battery work will be active throughout.

8. The IXth Corps will co-operate by shelling the dugouts in the DAM STRASSE from O 9 c 10.80 to O 9 c 90.30.

9. The Corps on the flanks have been asked to carry out active counter battery work on their respective fronts.

10. The O.C., 11th Royal West Kent Regiment will arrange to reduce his garrison of the front line by 50% one hour before Zero time; the men thus removed will be accommodated in OLD FRENCH TRENCH and at SPOIL DUMP until bombardment ceases when they will return to their position in front line.
    Lewis Guns will remain in the Front line.

/11.-

11. O.C., 122nd Machine Gun Company will arrange to have at least 3 Vickers Machine Guns to cover the front of Left Battalion (i.e. from junction of trenches O 34 and 35 to Canal) during the operation.

12. Zero time will be notified later in following message "Submit indent at.......today".

13. Acknowledge.

Note.- The Siege Artillery will register during the morning of the day of the bombardment.

Issued at........

29th October 191 .

Captain.
Brigade Major.
122nd Infantry Brigade.

```
Copy No. 1 Filed.
     No. 2 War Diary.
     No. 3 41st Division.
     No. 4 12th East Surrey Regt.
     No. 5 15th Hants. Regt.
     No. 6 11th R.W.Kent Regt.
     No. 7 18th K.R.R.Corps.
     No. 8 122nd M.G.Company.
     No. 9 122nd T.M.Battery.
     No.10 124th Inf.Bde.
     No.11 141st Inf.Bde.
     No.12 233rd Field Coy.R.E.
     No.13 St.Eloi Group Artillery.
```

EV13

"C" Form (Original).
MESSAGES AND SIGNALS.
Army Form C. 2123.
(In books of 50's in duplicate.)
No. of Message..................

Prefix......Code......Words......	Received	Sent, or sent out	Office Stamp.
£ s. d.	From..................	At..............m.	
Charges to collect	By..................	To..................	
Service Instructions.		By..................	

Handed in at.................... Office..........m. Received..........m.

TO

| *Sender's Number | Day of Month | In reply to Number | A A A |

Submit list of deficien at
2 p.m. today.

E v. 49.

FROM
PLACE & TIME

* This line should be erased if not required.
Wt. 432—M437 500,000 Pads. HWV 5 16 Forms C.2123.

"A" Form
MESSAGES AND SIGNALS.

Army Form C. 2121

Prefix......Code......m.	Words	Charge.	This message is on a/c of:	Recd. at ......m.
Office of Origin and Service Instructions.	Sent At ......m. To By		......Service. (Signature of "Franking Officer.")	Date...... From...... By......

TO	~~JACKAL~~ ~~JACKDAW~~ JAM	~~JAR~~		

Sender's Number.	Day of Month.	In reply to Number.	AAA
* BM 500	6-10-16		

Reference	BM	493	X	equals
20	Y	equals	14	Z
equals	20	aaa	Reference	BM
492	this	should	read	13
Officers	and	45	men	aaa
Acknowledge	aaa			

From: TAY
Place:
Time: 11/40 pm

"A" Form
MESSAGES AND SIGNALS.

Army Form C. 2121

Prefix......Code......m.	Words	Charge.	This message is on a/c of:	Recd. at......m.
Office of Origin and Service Instructions.	Sent			Date
	At......m.		......Service.	From
	To			
	By		(Signature of "Franking Officer.")	By

TO JACKAL   JAR
    JACKDAW
    JAM

Sender's Number.	Day of Month.	In reply to Number.	A A A
BM 492	6.10.16		

One Officer 45 men AAA
ask ...

From JAY
Place
Time 1/30 pm

Army Form C. 2118

WAR DIARY
or
INTELLIGENCE SUMMARY

(Erase heading not required.)

Instructions regarding War Diaries and Intelligence Summaries are contained in F. S. Regs., Part II. and the Staff Manual respectively. Title Pages will be prepared in manuscript.

Place	Date	Hour	Summary of Events and Information	Remarks and references to Appendices
ST. ELOI.	1/11/16.		Battalion in trenches in VOORMEZEELE sector. 2/Lt. Croneen evacuated. 2/Lts. Knight and Dean took out reconnoitring patrols of 1 N.C.O. and man respectively. 2/Lt. KNIGHT failed to return (presumed a prisoner). 2/Lts. MORGAN and BLOODWORTH took out reconnoitring patrol of 1 N.C.O., all returning safely. Strength of Battalion Officers 35. O.R. 786.	
RENING-HELST.	2/11/16.		4 p.m. Battalion relieved in trenches by 11th Q.R.W.Surreys, and proceeded by route march to old camp. Operation Order 27 attached. 12 p.m. Battalion arrived at ALBERTA Camp, RENINGHELST.	
	3/11/16.		Battalion engaged in fatigue parties. 2/Lt. CARTMELL reported for duty from Field Ambulance. Order from 4th Army attached re good work done on SOMME front by 41st Division.	
	4/11/16.		Rest Day for Battalion. DUKE of CONNAUGHT visited troops at RENINGHELST. Strength of Battalion Officers 36. O.R. 779.	
	5/11/16.		Sunday, day of rest.	
	6/11/16		O.C.'s Companies visited trenches. Company training, and instruction in use of small box respirator by GAS school 41st Division. Inspection of camp by D.M.S., 2nd Army, and AREA Commandant.	
	7/11/16.		Company training. 2/Lt. Cotton-Cooke, attached to 11th Queens R.W.Surrey Regt., as Transport Officer. 2/Lt. T.C. Wright returned to duty from leave.	
ST. ELOI.	8/11/16.		Battalion relieved the 11th Q.R.W.S. Regt. in trenches at VOORMEZEELE, relief completed by 6.30 p.m., Operation Order 28 attached.	
	9/11/16 10/11/16.		Battalion in trenches. Lieut. Gordon-Smith returned to Battalion from hospital. Battalion in trenches.	
	11/11/16.		2/Lt. R.O.RUSSELL rejoined for duty from 18th K.R.R.C. Strength of Battalion Officers 35. O.R. 803.	

Army Form C. 2118

WAR DIARY
or
INTELLIGENCE SUMMARY
(Erase heading not required.)

Instructions regarding War Diaries and Intelligence Summaries are contained in F.S. Regs., Part II. and the Staff Manual respectively. Title Pages will be prepared in manuscript.

Place	Date	Hour	Summary of Events and Information	Remarks and references to Appendices
ST. ELOI.	12/11/16.		Battalion in trenches.	
	13/11/16.		do	
	14/11/16.		do	
RENING-HELST.	15/11/16.		2/Lt. BLOODWORTH evacuated to Field Ambulance. Battalion relieved by 11th Q.R.W.R. in trenches, and proceeded by route march to ALBERTA Camp, RENINGHELST. 9.30 p.m. arrived in camp. Operation Order 29 attached.	
	16/11/16.		2/Lts. MALTBY and BERGER joined the Battalion for duty.	
	17/11/16.		Battalion engaged in fatigues.	
	18/11/16.		Day of Rest. 9 a.m. Inspection of transport by Col MALONEY, O.C. Divisional Train. Company training. Strength of Battalion Officers 37. O.R.'s 796.	
	19/11/16.		Sunday, rest day. 2/Lts. H.D.P.Hall and K.THOMPSON-SMITH evacuated to Field Ambulance.	
	20/11/16.		Company training and fatigues. 11 a.m. Presentation of medal ribbons by Corps Commander. 2/Lt. HOWLAND reported for duty from G.H.Q. Cadet School.	
	21/11/16.		Company training and baths.	
ST. ELOI.	22/11/16.		Battalion relieved 11th QUEENS in the line in sector previously occupied by Battalion. Relief completed by 5 p.m. Operation Order 30 attd.	
	23/11/16.		Battalion in trenches.	
	24/11/16.		do	
	25/11/16.		do	
	26/11/16.		Strength of Battalion Officers 36. O.R. 787.	
	27/11/16.		Battalion in trenches. No.17467, Pte. J. ROGERS killed.	
RENING-HELST.	28/11/16.		4 p.m. Battalion relieved by 11th QUEENS and proceeded by route march to camp previously occupied at RENINGHELST, arriving 9 p.m. Vide Operation Order 31 attached.	
	29/11/16.		Battalion engaged on fatigues. Rest day and baths.	
	30/11/16.		Company training. Strength of Battalion Officers 36. O.R. 779.	

Lieut.
Commanding 11th Bn. Royal West Kent Regt

1/12/16

S E C R E T.   OPERATION ORDER No.27   Copy No. 8
by Lieut. Col. A.C.Corfe,
Commanding BOW Battalion.

2nd November, 1916.

1. The Battalion will be relieved by the 11th Queen's today, relief starting at 4 p.m.

2. Opposite numbers will take over in the order in which they relieve, and Platoons will march off independently with the guides already detailed leading. Company Commanders will report to Battalion Headquarters as soon as relief is complete.

3. All movement will be by platoons at not less than 100 yards distance.

4. Maps, Aeroplane photographs and Trench Stores, are to be handed over to incoming unit, and a copy of receipts for Trench Stores handed in to Battalion Headquarters after relief.
Periscopes & Sniperscopes, may be handed over to opposite number at the discretion of Company Commanders, a separate receipt in duplicate for these being obtained. (These must not be confounded with TRENCH STORE RETURNS.).

5. Officers Trench Bundles, Mess Boxes, etc, will be sent to Battalion Headquarters by 3 p.m. - each company being responsible for a fatigue party for this, and 4 men per company to accompany Transport back to Camp in charge of their own Company property.

6. O.C. "C" Company will detail a fatigue party of 20 men and 1 Officer to report at Battn. Headqrs. at 4 p.m. and will receive instructions there. These men must report with full equipment ready for moving off.

7. Company Cookers and Transport, under Coy.Quartermaster Sergts., will meet the Battalion on the road behind DICKEBUSCH about H.27.c.9.5., where men will rest, have tea, and packs will be placed on the limbers.

8. Companies will occupy exactly the same accommodation as they left at ALBERTA CAMP.

9. Trenches must be left clean and in good order. A certificate signed by the Officer Commanding opposite number to be obtained and handed in to the Orderly Room with the Trench Stores Returns on arrival at Rest Billet.

10. Company Commanders are responsible that all Gum Boots are handed over in as dry a condition as possible (in the manner in which they would like to receive them). On no account are any Gum Boots to be taken out of the trenches.

(Sgd) A. C. Corfe, Lieut. Col.
Commanding BOW Battalion.

Copy No. 1 C.O.   9. Lewis Gun Offr.
        2 Adjutant.   10. Sniping N.C.O.
        3 O.C. "A" Coy.   11. Quartermaster.
        4 O.C. "B" Coy.   12. Transport Offr.
        5 O.C. "C" "
        6 O.C. "D" "
        7 Office Diary. Copy.
        8 War Diary.

WAR DIARY or INTELLIGENCE SUMMARY

Army Form C. 2118

XI R W Kent Regt Vol 8

(Erase heading not required.)

Place	Date	Hour	Summary of Events and Information	Remarks and references to Appendices
St.Eloi. Left.	1/12/16		Battalion in rest at ALBERTA Camp, RENINGHELST. Strength of Battalion. 36 Officers, 779 Other Ranks.	
	2/12/16		Battalion relieved 11th "Queen's" in the line previously occupied, relief completed 4 p.m. Vide Operation Order 32 attached. Strength of Battalion. Officers 36. Other Ranks 773.	
	3/12/16		Battalion in trenches. 2/Lt. W.N.Hall reported for duty from Hospital.	
	4/12/16		do	
	5/12/16		do	
	6/12/16		do	
	7/12/16		do	
RENING-HELST.	8/12/16		Battalion relieved by 11th "Queen's" and proceeded by route march to old Camp at RENINGHELST, arriving 9 p.m.. See Operation Order 33 attd. Casualties for period in trenches, December 2-8 - 1 man slightly wounded.	
	9/12/16		Strength of Battalion. Officers 36. Other Ranks 825. 2/Lts. A.Drumgold, F.C.Westmacott, and L.E.Mumford arrived and taken on strength.	
	10/12/16		Battalion engaged in fatigues.	
	11/12/16		Draft of 50 Other Ranks arrived from Base.	
	12/12/16		Sunday. Rest Day.	
	13/12/16		Company Training and baths.	
ST. ELOI LEFT	14/12/16.		" " and fatigues.	
	15/12/16		Battalion relieved the 11th Queen's in sector of line previously occupied. Vide Operation Order 34. Relief completed 4.30 p.m. Battalion in trenches. Strength of Battalion Officers 37. O.R.'s 821	
	16/12/16		do	
	17/12/16		do	
	18/12/16		do	
	19/12/16		2/Lts. W.H.Glover, A.J.Chandler, and R.S.French joined for duty from Base	
	20/12/16		Battalion in trenches.	
	21/12/16		Capt. S.L.Simmonds proceeded to join 19th Bn. R. Scots.	

Army Form C. 2118

WAR DIARY
or
INTELLIGENCE SUMMARY

(Erase heading not required.)

Instructions regarding War Diaries and Intelligence Summaries are contained in F. S. Regs., Part II. and the Staff Manual respectively. Title Pages will be prepared in manuscript.

Place	Date	Hour	Summary of Events and Information	Remarks and references to Appendices
RENING-HELST.	22/12/16.		Battalion relieved by the 11th "Queen's" and proceeded by route march to ALBERTA Camp, RENINGHELST. Vide Operation Order 35 attached. Arrived in Camp 1 a.m. Rest Day. Casualties for period 14-21st December, 3 Other Ranks killed, 2 Other Ranks wounded. Temp. Lieut. F.G.Fraser, and Temp. 2/Lt. T.C.Wright appointed Acting Captains while commanding Companies. Temp. Lieut. A.W. Puttick promoted to be Temp. Captain, and Temp. 2/Lt. R. Kerr promoted to be Temp. Lieut.	
	23/12/16.		Company Training. 2/Lt. A.R. Morgan joined Heavy Section, M.G.C., BERMICOURT. Draft of 11 Other Ranks arrived from Base & Hospital, and taken on strength of Battalion. Officers 38. Other Ranks 813.	
	24/12/16.		Sunday. Rest Day and baths at RENINGHELST. Medal ribbons presented to recipients from 122nd Brigade including, Capt. G.D.Henderson, Ptes. J.Woods, A. Webb, and J.H.Goodison, of this Battalion by G.O.C., 41st Division. 2/Lt. W. Donnet proceeded to join Heavy Section, M.G.C., at BERMICOURT.	
	25/12/16.		Christmas Day. 10 a.m. G.O.C., Division, visited Camp to wish men Happy Christmas. 12 noon G.O.C., Brigade, visited Camp to wish men Happy Christmas. 1 p.m. The Commanding Officer visited each hut in the Camp while the men were having their Christmas Dinner, to wish them a Happy Christmas. Copy of Christmas Order read out in each hut attached. Special Order of the Day by General Sir Douglas Haig, G.O.C., British Armies in France, and telegram, also Greetings from the Army Commander and Staff, 2nd Army, received; copies attached.	
	26/12/16.		Company Training. 2.30 p.m. Inspection Transport by G.O.C., Division. On this occasion our Transport was rated the best in the Brigade by the General.	
	27/12/16.		Battalion engaged in fatigues.	

Army Form C. 2118.

WAR DIARY
or
INTELLIGENCE SUMMARY

(Erase heading not required.)

Instructions regarding War Diaries and Intelligence Summaries are contained in F. S. Regs., Part II. and the Staff Manual respectively. Title Pages will be prepared in manuscript.

Place	Date	Hour	Summary of Events and Information	Remarks and references to Appendices
ST.ELOI LEFT.	28/12/16.		Battalion relieved 11th "Queen's" in the line. Relief complete 5 p.m. Vide Operation Order 36 attached.	
	29/12/16.		Battalion in trenches.	
	30/12/16		do	
	31/12/16		do	
			Draft of 47 Other Ranks arrived from Base, and taken on strength. Casualties for period December 28 – 31st, Nil. Strength of Battalion. Officers 36. Other Ranks 848.	

John C Beadle Capt.

Lieut. Colonel,
Commanding 11th Bn. The Queen's Own
(Royal West Kent) Regt. (Lewisham).

S E C R E T.   OPERATION ORDER No. 31.   Copy No. 4

by Lieut. A.W. Puttick,
Commanding 11th Bn. Royal West Kent Regt.

1st December, 1916.

1. The Battalion will relieve the 11th Queen's Royal West Surrey Rgt. tomorrow, and will take over trenches as hereunder, namely:-

    Right Front Coy.   "C" Coy.
    Left Front Coy.   "B" Coy.
    Right Support Coy.   "A" Coy.
    Left Support Coy.   "D" Coy.

2. Reveille 7.15 a.m.
3. Breakfasts 7.45 a.m.
4. Order and time of March:-

    Lewis Gunners will move off at ......9.15 a.m.
    Signallers (Hd.Qrs.) " " " ......9.20 a.m.
    "B" Coy will " " " ......9.25 a.m.
    "C" Coy. " " " " ......9.35 a.m.
    "D" Coy. " " " " ......9.50 a.m.
    Headquarters " " " ......10 a.m.
    "A" Coy " " " ......10.10 a.m.

Company Signallers will report to the O.C. Companies to which they are attached and will march with their companies.

Snipers will move as a Platoon of "C" Company.

Platoon Commanders must not, on any pretext, halt their men in DICKEBUSCHE.

Platoons to march at 100 yards distance.

Company Commanders will insist that these orders are observed. They are reminded that these are Divisional Orders.

5. The Battalion will halt and rest at H.27.d.4.1. The Cookers will be sent on earlier, and will have a hot meal ready for the men.

O.C. Companies are responsible that all papers, tins, etc, are buried.

6. The Companies will move off from here as follows:-

    Lewis Gunners...........at 11.45 a.m. (under Lieut.G.Gordon-Smith.
    Signallers (Headquarters) 12 a.m.
    "B" Coy....................12.15 a.m.
    "C" Coy....................12.25 a.m.
    "D" Coy....................12.40 a.m.
    Headquarters...............12.50 a.m.
    "A" Coy....................1 p.m.

7. The Lewis Guns will be taken up by Transport this afternoon, with 2 men per gun. Cpl. Nightingale will be in charge of this party.

He will arrange to change over the "Queens" guns for our own, during the course of tomorrow morning.

8. Officers Mess Boxes, and Trench Bundles, will be stacked in "A" Coys Officer's hut. Officers Servants will remain behind with these and come up with the Transport in the evening, and they will also act as a loading party.

9. Blankets in <u>bundles</u> of <u>10</u> and mens' packs <u>properly labelled</u> will be stacked before moving off, as previously.

O.C. Coys. will see that Officers Valises are given over to their C.Q.M.S.'s, and stacked in "D" Coys stores, before moving off.

10. List of Trench Stores taken over will be forwarded to the Adjutant immediately after the relief is completed.

11. The relief will be carried out as quietly and carefully as possible, and completion reported to Battalion H.Q. by phone Code Word "WETTER".

                                              P.T.O.

-2-

12. All waterbottles will be filled before moving off.

13. Company Commanders will be held responsible for the cleanliness of their Huts, Lines, Latrines, Wash-houses, etc.

14. Company Commanders should hand their Company Conduct Sheets into the Orderly Room this evening, and obtain a receipt for same.

15. O.C. "A" Company will please detail a fatigue party of 30 men under an Officer, to report to the Asst. Adjutant at Battalion Headquarters at 5 p.m. tomorrow.

16. O.C. "B", "C", & "D" Coys will arrange each for a guide to report to the Asst. Adjutant at 6 p.m. tomorrow, at Battalion Headquarters to guide ration party to Companies.

17. O.C. "B" and "C" Coys. will please arrange to have a "TEST S.O.S." during the first night in the trenches.

A full report should be forwarded to Battalion Headquarters, stating the time taken - from handing in the telephone message until the shell passes over the trench.

              (Sgd). A. W. Puttick. Lieut.
      Commanding 11th Bn. Royal West Kent Regt.
                   (Lewisham).

Copy No.		No.	
1.	C.O.	9.	Lewis Gun Offr.
2.	Asst. Adjutant.	10.	Medical Offr.
3.	Office Copy.	11.	Quartermaster.
4.	War Diary.	12.	Transport Offr.
5.	O.C. "A" Coy.	13.	Sniping Cpl.
6.	O.C. "B" "	14.	Signalling Offr.
7.	O.C. "C" "	15.	R. S. M.
8.	O.C. "D" "	16.	O.C. 11th R.W. Surrey Rgt.

War Diary

SECRET.　　　OPERATION ORDERS No.26.　　　Copy No. 4
　　　　　　　　By Lieut.Col. A.C.Corfe,
　　　　　　　　　Commanding 11th Bn.R.West Kent Regt.

　　　　　　　　　　　　　　　　　　7th November, 1916.

1. The Battalion will relieve the 11th Queen's Royal West Surrey Regt. tomorrow, and will take over trenches as last time, namely :-
    - Right Front Coy.　　"A" Coy.
    - Left Front Coy.　　 "D" "
    - Right Support Coy.　"C" "
    - Left Support Coy.　 "B" "

2. Reveille 6.15 a.m.

3. Breakfasts 6.45 a.m.

4. Order and time of March :-
    - Lewis Gunners will move off at ...7.50 a.m.
    - "D" Coy.　"　"　"　"　...8.0 a.m.
    - "A" "　　 "　"　"　"　...8.15 a.m.
    - "B" "　　 "　"　"　"　...8.25 a.m.
    - "C" "　　 "　"　"　"　...8.35 a.m.
    - Headquarters "　"　"　"　...8.45 a.m.

    Signallers will report to the O.C. Companies to which they are attached and will march with their Companies.
    Snipers will move as a Platoon of "A" Coy.
    Platoons to march at 100 yards distance.
    Company Commanders will insist that this interval is kept. They are reminded that this is a Divisional order

5. The Battalion will halt and rest at H.27.d.4.1. The Cookers will be sent on earlier, and will have a hot meal ready for the men.

6. The Companies will move off from here as follows :-
    - Lewis Gunners at 12 noon (under 2/Lieut.Donnet).
    - "D" Coy.　　"　12.30 p.m.
    - "A" "　　　 "　12.40 p.m.
    - "B" "　　　 "　12.50 p.m.
    - "C" "　　　 "　1 p.m.
    - Headquarters "　1.10 p.m.

7. The Lewis Guns will be taken up by Transport this afternoon, with 2 men per Gun. Corpl. Hayden, will be in charge of this party.
    He will arrange to change over the "Queen's" Guns for our own, during the course of tomorrow morning.

8. Officers Mess Boxes and Trench Bundles, will be stacked at the Q.M. Stores before moving off. Officers servants will remain behind with these and come up with the Transport in the evening, and they will also act as a loading party.

9. Blankets in bundles of 10, and mens' packs properly labelled, will be stacked before moving off, in accordance with details already arranged. O.C. Coys. will see that officers Valises are given over to their C.Q.M.S's, and stacked in "D" Coys. Stores, before moving off.

10. A list of Trench Stores taken over will be forwarded to the Adjutant immediately after the relief is completed.

11. The relief will be carried out as quietly and carefully as possible, and completion reported to Battalion H.Q. by phone, Code Word "WETTER".

12. All waterbottles will be filled before moving off.

13. Company Commanders will be held responsible for the cleanliness of their Huts, Lines, Latrines, Washhouses, etc.

14. Company Commanders should hand their Company Conduct Sheets into the Orderly Room this evening, and obtain a receipt for same.

15. O.C. "C" Company will please detail a fatigue party of 30 men under an Officer, to report to the Assistant Adjutant at Battalion Head-Quarters at 5.30 p.m. tomorrow.　　　　　　　　　　　　　P.T.O.

16. O.C. "A", "B" & "D" Coys., will arrange each for a guide to report to the Asst. Adjutant, at 6.30 p.m. tomorrow, at Battalion Headquarters, to guide ration party to Companies.

       (Sgd) A. C. Corfe, Lt. Colonel.
         Commanding 11th Bn. R. West Kent Regt.

Copy No. 1	C.O.	No. 9.	Lewis Gun Offr.
2	Adjutant.	10.	Medical Offr.
3	Office Copy.	11.	Quartermaster.
4	War Diary.	12.	Transport Sgt.
5	O.C. "A" Coy.	13.	Sniping Sgt.
6	O.C. "B" "	14.	Signalling Sgt.
7	O.C. "C" "	15.	Asst. Adjutant.
8	O.C. "D" "		

SECRET.   OPERATION ORDER NO. 33.   Copy No. 4
by Lieut. A.W.Puttick,
Commanding 11th Bn.R.West Kent Rgt.

7th December, 1916.

1. The Battalion will be relieved by the 11th "Queen's" tomorrow, relief starting at 4.30 p.m.

2. Opposite numbers will take over in the order in which they relieve, and Platoons will march off independently. Company Commanders will report to Battalion Headquarters as soon as relief is complete. Code words "O.O.33 complied with".

3. All movement will be by platoons at not less than 100 yards distance

4. Maps, Aeroplane Photographs and Trench Stores, are to be handed over to incoming Unit, and a copy of receipts for Trench Stores handed in to Battalion Headquarters after relief.
Periscopes and Sniperscopes, may be handed over to opposite number at the discretion of Company Commanders, a separate receipt in duplicate for these being obtained. (These must NOT be confounded with Trench Store Returns.)

5. Officers Trench Bundles, Mess Boxes, Blankets, etc, will be sent to Battalion Headquarters by 2 p.m. - each Company will detail a fatigue party for this, and also 4 men per Company to accompany Transport back to Camp in charge of their own Company property.

6. O.C. "A" Company will detail a fatigue party of 1 Officer & 20 men to report at Battalion Headquarters at 3 p.m., and will receive instructions there. These men must report with full equipment ready for moving off.

7. Company Cookers and Transport, under Coy.Quartermaster Sergts. will meet the Battalion on the road behind DICKEBUSCH about H.27.c.9.5., where men will rest and have tea.

8. Two cooks per company under Sgt.Finch, will report to Battalion Headquarters at 2 p.m. and will proceed to H.27.c.9.5.

9. Companies will occupy exactly the same accommodation as they left at ALBERTA CAMP.

10. Trenches must be left clean and in good order. A certificate signed by the Officer Commanding opposite number to be obtained and handed in to the Orderly Room with the Trench Store Returns on arrival at Rest Billet. Fires will be left in the Cook-houses, also tins of water.

11. Company Commanders are responsible that all Gum Boots are handed over in as dry a condition as possible (in the manner in which they would like to receive them). On no account are any Gum Boots to be taken out of the Trenches.

12. Surplus blankets etc., will be brought to Battalion H.Q. by 3 p.m. today, to relieve the pressure tomorrow night.

(Sgd) A.W.Puttick. Lieut.
Commanding 11th Bn.R.West Kent Regt.
(Lewisham)

Copy No.1 C.O.
2. Adjutant.   No.9. O.C. "D" Coy.
3. Asst.Adjt.   10. Lewis Gun Offr.
4. War Diary.   11. Signalling Offr.
5. Office Copy.   12. Sniping N.C.O.
6. O.C. "A" Coy.   13. Quartermaster.
7. O.C. "B" "   14. Transport Offr.
8. O.C. "C" "   15. R.S.M.
                            16. O.C. 11th "Queen's" R.W.S.Rgt.

SECRET.   OPERATION ORDER NO.34   Copy No. 5
by Lieut.Col.A.C.Corfe,
Commanding 11th Battn. "The Queen's Own"
Royal West Kent Regt. (Lewisham).

13th December, 1916.

1. The Battalion will relieve the 11th "Queen's" Royal West Surrey Regt. tomorrow, and will take over trenches as hereunder, namely:-
   - Right Front Coy.   "A" Coy.
   - Left Front Coy.   "B" "
   - Right Support Coy. "C" "
   - Left Support Coy.   "D" "

2. Reveille 7.15 a.m.
3. Breakfasts 7.45 a.m.
4. Order and time of March:-
   - Lewis Gunners will move off at .... 9.30 a.m.
   - Signallers (Headqrs) " " " .... 9.35 a.m.
   - "B" Coy. will move off at .... 9.40 a.m.
   - "A" "   "   "   "   " .... 9.50 a.m.
   - "D" "   "   "   "   " .... 10.5 a.m.
   - Headquarters " " " .... 10.15 a.m.
   - "C" Coy.   " " " .... 10.25 a.m.

   Company Signallers will report to the O.C. Companies to which they are attached, and will march with their company.
   Snipers will move as a Platoon of "A" Company.
   Platoon Commanders must not on any pretext halt their men in DICKEBUSCH.   Platoons to march at 100 yards distance.
   Company Commanders will insist that these orders are observed. They are reminded that these are Divisional Orders.

5. The Battalion will halt and rest at H.27.c.4.1.   The Cookers will be sent on earlier and will have a hot meal ready for the men.
   O.C. Companies are responsible that all papers, tins, etc., are buried.

6. The Companies will move off from here as follows:-
   - Lewis Gunners at 11.45 a.m. under Lt.G.Gordon-Smith.
   - Signallers (Headqrs)   12 noon.
   - "B" Coy.   12.15 p.m.
   - "A" "   12.25 p.m.
   - "D" "   12.40 p.m.
   - Headquarters   12.50 p.m.
   - "C" Coy.   1 p.m.

7. The Lewis Guns will be taken up by Transport this afternoon with 2 men per gun. Sgt. Hayden will be in charge of this party. He will arrange to change over the "Queen's" Guns for our own, during the course of tomorrow morning.

8. Officers Mess Boxes and Trench Bundles will be stacked in "A" Coys Officers Hut. Officers servants will remain behind with these and come up with the Transport in the evening, and they will also act as a loading party.

9. Each man will carry his pack, and leave his surplus kit in a sandbag.
   Blankets in bundles of 10 and sandbags properly labelled, will be stacked before moving off.   O.C. Companies will see that Officers Valises are given over to their C.Q.M.S's, and stacked in "D" Coys' stores before moving off.

10. List of Trench Stores taken over will be forwarded to the Adjutant immediately after the relief is completed.

P.T.O.

- 2 -

11. The relief will be carried out as quietly and carefully as possible, and completion reported to Battalion H.Q. by phone, Code Word "WETTER".

12. All waterbottles will be filled before moving off.

13. Company Commanders will be held responsible for the cleanliness of their Huts, Lines, Latrines, Wash-houses, Officers Mess Cook-houses etc.

14. Company Commanders will hand their Company Conduct Sheets into the Orderly Room this evening and obtain a receipt for same.

15. O.C. "C" Company will please detail a fatigue of 30 men under an Officer, to report to the Assistant Adjutant at Battalion H.Q. at 5 p.m. tomorrow.

16. O.C. "A", "B" & "D" Companies, will arrange each for a guide to report to the Assistant Adjutant at 7 p.m. tomorrow at Battalion Headqrs. to guide ration parties to companies.

17. O.C. "A" & "B" Coys., will please arrange to have a test "S.O.S." each night in the trenches. A full report on each occasion should be forwarded to Battalion Headqrs. by 9 a.m., stating the time taken from handing in the telephone message until the shell passes over the trench.

(Sgd) A.C.Corfe. Lt.Col.
Commanding 11th Battn."The Queen'sOwn"
Royal West Kent Regt. (Lewisham).

Copy No. 1 C.O.   9. O.C. "D" Coy.
        2. Adjutant,   10. Lewis Gun Offr.
        3. Asst. Adjt.   11. Quartermaster,
        4. Office Copy.   12. Transport Offr.
        5. War Diary.   13. Sniping Sergt.
        6. O.C. "A" Coy   14. Signalling Offr.
        7. O.C. "B" "   15. R.S.M.
        8. O.C. "C" "   16. O.C. 11th Queen's.R.W.S.Rgt.

S E C R E T.   OPERATION ORDER NO.35   Copy No. 4
              by Lieut. Col. A. C. Corfe
              Commanding 11th Bn. The "Queens Own"
                     Royal West Kent Regt.

                                        20th December, 1916.

1. The Battalion will be relieved by the 11th "Queens" tomorrow, relief starting at a time to be notified later.

2. Opposite numbers will take over in the order in which they relieve, and platoons will march off independently. Company Commanders will report to Battalion Headquarters as soon as relief is complete. Code words "O.O. 35 complied with."

3. All movement will be by platoons at not less than 100 yards distance.

4. Maps, aeroplane photographs, trench stores, are to be handed over to incoming unit, and a copy of receipts for Trench Stores handed in to Battalion Headquarters after relief. Periscopes & sniperscopes may be handed over to opposite number at the discretion of Company Commanders, a separate receipt in duplicate for these being obtained. (These must not be confounded with Trench Store Returns.)

5. Officers trench bundles, mess boxes, blankets, etc, will be sent to Battalion Headquarters by 2 p.m.- Each Company will detail a fatigue party for this, and also 4 men per Company, Headquarters included, to accompany Transport back to Camp in charge of their own Company property.

6. O.C. "C" Company will detail a fatigue party of 1 Officer and 20 men to report at Battalion Headquarters at a time to be notified later, and will receive instructions there. These men must report with full equipment ready for moving off.

7. Company cookers and transport, under Company Quartermaster Sergeants, will meet the Battalion on the road behind DICKEBUSCH about H.27.c.9.5., there men will rest and have tea.

8. Two cooks per Company under Sergt. Finch will report to Battalion Headquarters at 3 p.m. and will proceed to H.27.c.9.5.

9. Companies will occupy exactly the same accommodation as they left at ALBERTA CAMP.

10. Trenches must be left clean and in good order. A certificate signed by the Officer commanding Company taking over to be obtained and handed in to the Orderly Room with the Trench Store Returns on arrival at Rest Billet. Fires will be left in the cookhouses, also tins of water.

11. Company Commanders are responsible that all gum boots are handed over in as dry a condition as possible . (in the manner in which they would like to receive them). On no account are any gum boots to be taken out of the trenches.

12. Surplus blankets etc., will be brought to Battalion Headquarters by 3 p.m. to-day to relieve the pressure tomorrow night.

13. Immediately on return to camp O.C. Companies will render a return showing approximate number of all men available for fatigues in their Companies.

              (Sgd) A. C. Corfe, Lieut. Colonel,
                 Commanding 11th Bn. The "Queens Own" Royal
                        West Kent Regiment. (Lewisham).

Copy No. 1. C.O.   6. O.C. "A" Coy.   11. S.O.   16. O.C.
         2. Adjt.   7. C.C. "B" "   12. Snip. N.C.O.   11th Queens.
         3. Asst. Adjt.   8. C.C. "C" "   13. Q.M.   17. M.O.
         4. War Diary.   9. C.C. "D" "   14. T.O.
         5. Office Copy.   10. L.G.O.   15. R.S.M.

CHRISTMAS ORDER.

I wish to convey to all Officers, N.C.O.'s, and men of the Battalion under my Command, my heartiest Christmas Greetings. Although it is impossible to give you all the good things you deserve, and are accustomed to have at Christmas time, I trust you will take the will for the deed, and make the most of any little comforts that have been provided for you.

I take this opportunity of thanking you all for your very loyal devotion to duty - by which you have gained for the Battalion a reputation second to none in the Division. To those old members of the 11th, and more especially the Warrant Officers, and N.C.O.'s who spent last Christmas with us at Aldershot I would tender my special thanks. To the new drafts who have so speedily become acclimatised to Trench life, and who have so well upheld the name of the Regiment my thanks are also due. There may be much hard, and dreary work in front of us, but if it is faced by all ranks with the same spirit that you have always shown, then the work will seem, not quite so hard and dreary, and the night less dark and long.

Again wishing you all the best of Christmas Greetings, and with the hope that next Christmas may see us all at home with our loved ones, and a lasting victory gained by us.

[signature] Lt. Colonel.

Commanding 11th Bn. "The Queens Own" Royal West Kent Regiment. (Lewisham).

25th December, 1916.

S E C R E T. OPERATION ORDER No. 56.   Copy No. 5
by Lieut. Col. A.C. Corfe,
Commanding 11th Bn. "The Queen's Own
Royal West Kent Regiment.(Lewisham).

27th December, 1916.

1. The Battalion will relieve the 11th "Queen's" Royal West Surrey Regt tomorrow, and will take over trenches as hereunder, namely:-
   Right Front Coy.   "A" Coy.
   Left Front Coy.   "D" "
   Right Support Coy.   "C" "
   Left Support Coy.   "B" "

2. Reveille 7.15 a.m.
3. Breakfasts 7.45 a.m.

4. Order and time of march:-
   Lewis Gunners will move off at .... 10 a.m.
   Signallers (Headqrs.) " " " .... 10.5 a.m.
   "D" Coy.   " " " " .... 10.10 a.m.
   "A" "   " " " " .... 10.20 a.m.
   "B" "   " " " " .... 10.35 a.m.
   Headquarters   " " " " .... 10.45 a.m.
   "C" Coy.   " " " " .... 10.55 a.m.

   Company Signallers will report to the O.C. Companies to which they are attached, and will march with their Company.
   Snipers will move as a Platoon of "A" Company.
   Platoon Commanders must not on any pretext halt their men in DICKEBUSCH. Platoons to march at 100 yards distance.
   Company Commanders will insist that these orders are observed. They are reminded that these are Divisional Orders.

5. The Battalion will halt and rest at H.27.d.4.1.. The cookers will be sent on earlier and will have a hot meal ready for the men.
   O.C. Companies are responsible that all papers, tins, etc, are buried.

6. The Companies will move off from here as follows:-
   Lewis Gunners at 12.15 p.m. under Lt. G. Gordon-Smith.
   Signallers (Headqrs.)   12.30 p.m.
   "D" Coy.   12.45 p.m.
   "A" "   12.55 p.m.
   "B" "   1.10 p.m.
   Headquarters.   1.20 p.m.
   "C" Coy.   1.30 p.m.

7. The Lewis Guns will be taken up by Transport this afternoon with 2 men per gun. Cpl. Nightingale will be in charge of this party. He will arrange to change over the "Queen's" guns for our own, during the course of tomorrow morning.

8. Officers Mess Boxes and Trench Bundles will be stacked in "A" Coys. Officers Hut. Officers servants will remain behind with these and come up with the Transport in the evening, and they will also act as a loading party.

9. Each man will carry his pack, and leave his surplus kit in a sandbag.
   Blankets in bundles of 10 and sandbags properly labelled, will be stacked before moving off. O.C. Companies will see that Officers Valises are given over to their C.Q.M.S.'s, and stacked in "D" Coys. stores before moving off.

10. List of Trench Stores taken over will be forwarded to the Adjutant immediately after the relief is completed.

11. The relief will be carried out as quietly and carefully as possible, & completion reported to Battalion H.Q. by 'phone, Code Word "DRIER".

P.T.O.

12. All waterbottles will be filled before moving off.

13. Company Commanders will be held responsible for the cleanliness of their Huts, Lines, Latrines, Wash-houses, Officers Mess Cook-houses etc.

14. Company Commanders will hand their Company Conduct Sheets into the Orderly Room this evening and obtain a receipt for same.

15. O.C. "C" Company will please detail a fatigue party of 20 men under an Officer, to report to the Assistant Adjutant at Battalion H.Q. at 5 p.m. tomorrow.

16. O.C. "A", "B", & "D" Companies, will arrange each for a guide to report to the Assistant Adjutant at 5 p.m. tomorrow at Battalion Headquarters to accompany ration party, take over from his C.Q.M.S., and guide ration party to Company.

17. O.C. "A" & "D" Companies, will please arrange to have a test "S.O.S." each night in the trenches. A full report on each occasion should be forwarded to Battalion Headquarters by 9 a.m., stating the time taken from handing in the telephone message until the shell passes over the trench

(Sgd). A.C.Corfe,Lt. Colonel
Commanding 11th Battn. "The Queen's Own" Royal
West Kent Regiment. (Lewisham).

Copy No. 1. C. O.
2. Adjutant.
3. Asst. Adjt.
4. Office Copy.
5. War Diary.
6. O.C. "A" Coy.
7. O.C. "B" "
8. O.C. "C" "
9. O.C. "D" "
10. Lewis Gun Officer.
11. Quartermaster.
12. Transport Officer.
13. Sniping Sergeant.
14. Signalling Officer.
15. R.S.M.
16. O.C. 11th "Queen's"R.W.S.Rgt.
17. Medical Officer.

SPECIAL ORDER OF THE DAY
by
General Sir Douglas Haig,
G.C.B.,G.C.V.O.,K.C.I.E.,A.D.C.,
Commander-in-Chief British Armies in France.

CHRISTMAS MESSAGES FROM HIS MAJESTY THE KING.

No. 1.

I send you my sailors and soldiers hearty good wishes for Christmas and the New Year. My grateful thoughts are ever with you for victories gained, for hardships endured, and for your unfailing cheeriness. Another Christmas has come round and we are still at War, but the Empire confident in you remains determined to win.

MAY GOD BLESS AND PROTECT YOU.

GEORGE R.I.

No. 2.

At this Christmastide, the Queen and I are thinking more than ever of the sick and wounded among my sailors and soldiers. From our hearts we wish them strength to bear their sufferings, speedy restoration to health, a peaceful Christmas and many happier years to come.

GEORGE R.I.

D. Haig, Genl.
Commander-in-Chief,
British Armies in
France.

The following wire was received from Sir Douglas Haig to-day.-
"I desire to convey to all ranks under my Command my hearty good wishes for Christmas and the New Year. It is indeed a pleasure to command such Officers and men, and feel confident that the magnificent qualities they have already shown in the face of the enemy will carry our arms to ultimate victory."

The Army Commander and Staff, Second Army, send their Best Wishes for 'Xmas to all ranks of the Second Army, and wish them continued success in the New Year. Christmas, 1916. H. Q., Second Army.

11 R W Kent Regt
Vol 9

Army Form C. 2118.

SUMMARY

(heading not required.)

	Summary of Events and Information	Remarks and references to Appendices

...L BANK Sector. Strength of Battalion, Officers
... by 11th "Queen's" R.W. Surrey Regt., & proceeded by
...ALBERTA CAMP, RENINGHELST. Vide O.O. 37 attached.
...r period 1st & 2nd January, 2 Other Ranks killed, 5 wounded.
...A. SIMPSON and A.J. ELLERAY joined for duty from G.H.Q.
...el.
...n engaged on fatigues for R.E. Draft of 29 Other Ranks arrived
...ase and taken on strength.
..., Day, and Baths at RENINGHELST.
...tice of scheme of work, attached, for inspection by G.O.C., Division.
...talion inspected on work, as per attached schedule, by G.O.C., 41st
...vision. Strength of Battalion, Officers 36, Other Ranks 875.
Draft of 16 Other Ranks arrived from Base & taken on strength.
Battalion relieved the 11th "Queen's" in the SPOIL BANK Sector. Vide O.O.
38 attached.
Draft of 132 for the Battalion in training at STEENVOORDE.
Battalion in trenches.
Lieut. R.G. ROGERS rejoined the Battalion for duty from the Base.
Notice received of Capt. G.F. PRAGNELL being appointed Staff Captain.
Strength of Battalion, Officers 35, Other Ranks 1015.
Battalion relieved by the 11th "Queen's" & proceeded by route march to
ALBERTA CAMP, RENINGHELST, vide O.O. 39 attached.
Casualties for period January 7 – 14th, 2 Other Ranks wounded.
Rest Day, except for a fatigue party of 60 Other Ranks.
Company Training.
Lieut. F. GAMM, R.A.M.C., appointed M.O. of the Battalion vice Captain
T. McCririck, R.A.M.C., sick to Hospital
Battalion engaged on fatigues.
Lieut. J.H. ASHTON to M.G. Corps.
2/Lieut. H.W.H. BOTHAMLEY, sick to England.
Lieut. Col. A.C. CORFE having proceeded to England on leave, Captain
J.C. Beadle assumed Command.
Battalion bathing, and Company Training.

...GHELST	14/1/17	
	15/1/17	
	16/1/17	
	17/1/17	
	18/1/17	

WAR DIARY
or
INTELLIGENCE SUMMARY

(Erase heading not required.)

Army Form C. 2118.

Place	Date	Hour	Summary of Events and Information	Remarks and references to Appendices
RENINGHELST	19/1/17		Lieut. R. KERR temporary attached to 122nd Infantry Brigade for instructional purposes.	2
	20/1/17		Battalion partially engaged in fatigues, and also in bombing practice. 2/Lieuts. E.O.E.AYLETT, L.W. HUDSON, & E.C.H. SALMON joined for duty from the Base.	
	21/1/17		Company Training. Strength of Battalion, Officers 38, Other Ranks, 1005. Battalion relieved the 11th "Queen's" R.W. Surrey Regt. in the trenches. O.O. 40 attached.	
ST. ELOI	22/1/17		Battalion in trenches.	
	23/1/17		do	
	24/1/17		do	
	25/1/17		do	
	26/1/17		do Casualties for period 21-26/1/17, 1 O.R.killed, 1 O.R. wded.	
RENINGHELST	27/1/17		Battalion relieved in) trenches by the 11th "Queen's" R.W. Surrey Regt. and proceeded by route march to ALBERTA CAMP, RENINGHELST, arriving in Camp at 8.30 p.m. Vide O.O. No. 41 attached. Strength of Battalion, Officers 38, Other Ranks 998.	
	28/1/17		Battalion engaged on fatigues.	
	29/1/17		Company Training and baths.	
	30/1/17		Company Training and fatigues. details attached	
	31/1/17		Battalion engaged in tactical operation during morning Company Training in the afternoon.	

1/2/17.

[signature]
Captain,
Commanding 11th Bn. The Queen's Own (Royal West Kent) Regiment.

S E C R E T.   OPERATION ORDER No. 37.   Copy No. 4
by Lieut. Col. A.C. Corfe,
Commanding 11th Bn. The Queen's Own
(Royal West Kent) Regiment.

1st January, 1918.

1. The Battalion will be relieved by the 11th "Queen's" tomorrow, relief starting at 4.30 p.m.

2. Opposite numbers will take over in the order in which they relieve, and platoons will march off independently. Company Commanders will report to Battalion Headquarters as soon as relief is complete. Code words " O.O. 37 complied with."

3. All movement will be by platoons at not less than 100 yards distance

4. Maps, aeroplane photographs, trench stores, are to be handed over to incoming unit, and a copy of receipts for Trench Stores handed in to Battalion Headquarters after relief. Periscopes & sniperscopes may be handed over to opposite number at the discretion of Company Commanders, a separate receipt in duplicate for these being obtained. (These must not be confounded with Trench Store Returns.)

5. Officers trench bundles, mess boxes, blankets, etc, will be sent to Battalion Headquarters by 2 p.m.. Each Company will detail a fatigue party for this, and also 4 men per Company, Headquarters included, to accompany Transport back to Camp in charge of their own Company property.

6. O.C. "A" Company will detail a fatigue party of 1 Officer & 20 men to report at Battalion Headquarters at 3 p.m., and will receive instructions there. These men must report with full equipment ready for moving off.

7. Company cookers and transport, under Company Quartermaster Sergeants, will meet the Battalion on the road behind DICKEBUSCH about H.27.d.8.2., there men will rest and have tea.

8. Two cooks per Company, under Sergt. Finch, will report to Battalion Headquarters at 2 p.m., and will proceed to H.27.d.8.2..

9. Companies will occupy exactly the same accommodation as they left at ALBERTA CAMP.

10. Trenches must be left clean and in good order. A certificate to this effect signed by the Officer commanding Company taking over to be obtained & handed in to the Orderly Room with the Trench Store Returns on arrival at Rest Billet. Fires will be left in the cookhouses, also tins of water.

11. Company Commanders are responsible that all gum boots are handed over in as dry a condition as possible. (in the manner in which they would like to receive them). On no account are any gum boots to be taken out of the trenches.

12. Surplus blankets, etc. will be brought to Battalion Headquarters by 3.45 p.m. to-day to relieve the pressure tomorrow night.

13. Immediately on return to Camp, O.C. Companies will render a return showing approximate number of all men available for fatigues in their Companies.

(Sgd) A. C. Corfe, Lieut. Colonel,
Commanding 11th Bn. The Queen's Own
(Royal West Kent) Regiment.(Lewisham)

Copy No.1. C.O.   6. O.C. "A" Coy.   11. S.O.
        2. Adjt.   7. O.C. "B" "   12. Snip. N.C.O.
        3. Asst. Adjt. 8. O.C. "C" "   13. Q.M.
        4. War Diary.   9. O.C. "D" "   14. T.O.
        5. Office Copy. 10. L.G.O.   15. R.S.M.
                                             16. O.C. 11th "QUEEN'S.
                                             17. M.O.

11TH BATTALION ROYAL WEST KENT REGIMENT.

PROGRAMME OF WORK FOR 5TH & 6TH JAN. '17.

"A" Coy.

9 a.m. to 1 p.m.
Route March with Coy. Lewis Guns. Attack scheme during March.

2 to 4.30 p.m.
Bayonet Fighting 2 to 3 p.m.
Musketry –
Fire Control)
Fire Discipline) 3 to 4.30 p.m.

"B" Coy.

9 a.m. – 10.30 a.m.
2 Platoons Bombing at Bde.T.W.Sch.
1 Platoon Bayonet Fighting.
1 Platoon Rapid Loading.

10.30 – 12 noon.
2 Platoons Bombing at Bde.T.W.Sch.
1 Platoon Bayonet Fighting.
1 Platoon Rapid Loading.

12-1
Gas Helmet Drill
Gas Lecture.

2 – 4.30 p.m.
Practise attack, Open warfare, extended order.

"C" Coy.

9 – 11 a.m.
1 Platoon Gas Helmet Drill & Gas Lecture.
1 Platoon Wiring.
2 Platoons Musketry, Fire Control, Fire discipline.

11 a.m. – 1 p.m.
4 Platoons Attack Practise.

2 – 4.30 p.m.
Visual training & extended order drill – 2 platoons.
Bombing 2 "

"D" Coy.

9 – 11 a.m.
Practise attack Open Warfare with Lewis Guns.

11 – 12
Bayonet Fighting 3 Platoons.
Wiring – 1 Platoon.

12 noon – 1 p.m.
Gas Helmet Drill.
Gas Lecture.

2 – 4.30 p.m.
Musketry – Rapid Loading.
Fire Control.
" Discipline.

SIGNAL SECTION.

	SENIOR CLASS.	**JUNIOR CLASS.**
9 – 10 a.m.	Flag Drill.	Flag Drill.
10 – 11 a.m.	Lamp Reading by day.	Station Work – Flags.
11 – 12 noon	Practise with discs & shutters.	Practise with discs and shutters.
12 – 1 p.m.	Station work with discs and shutters.	Station work with discs and shutters.
2 – 3 p.m.	Buzzing for both classes.	
3 – 4.30 p.m.	Lecture. Map reading as affecting signalling.	

LEWIS GUNNERS.

Lewis Gunners when not with their companies, will parade under arrangements made by Lieut. G. Gordon-Smith.

(Signed) A. Cox

Lt. Colonel.
Commanding 11th Bn. Royal West Kent Regiment.

SECRET.   OPERATION ORDER No.38.   Copy No. 5.
by Lieut. Col. A.C. Corfe,
Commanding 11th Bn. The Queen's Own
(Royal West Kent) Regt.(Lewisham).

6th January, 1917.

1. The Battalion will relieve the 11th "Queen's" Royal West Surrey Regt. tomorrow, and will take over trenches as hereunder, namely:-
    Right Front Company   "C" Coy.
    Left Front Company   "B" "
    Right Support Coy.   "A" "
    Left Support Company.   "D" "

2. Reveille 7.15 a.m.
3. Breakfasts 7.45 a.m.

4. Order and time of march:-
    Signallers (Headqrs)..........................10.5 a.m.
    "B" Company...................................10.10 a.m.
    "C" " ....10.20 a.m.
    "D" " ....10.35 a.m.
    Headquarters..................................10.45 a.m.
    "A" Company...................................10.55 a.m.
   Lewis Gunners and Company Signallers will report to the O.C. Companies to which they are attached, and will march witht their Companies.
   Snipers will move as a platoon of "C" Company.
   Platoon Commanders must not on any pretext halt their men in DICKEBUSCH. Platoons to march at 100 yards distance.
   Company Commanders will insist that these orders are observed, They are reminded that these are Divisional Orders.

5. The Battalion will halt and rest at H.27.d.8.2.. The cookers will be sent on earlier and will have a hot meal ready for the men.
   O.C. Companies are responsible that all papers, tins, etc, are buried.

6. The Companies will move off from here as follows:-
    Signallers (Headqrs.).........................12.30 p.m.
    "B" Company...................................12.45 p.m.
    "C" " ....12.55 p.m.
    "D" " ....1.10 p.m.
    Headquarters..................................1.20 p.m.
    "A" Company...................................1.30 p.m.

7. The Lewis Guns will be taken up by Transport this afternoon with 2 men per gun. L/Cs Mackey and Dunn will be in charge of this party. They will arrange to change over the "Queen's" guns for our own during the course of tomorrow morning.

8. Officers Mess Boxes and Trench Bundles will be stacked in Medical Inspection Hut. Officers servants will remain behind with these and come up with the Transport in the evening, and they will also act as a loading party.

9. Each man will carry his pack, and leave his surplus kit in a sandbag.
   Blankets <u>in bundles of 10</u> and sandbags <u>properly labelled</u>, will be stacked before moving off. O.C. Companies will see that Officers Valises are given over to their C.Q.M.S.'s, and stacked in "D" Coy.'s stores before moving off.

10. List of trench stores taken over will be forwarded to the Adjutant immediately after the relief is completed.

11. The relief will be carried out as quietly and carefully as possible & completion reported to Battalion H.Q. by 'phone, Code Word "TIRED."

P.T.O.

-2-

12. All waterbottles will be filled before moving off.

13. Company Commanders will be held responsible for the cleanliness of their Huts, Lines, Latrines, Wash-houses, Officers Mess Cook-houses, etc.

14. Company Commanders will hand their Company Conduct Sheets into the Orderly Room this evening and obtain a receipt for same.

15. O.C. "A" Company will please detail a fatigue party of 20 men under an Officer, to report to the Asst. Adjutant at Battalion H.Q. at 5 p.m. tomorrow.

16. O.C. "B", "C", and "D" Companies, will arrange each for a guide to report to the Asst. Adjutant at 5 p.m. tomorrow at Battalion H.Q. to accompany ration party, take over from his C.Q.M.S., and guide ration party to Company.

17. O.C. "B" and "C" Companies will please arrange to have a test S.O.S. each night in the trenches. A full report on each occasion should be forwarded to Battalion Headquarters by 9 a.m. stating the time taken from handing in the telephone message until the shell passes over the trench.

         (Sgd) A. C. Corfe, Lieut. Colonel,
   Commanding 11th Bn. The Queen's Own (Royal West Kent)
          Regiment. (Lewisham).

Copy No.
1. C.O.
2. Adjutant.
3. Asst. Adjt.
4. Office Copy.
5. War Diary.
6. O.C. "A" Coy.
7. O.C. "B" "
8. O.C. "C" "
9. O.C. "D" "
10. Lewis Gun Officer.
11. Quartermaster.
12. Transport Officer.
13. Sniping Sergeant.
14. Signalling Officer.
15. R.S.M.
16. O.C., 11th "Queen's" R.W.S.R.
17. Medical Officer.

S E C R E T.   OPERATION ORDER NO.39   Copy No. 5.
by Lieut.Col. A.C.Corfe,
Commanding 11th Bn. "The Queen's Own"
Royal West Kent Regiment.

13th January, 1917.

1. The Battalion will be relieved by the 11th "Queen's" tomorrow, relief starting at 4.30 p.m.

2. Opposite numbers will take over in the order in which they relieve, and platoons will march off independently. Company Commanders will report to Battalion Headquarters as soon as relief is complete. Code Words "O.O.39 complied with"

3. All movement will be by platoons at not less than 100 yards distance.

4. Maps, Aeroplane photographs, trench stores, are to be handed over to incoming unit, and a copy of receipts for trench stores handed in to Battalion Headquarters after relief. Periscopes and Sniperscopes may be handed over to opposite number at the discretion of Company Commanders, a separate receipt in duplicate for these being obtained. (These must not be confounded with Trench Store Returns.).

5. Officers Trench Bundles, Mess Boxes, blankets, etc, will be sent to Battalion Headquarters by 2 p.m. Each Company will detail a fatigue party for this and also 4 men per company, Headquarters included, to accompany transport back to camp in charge of their own Company property.

6. C.C. "A" Company will detail a fatigue party of 1 Officer & 20 men to report at Battalion Headquarters at 3 p.m., and will receive instructions there. These men must report with full equipment ready for moving off.

7. Company Cookers and Transport, under Company Quartermaster Sergeant will meet the Battalion on the road behind DICKEBUSCH about H.27.d.8.2 There men will rest and have tea.

8. 2 cooks per Company under Sergt.Finch, will report at Battalion Headquarters at 2 p.m. and will proceed to H.27.d.8.2.

9. Companies will occupy exactly the same accommodation as they left at ALBERTA CAMP.

10. Trenches must be left clean and in good order. A certificate to this effect signed by the Officer Commanding Company taking over, to be obtained and handed into the Orderly Room with the Trench Store Returns on arrival at Rest Billet. Fires will be left in the Cookhouses, also tins of water.

11. Company Commanders are responsible that all gum boots are handed over in as dry a condition as possible, (in the manner in which they would like to receive them. On no account are any gum boots to be taken out of the trenches.

12. Surplus blankets and etc, will be brought to Battalion Headqrs. by 3.45 p.m. today to relieve the pressure tomorrow night.

13. Immediately on return to Camp, O.C. Companies will render a return shewing approximate number of all men available for fatigues in their Companies.

(Sgd) A. C. Corfe, Lieut. Colonel.
Commanding 11th Bn. "The Queen's Own"
(Royal West Kent Regt,) (Lewisham)

Copy No. 1. C.C.
2. A/2nd in Command.
3. Adjutant.
4. Asst.Adjt.
5. War Diary.
6. Office Copy.
7. O.C. "A" Coy.
8. O.C. "B" "
9. O.C. "C" "

No.10 O.C. "D" Coy.
11 Sig.Offr.
12 Sniping N.C.O.
13 Lewis Gun Sgt.
14 Q.M.
15 Transport Offr.
16 Medical Offr.
17 D.S.M.
18 O.C. 11th "Queen's"

1177 BM
17

To:-
Headquarters,
122nd Infantry Brigade.

Report on Raid.

This morning an attempt was made to enter the enemy lines.

Object:- To obtain prisoners and all information possible about the enemy trenches.

Organisation.:- The party consisted of 2 Officers, 1 Sergeant, and 15 other ranks. 12 of these carried improvised knobkerries. All other ranks carried rifles and 4 bombs. 2 Officers and 8 men to enter trench, remainder to act as covering party.

Place of departure:- O.3.b.5.2.

Point reached :- O.3.b.6.1.

General Remarks :- The attempt was a regrettable but unavoidable failure. This was due to the snow which fell during the night. The enemy spotted the party almost immediately it got over the parapet, and by the time it reached enemy wire, the enemy were lining the parapet to receive it. 2 Machine Guns opened fire, a number of bombs were thrown, and there was continuous rifle fire.

As the raid was intended to take the enemy entirely by surprise it was decided to abandon the attempt for the night. All ranks returned safely in spite of a continuous fire.

Information :- The enemy line seems to be more thickly held than previously supposed. Enemy wire has been damaged here, but still creates an obstacle, most of it seems to be right on top of his parapet. No Man's alnd is wet but very fair going, plenty of cover, i.e. shell holes, old

old trenches, and a certain amount of dead ground.

Lt. Colonel.
Commanding 11th Battalion "The Queen's Own"
(Royal West Kent Regt) (Lewisham).

13/1/17.

SECRET.   OPERATION ORDER No. 40.   Copy No......
by Captain J.C. Beadle,
Commanding 11th Bn. The Queen's Own
(Royal West Kent) Regiment. (Lewisham).

20th January, 1917.

1. The Battalion will relieve the 11th "Queen's" Royal West Surrey Regt. tomorrow, and will take over trenches as hereunder, namely:-
   Right Front Company   "A" Company.
   Left Front Company   "D"   "
   Right Support Company   "C"   "
   Left Support Company   "B"   "

2. Reveille   7.15 a.m.

3. Breakfasts 7.45 a.m.

4. Order and time of march :-
   Signallers (Headquarters).............10.5 a.m.
   "D" Coy..............................10.10 a.m.
   "A" " ....10.20 a.m.
   "B" " ....10.35 a.m.
   Headquarters.........................10.45 a.m.
   "C" Coy..............................10.55 a.m.

   Lewis Gunners and Company Signallers will report to the O.C. Companies to which they are attached, and will march with their Companies.
   Snipers will move as a platoon of "A" Company.
   Platoon Commanders must not on any pretext halt their men in DICKEBUSCH. Platoons to march at 100 yards distance.
   Company Commanders will insist that these orders are observed. They are reminded that these are Divisional Orders.

5. The Battalion will halt and rest at H.27.d.8.2.. The cookers will be sent on earlier and will have a hot meal ready for the men.
   O.C. Companies are responsible that all papers, tins, etc, are buried.

6. The Companies will move off from here as follows :-
   Signallers (Headquarters).............12.30 p.m.
   "D" Coy..............................12.45 p.m.
   "A" Coy..............................12.55 p.m.
   "B" Coy..............................1.10 p.m.
   Headquarters.........................1.20 p.m.
   "C" Coy..............................1.30 p.m.

7. The Lewis Guns will be taken up by Transport this afternoon with 2 men per gun. L/Cps Hackey and Dunn will be in charge of this party. They will arrange to change over the "Queen's" guns for our own during the course of tomorrow morning.

8. Officers Mess Boxes and Trench Bundles will be stacked in the Mess Room of the Details Hut.. Officers servants will remain behind with these and come up with the Transport in the evening, and they will also act as a loading party.

9. Each man will carry his pack, and leave his surplus kit in a sandbag.
   Blankets in bundles of 10 and sandbags properly labelled, will be stacked before moving off. O.C. Companies will see that Officers Valises are given over to their C.Q.M.S.'s, and stacked in "D" Coy.'s stores before moving off.

10. List of trench stores taken over will be forwarded to the Adjutant immediately after the relief is completed.

11. The relief will be carried out as quietly and carefully as possible, and completion reported to Battalion H.Q. by 'phone, Code Word, "SNOW".

F.T.

-2-

12. All waterbottles will be filled before moving off.

13. Company Commanders will be held responsible for the cleanliness of their Huts, Lines, Latrines, Wash-houses, Officers Mess Cook-houses, etc.

14. Company Commanders will hand their Company Conduct Sheets into the Orderly Room this evening and obtain a receipt for same.

15. O.C. "C" Company will please detail a fatigue party of 20 men under an Officer, to report to the Adjutant at Battalion H.Q. at 5 p.m. tomorrow.

16. O.C. "A", "B", and "D" Companies will arrange each for a guide to report to the Adjutant at 5 p.m. tomorrow at Battalion H.Q. to accompany ration party, take over from his C.Q.M.S., and guide ration party to Company.

17. O.C. "A" and "D" Companies will please arrange to have a test S.O.S. each night in the trenches. A full report on each occasion should be forwarded to Battalion Headquarters by 9 a.m. stating the time taken from handing in the telephone message until the shell passes over the trench.

(Sgd) J. C. Beadle, Captain,
Commanding 11th Bn. The Queen's Own (Royal West Kent)
Regiment. (Lewisham).

Copy No. 1. C.O.
2. Adjutant.
3. Office Copy.
4. War Diary.
5. O.C. "A" Coy.
6. O.C. "B" Coy.
7. O.C. "C" Coy.
8. O.C. "D" Coy.
9. Lewis Gun Officer.
10. Quartermaster.
11. Transport Officer.
12. Intelligence Officer.
13. Signalling Officer.
14. R.S.M.
15. O.C., 11th "Queen's" R.W.S.R
16. Medical Officer.

SECRET. OPERATION ORDER NO.41. Copy No...3...
by Captain J.C. Beadle,
Commanding 11th Bn. The Queen's Own
(Royal West Kent) Regiment.

26th January, 1917

1. The Battalion will be relieved by the 11th "Queen's" tomorrow, relief starting at 4.30 p.m.

2. Opposite numbers will take over in the order in which they relieve, and platoons will march off independently. Company Commanders will report to Battalion Headquarters as soon as relief is complete. Code word, "FROST".

3. All movement will be by platoons at not less than 100 yards distance.

4. Maps, aeroplanes photographs, trench stores, are to be handed over to incoming unit, and a copy of receipts for Trench Stores handed in to Battalion Headquarters after relief. Periscopes & sniperscopes may be handed over to opposite number at the discretion of Company Commanders, a separate receipt <u>in duplicate</u> for these being obtained. (These must <u>not</u> be confounded with Trench Store Returns.)

5. Officers trench bundles, mess boxes, blankets, (properly labelled), etc., will be sent to Battalion Headquarters by 2 p.m.. Each Company will detail a fatigue party for this, & also 4 men per Company, Headquarters included, to accompany Transport back to Camp in charge of their own Company property.

6. O.C. "C" Company will detail a fatigue party of 1 Officer & 20 men to report at Battalion Headquarters at 4.30 p.m. and will take all trench bundles, etc., down to VOORMEZEELE DUMP so as to reach there by 5.15 p.m. These men must report with full equipment ready for moving off.

7. Company cookers and Transport, under Company Quartermaster Sergeants will meet the Battalion on the road behind DICKEBUSCH about H.27.d.8.2., there men will rest and have tea.

8. One cook per Company, under Sergt. Finch, will report to Battalion Headquarters at 4.30 to-day, & will proceed to ALBERTA CAMP.

9. Companies will occupy exactly the same accommodation as they left at ALBERTA CAMP.

10. Trenches must be left clean & in good order. A certificate to this effect signed by the Officer Commanding Company taking over to be obtained and handed in to the Orderly Room with the Trench Store Returns on arrival at Rest Billet. Fires will be left in the cookhouses, also tins of water.

11. The L.G.O. will arrange for one man from each Lewis Gun team to accompany the Transport & take over their Company guns on arrival at Camp, and the L.G.O. will detail one N.C.O. to be in charge of this party.

12. Company Commanders are responsible that all gum boots are handed over in as <u>dry a condition as possible</u> (in the manner in which they would like to receive them). On no account are any gum boots to be taken out of the trenches.

13. <u>Surplus</u> blankets, properly labelled, will be brought to Battalion Headquarters by 3.45 p.m. to-day to relieve the pressure tomorrow night

14. <u>Immediately on return</u> to Camp, O.C. Companies will render a return showing approximate number of all men available for fatigues in their Companies.

P.T.O.

(Sgd) J.C. Beadle, Captain.
Commanding 11th Bn. The Queen's Own (Royal West Kent)
Regiment. (Lewisham).

Copy No. 1.	C.O.	9.	L.G.O.
2.	Adjt.	10.	S.O.
3.	War Diary.	11.	Int. Officer.
4.	Office Copy.	12.	Q.M.
5.	O.C. "A" Coy.	13.	T.O.
6.	O.C. "B" Coy.	14.	R.S.M.
7.	O.C. "C" Coy.	15.	O.C. 11th "Queen's."
8.	O.C. "D" Coy.	16.	M.O.

SPECIAL IDEA.

Sheet 28.
140000.

Order for O.C. of Defending Company.

You will move with your Company at 9.30 a.m. on the morning of the 31st January, 1917.
Information to hand is that the enemy is advancing rapidly from DICKEBUSCH S.E. towards the road running N.W. from LA CLYTTE.
You will take up a position in advance of the RENINGHELST-LOCRE Road and hold up the enemy at all cost. Your boundary on the North will be O.35.d.10.2. to M.9.a.2.6/1, and on the South M.6.d.5.10. to M.9.c.3.1..
You will take three Lewis Guns with you and Company Signallers.
No ball ammunition to be carried.

Fighting Order.

Report in writing to the Windmill, (M.5.a.2.5.).

SPECIAL IDEA.

Sheet 28.
140000.

GERMAN
Order to O.C. Advanced Guard
3 Companies.

You will act as Advance Guard to the Brigade. On the morning of the 31st January, 1917, you will proceed at 10 a.m. from points O.35.d.10.2. to M.9.a.2.6. on the North Boundary and M.6.d.5.10 to M.9.c.3.1 on the South Boundary, travelling S.W. You will make good the country to WESTOUTRE, and report to Brigade H.Q. at LA CLYTTE when the country is clear of the enemy.

A direct line between the northern and southern points in each case represents the boundaries.

You will take 9 Lewis Guns and Signallers with you. No ball ammunition to be carried.

Fighting Order.

GENERAL IDEA.   Sheet 28.
                                           140000.

The Germans have broken through the line from North of YPRES to MESSINES and have overpowered our supports.

PARIS appears to be their objective. Our 6th Army is lying at CASTRE and is advancing with the idea of fighting a general action on a line from POPERINGHE, RENINGHELST, LOCRE.

Army Form C. 2118

11th R.W. Kent

Vol 10

WAR DIARY or INTELLIGENCE SUMMARY

(Erase heading not required.)

Place	Date	Hour	Summary of Events and Information	Remarks and references to Appendices
RENINGHELST.	1/2/17.		Battalion in rest. Company Training.	
ST. ELOI.	2/2/17.		Lt. Col. A.C. CORFE returned from leave and took over Command from Capt. J.C. BEADLE. Battalion relieved 11th Bn. Queen's R.W. Surrey Regt. in SPOIL BANK Sector. Vide O.O. 42 attached. 60 men under LIEUT. R.G.ROGERS, 2/LIEUT W.O.C.SEWELL, and 2/LIEUT. R.S.FRENCH left at RENINGHELST Camp in training for raid.	
	3/2/17.		Battalion in trenches. Strength, 38 Officers, 1011 Other Ranks.	
	4/2/17.		Battalion in trenches. Cook-house in ESTAMINET LANE blown in - 9 resultant casualties.	
	5/2/17.		Battalion in trenches.	
	6/2/17.		do	
	7/2/17.		do	
	8/2/17.		do Raid carried out by the Battalion vide O.O.43 & 44 attached. 12 German soldiers were taken prisoners, and 9 were known to be killed. O.C. Raid, 2/LIEUT. R.S. FRENCH was wounded before reaching the enemy line, but carried on until all were back into our own trench. 16 Other Ranks were also casualties. In second Raid, the party were unable to get into enemy trench but withdrew without sustaining any casualties.	
RENINGHELST.	9/2/17.		Battalion relieved in trenches by 11th Bn. The Queen's R.W. Surrey Regt, returning to ALBERTA CAMP, RENINGHELST, by route march. Vide O.O.45 attached. Casualties for period 2 - 9th Feb. Officers - wounded 2. Other Ranks, Missing 2, killed 6, wounded 23.	
	10/2/17.		Draft of 118 returned from Musketry Course at TILQUES. Battalion engaged in R.E. fatigues. G.O.C., 41st Division, congratulated raiders on successful raid. Strength of Battalion, 36 Officers, 959 Other Ranks.	
	11/2/17.		Usual Sunday parade service and rest day. 2/LIEUT. J.H. GREENWOOD joined the Battalion for duty from G.H.Q. Cadet School.	
	12/2/17.		R.E. fatigues and Company training. G.O.C. 122nd Inf. Brigade congratulated the raiding party before the Battalion.	
	13/2/17.		Baths, and inspection by Medical Officer. Rest Day.	

WAR DIARY
or
INTELLIGENCE SUMMARY

(Erase heading not required.)

Army Form C. 2118

Place	Date	Hour	Summary of Events and Information	Remarks and references to Appendices
ENINGHELST.	14/2/17.		2/LIEUTS. M. ROUGHLEY, L.G. PRESTON, and H.G. HARDING joined the Battalion for duty from G.H.Q. Cadet School. Company Training and R.E. fatigues. Recently arrived draft inspected by Commanding Officer and posted to Companies.	
	15/2/17.		Company Training.	
T. ELOI.	16/2/17.		The Battalion relieved the 11th Bn. The Queen's R.W. Surrey Regt. in the SPOIL BANK Sector. Vide O.O. 46 attached.	
	17/2/17.		Captain J.C. BEADLE granted Acting Rank of Major. Lt. COL. A.C. CORFE having proceeded on Commanding Officers Course at 2nd Army Central School, MAJOR J.C. BEADLE assumed Command of the Battn. Strength of Battalion 39 officers, 942 Other Ranks.	
	18/2/17.		2/LIEUTS C.E. MALPASS, T.G. PLATT, and H.A. GRAY joined the Battalion for duty from the Base.	
	19/2/17.		Battalion in trenches.	
	20/2/17.		do Extract from London Gazette d/20/2/17. - "R.W.Kent Regt.- Temp. Major, A.C. CORFE (Maj. S. Afr. Def. Force) to command a Battalion, and to be Temp. Lt. Col. (Sept. 16th 1916.)." Temp. Q.Mr. & Hon. Lt. W. BERNARD is transferred to Gen. List (Jan.13th). The 47th Division on the left made a raid on enemy trenches. The Battn. was to have co-operated (vide O.O. 0.47 attached) with a smoke barrage, but the wind was unfavourable. The raiders captured 105 prisoners, and 4 machine guns.	
ENINGHELST.	21/2/17.		The Battalion was relieved in trenches by the 11th Bn. The Queen's R.W. Surrey Regt. proceeding by route march to ALBERTA Camp, RENINGHELST, vide O.O.48 attached. Casualties for period 16 - 21st inclusive - 1 Officer accidentally wounded,. Other Ranks, 1 killed, 4 wounded.	
	22/2/17.		R.E. fatigues and Company Training. Draft of 25 Other Ranks joined from Base and were taken on strength.	
	23/2/17.		Company Training for two Companies. - Remainder at baths. No afternoon parades.	
	24/2/17.		LT. COL. A.C. CORFE having returned from Commanding officers Course took over the Command of the Battalion from MAJOR J.C. BEADLE. MAJOR L.H. HICKSON joined the Battalion for duty from the Base. 2/LIEUT. W. DONNET joined the Battalion for duty from M.G.C. (H.B.).	

Army Form C. 2118

WAR DIARY
or
INTELLIGENCE SUMMARY
(Erase heading not required.)

Instructions regarding War Diaries and Intelligence Summaries are contained in F. S. Regs., Part II. and the Staff Manual respectively. Title Pages will be prepared in manuscript.

Place	Date	Hour	Summary of Events and Information	Remarks and references to Appendices
RENINGHELST.	25/2/17.		Two Companies at Company Training.- Remainder of Battalion bathing. No afternoon parades.	
ST. ELOI.	26/2/17.		R.E. fatigues - remainder of Battalion on usual Sunday Parade Service. The Battalion relieved the 11th Bn. The Queen's R.W. Surrey Regt. in the SPOIL BANK Sector vide O.O. 49 attached.	
	27/2/17.		Battalion in trenches. 2/LIEUT. H.A. GRAY proceeded to join the 1st Bn. The Queen's Own (Royal West Kent) Regt..	
	28/2/17.		Battalion in trenches. Casualties from 26th to 28th inclusive, ORs Wounded 4.	

Robert [signature]
Lieut. Colonel,
Commanding 11th Bn. The Queen's Own (Royal West Kent) Rt.

1/3/17.

SECRET.   OPERATION ORDER No. 43.   Copy No....4....
                                by Captain J.C. Beadle,
                           Commanding 11th Bn. The Queen's own
                                (Royal West Kent) Regt.

                                                    1st February, 1917.

1.   The Battalion will relieve the 11th "Queen's" Royal West Surrey
Regt. tomorrow, and will take over trenches as hereunder, namely,-
                    Right Front Company   "C" Company
                    Left Front Company   "B"   "
                    Right Support Company   "A"   "
                    Left Support Company   "D"   "

2.   Reveille   7.15 a.m.
3.   Breakfasts 7.45 a.m.

4.   Order and time of march:-
                    Signallers (Headqtrs.)..........10.35 a.m.
                    "B" Company....................10.40 a.m.
                    "C" " ....10.50 a.m.
                    "D" " ....11.5 a.m.
                    Headquarters...................11.15 a.m.
                    "A" Company....................11.25 a.m.

        Lewis Gunners and Company Signallers will report to the O.C.
Companies to which they are attached, and will march with their
Companies.
        Snipers will move as a platoon of "B" Company.
        Platoon Commanders must not on any pretext halt their men in
DICKEBUSCH. Platoons to march at 100 yards distance.
        Company Commanders will insist that these orders are observed. They
are reminded that these are Divisional Orders.

5.   The Battalion will halt and rest at H.27.d.8.2. The cookers will be
sent on earlier and will have a hot meal ready for the men.
        O.C. Companies are responsible that all papers, tins, etc., are
buried.

6.   The Companies will move off from here as follows:-
                    Signallers (Headqtrs.)..............1   p.m.
                    "B" Company.........................1.15 p.m.
                    "C" " ....1.25 p.m.
                    "D" " ....1.40 p.m.
                    Headquarters.......................1.50 p.m.
                    "A" Company........................2   p.m.

7.   The Lewis Guns will be taken up by Transport this afternoon with 2
men per gun. The Lewis Gun Officer will detail 2 N.C.O.'s to be in
charge of this party. The Transport Officer will please arrange for 2
limbers to be ready outside Battalion Headquarters at 4 p.m. They will
arrange to change over the "Queen's" guns for our own during the
course of tomorrow morning.

8.   Officers Mess Boxes and Trench Bundles will be stacked in the Mess
Room of the Details Hut. Officers Servants will remain behind with
these and come up with the Transport in the evening, and they will also
act as a loading party.

9.   Each man will carry his pack, and leave his surplus kit in a sandbag.
Blankets in bundles of 10 and sandbags properly labelled will be
stacked before moving off. O.C. Companies will see that Officers
Valises are given over to their C.Q.M.S.'s, & stacked in "D" Company's
stores before moving off.

10.   List of trench stores taken over will be forwarded to the Adjutant
immediately after the relief is completed.

11.   The relief will be carried out as quietly and carefully as possible,
and completion reported to Battalion H.Q. by 'phone, Code Word,
"WRONG."

12.   All waterbottles will be filled before moving off.

                                                            P.T.O.

13. Company Commanders will be held responsible for the cleanliness of their Huts, Lines, Latrines, Wash-houses, Officers Mess Cook-houses, etc.

14. Company Commanders will hand their Company Conduct Sheets into the Orderly Room this evening and obtain a receipt for same.

15. O.C. "A" Company will please detail a fatigue party of 1 Officer & 30 men as a carrying party. This party will proceed from the Camp in advance of the Transport, and will move off at 5.30 p.m. Any details who have not proceeded with their Companies will go with this party & will report to the Officer in charge.

16. O.C. "B", "C", and "D" Companies will arrange each for a guide to report to the Adjutant at 5 p.m. tomorrow at Battalion Headquarters to accompany ration party, take over from his C.Q.M.S., and guide ration party to Company.

17. O.C. "B" and "C" Companies will please arrange to have a test S.O.S. each night in the trenches. A full report on each occasion should be forwarded to Battalion Headquarters by 8 a.m. the following morning stating the time taken from handing in the telephone message until the shell passes over the trench.

18. Company Commanders are requested to send in all returns punctually. Unpunctuality in this respect involves unnecessary correspondence.

                        (Sgd.) J. C. Beadle, Captain,
            Commanding 11th Bn. The Queen's Own (Royal
                   West Kent) Regiment. (Lewisham).

Copy No. 1. C.O.   9. Lewis Gun Offr.
        2. Adjutant.   10. Quartermaster.
        3. Office Copy.   11. Transport Offr.
        4. War Diary.   12. Intelligence Offr.
        5. O.C. "A" Coy.   13. Signalling Offr.
        6. O.C. "B" "   14. R.S.M.
        7. O.C. "C" "   15. O.C., 11th "Queen's" R.W.S.
        8. O.C. "D" "   Regt.
                                   16. Medical Offr.

SECRET.   OPERATION ORDER NO.43   Copy No........3
                            by Lieut.Col. A.C.Corfe,
                        Commanding 11th Bn. Royal West Kent Rgt.

                                                7th February, 1917.

Reference Sheet 28 S.W.2. - 1/10,000. Edition 3.E.

INTENTION. 1. A Raid will be carried out by the Battalion on a date to be notified later, on the enemy front line trenches from C.4.a.2.2½. to C.4.a.4.4.

INFORMATION. 2. The hostile trenches are at present reported to be held by the 413th Rgt. 204th Division.

OBJECT. 3. To obtain identifications and prisoners, and inflict loss on the enemy. Any mine shafts or emplacements will be destroyed and all portable equipment and documents will be brought back.

STRENGTH. 4. The strength of the party will be 2 Officers and 35 Other Ranks made up as follows:-
A. 2 Officers (one R.E.).
B. 27 O.R. (Divided into 3 Bombing Squads of 1 N.C.O. & 8 men each).
C. 4 Stretcher Bearers.
D. 4 O.R. (Tunnelling Co. R.E.).
E. 10 O.R. under 1 N.C.O. Covering Party.

EQUIPMENT. 5. A. Officers.
Dressed as Rank & File with badges of rank on shoulder.
Revolver and knobkerry.
Wire Cutters.
Gas Helmet.
Electric Torch.
2 Bombs (Mills No.5.)

B. Bombing Squads.
Knobkerry.
Bombing waistcoat to contain 10 Mills & 2 "P" Bombs.
Gas Helmet.
Wire Cutters at rate of 30%.
2 men of each Bombing Squad to carry a rifle, bayonet and 50 rounds of S.A.A.
1 Rifle Bomber with grenade rifle and 10 No.23 rifle grenades
2 Carriers in each squad to carry in addition a sandbag each containing 10 Mills Bombs.
1 Carrier in each squad to carry in addition 10 Mills No.23 Rifle Grenades.
N.C.O's - Revolver, Knobkerry and Electric Torch.

C. Stretcher Bearers.
2 improvised stretcher (made out of ground sheets).
Gas Helmet.
20 Mills No.23 Rifle Grenades and 1 "P" Bomb each.

N.B. All identification marks or badges on the clothing or uniform will be removed. Identity Discs will not be worn. Bayonets will be blackened. Faces and backs of hands will also be made black (or white - as the case may be) .If ground is covered with snow party will wear white overalls.

METHOD OF ATTACK. 6. The Raiding Party will leave our front line trench O.4. so as to be formed up in the dead ground in NO MAN'S LAND at 15 minutes before Zero. The party will be disposed in NO MAN'S Land as already arranged.
At 10 minutes before Zero the Artillery will bring an intense bombardment to bear on the enemy's front line at the point of entry for 10 minutes, commencing with H.E. for first 6 minutes and continuing with Shrapnel until Zero.

- 2 -

METHOD OF ATTACK CONTINUED.	6. ZERO. The Right Party will enter and block the trench at O.4.a.2.2½., clearing the dugouts about this point. The Left party will enter the trench at O.4.a.2½.4. and bomb down the trench to the dugouts at O.4.a.4.4. They will clear these and then block the trench at this point. The Centre party will enter the trench at O.4.a.2½.3½. They will clear the portion of the trench between this point and O.4.a.2.2½., and account for any of the enemy in the forward sap at O.4.a.2½.5½., being assisted by the Right party. O.C. Raid 2/Lieut. French, with 4 Stretcher Bearers, will station himself close to the parapet of enemy front line about the middle of the portion to be raided. The Demolition Party will accompany the Left bombing party and demolish any mine shafts or machine gun emplacements. Rifle Bombers will barrage the communication trenches which join the front line at O.4.a.2.2½., O.4.a.2½.3½., O.4.a.2½.4.
SIGNAL FOR ZERO HOUR & SIGNAL OF RECALL.	7. To assist Raiding Party in appreciating the exact moment of Zero, six RED Very Lights will be fired simultaneously 100 yards to the Left flank of trench O.4.1., on SPOIL BANK EXTENSION. O.C. Left front Company will detail one Officer for this duty who will report to the Infantry LIAISON Officer, Lt. ROGERS, one hour before zero, for the purpose of synchronising his watch.(He should have 2 watches). The Signal of Recall will be by long blasts on the whistle, given by O.C. Raid and Senior N.C.O., after 20 minutes from Zero. O.C. Left front Coy. will detail one Officer to be O.C. Flares. On hearing the Signal by whistle a YELLOW ground flare will be lighted on SPOIL BANK EXTENSION. on the extreme left of trench O.41. At the same time YELLOW ground flares will be lighted at two places in the old SUPPORT LINE, one behind 0.37, and one behind 0.35. O.C. Flares will make the necessary arrangements for the flares to be douched. after burning for 20 seconds.
RALLYING POINT.	8. Rallying Point for returning raiders will be Battalion Headquarters SPOIL BANK. All ranks on return to our trenches will make for this point direct, with the exception of men bringing prisoners, who will report to the LIAISON OFFICER.
LIAISON OFFICER.	9. Infantry LIAISON OFFICER, Lieut. ROGERS, will be in the Company Headquarters in Trench O.4.1., between ESTAMINET LANE and the CANAL. He will keep Battalion Headquarters informed of the situation by means of code. He will pass on prisoners and material to Battalion Headquarters SPOIL BANK.
ARTILLERY.	10. O.C. Raid and the Artillery LIAISON OFFICER will examine the wire on the morning of the raid, and report to Battalion Headquarters in writing whether they are satisfied that the wire has been effectively cut.
STOKES, VICKERS and LEWIS GUNS.	11. Stokes, Vickers and Lewis Guns will co-operate in the bombardment. The Vickers and Lewis Guns will continue to keep the top of the enemy's parapet under fire from Zero, on either side of the point to be raided and on salient O.3.b.6.½. to O.3.b.9.½. Lewis Gunners will watch for flashes from Hostile Machine Guns operating in "NO MAN'S LAND". (See appendix 3).
SMOKE BARRAGE.	12. Should the wind be favourable, that is from N.E. to N.W. a smoke barrage at 10 minutes before Zero will be formed to mask the salient at O.3.b.6.½. to O.3.b.9.½., or to cause a diversion from the actual raid.

continued:-

SECRET.   OPERATION ORDER NO. 44.   Copy No. 3
                 by Lieut.Col. A.C.Corfe,
                 Commanding 11th Bn. Royal West Kent Rgt.
                                                    5th Feb. 1917.

Ref:- Sheet 28 S.W.2 - 1/10,000 Edition 5 E.

INTENTION. 1. The Raid detailed in Operation Order No.43, will be repeated about six hours later on the enemy front line, from C.4.a.2.3. to C.4.a.4.4., at the discretion of the Commanding Officer.

OBJECT. 2. To obtain prisoners and inflict further loss on the enemy.

STRENGTH. 3. The party will be 1 Officer and 31 Other Ranks, made up as follows:-
   A. 1 Officer.
   B. 27 Other Ranks (Divided into 3 Bombing squads of 1 N.C.O. & 8 men each).
   C. 4 Stretcher Bearers.

EQUIPMENT. 4. Same as for first party.

METHOD OF ATTACK. 5. The party will leave our front line trench O.4.1. so as to be formed up as close to the enemy's front line as possible, at least 5 minutes before ZERO.
At ZERO the artillery will repeat barrage as for the first operation, and raiders will rush enemy front line. Parties will take same action as previously on entering enemy trench.

SIGNAL FOR ZERO HOUR AND SIGNAL OF RECALL. 6. No supplementary Signal for ZERO HOUR will be used. Signal of RECALL will be by long blasts on the whistle, given by O.C. RAID (Lieut. ROGERS).) and senior N.C.O. This will be supplemented by four RED Very Lights fired in succession from trench O.3.4. O.C. Right Front Coy. will detail one Officer for this duty.

STOKES VICKERS & LEWIS GUNS. 7. Vickers Guns will not co-operate. Lewis Gunners will watch for flashes of hostile machine guns and open fire on them. Stokes Guns will not co-operate but gun in position to cover enemy trench from O.4.a.80.47. to CANAL BANK will stand by as before.

COMMUNICATION. 8. ESTAMINET LANE and track South of SPOIL BANK will be kept clear from 2½ hours before ZERO of first operation till 1 hour after ZERO of second operation.
O.C. Left Support Coy., will make the same arrangements as for the first operation.

ZERO HOUR. 9. ZERO HOUR will be notified later as follows:-

   Extra leave train leaves POPERINGHE at.........

TIME TABLE. 10.
40 minutes before Zero   Raiders assemble in our front line trench.
20   "   "   "   Parties commence to get into NO MAN'S LAND.
5   "   "   "   Parties are formed up in NO MAN'S LAND as close to enemy line as possible.
Z E R O.   Barrage commences, Raiders rush trench.
ZERO plus 10 minutes   - Raiders return to our own trench
ZERO plus 15 minutes   - Barrage ceases.

11. Medical, Liaison and prisoners escort arrangements remain the same.

12. The Commanding Officer will notify all concerned if the operation will take place by code as follows:-
To take place - Tramway blocked, repairs in hand.
NOT to take place - Truck "B" lost. Please endeavour to trace.

P.T.O

- 2 -

<u>12 Cont:</u> This notification will be sent as soon as possible after completion of first operation.

      (Sgd) A.C.Corfe. Lieut. Colonel.
        Commanding 11th Royal West Kent Rgt.

Copy No. 1 C.O. & 2nd In Command.
    2. Adjutant & File Copy.
    3. War Diary.
    4. C.C. "A" Coy.
    5. O.C. "B" Coy.
    6. C.C. "C" Coy.
    7. O.C. "D" Coy.
    8. S.O., M.O., & R.S.M.
    9. Infantry Liaison Offr.
   10. Artillery Liaison Offr.
   11. 122nd M.G. Coy.
   12. 228th Field Coy. R.E.
   13. Canadian Tun. Coy.
   14. 122nd Trench Mortar Battery.
   15. L.G.C.

SMOKE BARRAGE CONTINUED.	12.	O.C. Smoke, 2/Lieut. DRUMGOLD, will have fifteen men under his Command. Ten of Pain's Triple Smoke Candles and 10 "P" Bombs will be lighted every two minutes on a front of 50 yards in trench O.33 from ZERO minus 10 minutes to ZERO plus 30 minutes. O.C. Smoke will report to Lieut. ROGERS, 1 hour before Zero to synchronise watches.
PRISONERS OF WAR.	13.	O.C. Prisoners of War after being searched will be marched without delay to Battalion Headquarters in SPOIL BANK. O.C. Right Support Company will detail 1 N.C.O. and 8 men to report to the Adjutant at Zero as prisoners escort.
MEDICAL ARRANGEMENTS.	14.	In addition to Stretcher Bearers with the raiding party, the Battalion Medical Officer will arrange to have stretchers in trench O.3.8. and Trench O.4.1. A stretcher path must be selected between ESTAMINET LANE and the CANAL.
COMMUNICATION.	15.	ESTAMINET LANE and the track S. of SPOIL BANK will be closed for ordinary traffic and reserved for raiders and runners from 2 hours before Zero till 1 hour after Zero. O.C. Left Support Company will detail one Officer as O.C. Traffic, and will arrange to police the above routes. The LIAISON Officer will be in direct communication by telephone with the Battalion Headquarters. Code will be used. See appendix.
ZERO HOUR.	16.	ZERO HOUR will be notified later as follows:- "Send Guides at..........(Time).
TIME TABLE.	17.	1 Hour and 10 minutes before Zero. — Raiders assemble in our front line trenches. 30 minutes before Zero — Parties commence to get into NO MAN'S LAND. 15 minutes before Zero — Parties are formed up in NO MAN'S LAND (not nearer to the enemy's parapet than 100 yards). 14 and 12 minutes before Zero — Dummy bombardments commence as shewn in appendix 5. 10 minutes before Zero — Bombardment of enemy's front line at point of attack. Smoke candles lighted. 4 minutes before Zero — Bombardment changes from H.E. to Shrapnel. Front line of riading party creep up to within 50 yards of enemy parapet. Z E R O. — Artillery lifts from enemy's front line at point of attack and forms a box barrage round raided trench; raiding party rushes trench. Zero plus 20 minutes — Raiders return to our own trenches. Zero plus 30 minutes — Smoke barrage ceases.
	19.	Men must be reminded that if captured they must not give any information beyond their rank and names.

(Sgd) A. C. Corfe, Lieut. Colonel.
Commanding 11th Bn. Royal West Kent Rgt.

Copy No. 1. C.O. & 2nd In Command.   No. 7. O.C. "D" Coy.
        2. Adjutant & File Copy.   8. S.O., M.O., & R.S.M.
        3. War Diary.   9. Infantry Liaison Offr.
        4. O.C. "A" Coy.   10. Artillery Liaison Offr.
        5. O.C. "B" "   11. 122nd M.G.Coy.
        6. O.C. "C" "   12. 226th Field Coy. R.E.
                                           13. Canadian Tun. Co.

o-------------X------------o

APPENDIX 4.

A. Raiders have left our trench.

B. Raiders are formed up in NO MAN'S LAND.

C. Raiders have entered enemy trench.

D. Raiders have returned (giving number).

E. Raiders under heavy Machine Gun and Rifle fire.

F. Raiders under heavy shell fire.

G. Enemy retaliating on trench.......

H. Prisoner(s) taken (giving number).

J. Officer prisoner(s) taken (giving number).

K. Estimated enemy casualties (Killed).

L. Estimated enemy casualties (Wounded).

M. Own casualties (killed).

N. Own casualties (wounded).

O. Raid successful.

P. Raid unsuccessful.

Q. More bombs required.

R. More stretcher bearers required.

S. Artillery has ceased fire.

T. Artillery shooting short.

U. Raiding party held up by enemy wire.

V. Officers missing (giving number).

W. Other Ranks missing (giving number).

--------------o--------------

SECRET.

OPERATION ORDER NO. 45
by Lt. Col. A.C. Corfe,
Commanding 11th Bn. The Queen's Own
(Royal West Kent) Regiment.

Copy No. 3

8th February, 1917.

1. The Battalion will be relieved by the 11th "Queen's" tomorrow, relief starting at 5 p.m.

2. Opposite numbers will take over in the order in which they relieve, & platoons will march off independently. Company Commanders will report to Battalion Headquarters as soon as relief is complete. Code word "FROST".

3. All movement will be by platoons at not less than 100 yards distance.

4. Maps, aeroplane photographs, trench stores, are to be handed over to incoming unit, & a copy of receipts for Trench Stores handed in to Battalion Headquarters after relief. Periscopes and sniperscopes may be handed over to opposite number at the discretion of Company Commanders, a separate receipt in duplicate for these being obtained. (These must not be confounded with Trench Store Returns).

5. Officers trench bundles, mess boxes, blankets, (properly labelled) etc., will be sent to Battalion Headquarters by 4.30 p.m.. Each Coy. will detail a fatigue party for this, and also 4 men per Company, Headquarters included, to accompany Transport back to Camp in charge of their own Company Property.

6. O.C. "C" Company will detail a fatigue party of 1 Officer & 20 men to report at Battalion Headquarters at 5 p.m. and will take all trench bundles, etc, down to VOORMEZEELE DUMP so as to reach there by 5.30 p.m. These men must report with full equipment ready for moving off.

7. Company cookers and Transport, under Company Quartermaster Sergeants will meet the Battalion on the road behind DICKEBUSCH about H.27.d.8.2 there men will rest and have tea.

8. One cook per Company, under Sergt. Finch, will report to Battalion Headquarters at 4.30 to-day, and will proceed to ALBERTA CAMP.

9. Companies will occupy exactly the same accommodation as they left at Alberta Camp.

10. Trenches must be left clean and in good order. A certificate to this effect signed by the Officer Commanding Company taking over to be obtained and handed in to the Orderly Room with the Trench Store Return on arrival at Rest Billet. Fires will be left in the cook-houses, also tins of water.

11. The L.G.O. will arrange for one man from each Lewis Gun team to accompany the Transport & take over their Company guns on arrival at Camp, and the L.G.O. will detail one N.C.O. to be in charge of this party.

12. Company Commanders are responsible that all gum boots are handed over in as dry a condition as possible. (in the manner in which they would like to receive them). On no account are any gum boots to be taken out of the trenches.

13. Immediately on return to Camp, O.C. Companies will render a return showing approximate number of all men available for fatigues in their Companies.

(Sgd) A.C. Corfe, Lt. Colonel.
Commanding 11th Bn. The "Queen's Own (Royal West Kent) Regt.

Copy No. 1. C.O.   5. O.C. "A" Coy. 9. L.G.O.   (Lewisham).
        2. Adjt.   6. O.C. "B" "   10. S.O.   13. T.O.
        3. War Diary.   7. O.C. "C" "   11. Int. Off. 14. R.S.M.
        4. Office Copy.   8. O.C. "D" "   12. Q.M.   15. O.C. 11th "Queens"
                                                          16. M.O.

SECRET.   OPERATION ORDER No. 46.   Copy No......
                              by Lieut. Col. A.C. Corfe,
                              Commanding 11th Bn. The Queen's Own
                                  (Royal West Kent) Regt.

                                                    15th February, 1917.

1.   The Battalion will relieve the 11th "Queen's" Royal West Surrey Regt.
     tomorrow, & will take over trenches as hereunder, namely:-
                    Right Front Company   "A" Company.
                    Left Front Company.   "D"   "
                    Right Support Company.   "C"   "
                    Left Support Company.   "B"   "

2.   Reveille   7.15 a.m.
3.   Breakfasts 7.45 a.m.

4.   Order and time of march:-
                    Signallers (Headqtrs.)............11.35 a.m.
                    "D" Company......................11.40 a.m.
                    "A" "   ....11.50 a.m.
                    "B" "   ....12.5 p.m.
                    Headquarters.....................12.15 p.m.
                    "C" Company......................12.25 a.m.
     Lewis Gunners and Company Signallers will report to the O.C. Companies
     to which they are attached, and will march with their Companies.
     Snipers will move as a platoon of "D" Company.
     Platoon Commanders must not on any pretext halt their men in DICKEBUSCH.
     Platoons to march at 100 yards distance.
     Company Commanders will insist that these orders are observed. They are
     reminded that these are Divisional Orders.

5.   The Battalion will halt and rest at N.27.d.6.2. The cookers will be sent
     on earlier & will have a hot meal ready for the men.
     O.C. Companies are responsible that all papers, tins, etc., are buried.

6.   The Companies will move off from here as follows:-
                    Signallers (Headqtrs.)............2 p.m.
                    "D" Company......................2.15 p.m.
                    "A" "   ....2.25 p.m.
                    "B" "   ....2.40 p.m.
                    Headquarters.....................2.50 p.m.
                    "C" Company......................3 p.m.

7.   The Lewis Guns will be taken up by Transport this afternoon with 2 men
     per gun. The Lewis Gun Officer will detail 2 N.C.O.'s to be in charge of
     this party. The Transport Officer will please arrange for 2 limbers to be
     ready outside Battalion Headquarters at 4.30 p.m. They will arrange to
     change over the "Queen's" guns for our own during the course of tomorrow
     morning.

8.   Officers Mess Boxes and Trench Bundles will be stacked in the Mess Room
     of the Details Hut. Officers servants will remain behind with these & come
     up with the Transport in the evening, and they will also act as a loading
     party.

9.   Each man will carry his pack, & leave his surplus kit in a sandbag.
     Blankets in bundles of 10 & sandbags properly labelled will be stacked
     before moving off. O.C. Companies will see that Officers Valises are given
     over to their C.Q.M.S.'s & stacked in "D" Company's stores before moving
     off.

10. List of trench stores taken over will be forwarded to the Adjutant
     immediately after the relief is completed.

11. The relief will be carried out as quietly & carefully as possible, and
     completion reported to Battalion H.Q. by 'phone, Code Word, "WONG".

12. All waterbottles will be filled before moving off.

13. Company Commanders will be held responsible for the cleanliness of their
     Huts, Lines, Latrines, Wash-houses, Officers Mess cook-houses, etc.

                                                              P.T.O.

14. Company Commanders will hand their Company Conduct Sheets into the Orderly Room this evening & obtain a receipt for same.

15. O.C. "C" Company will please detail a fatigue party of 1 Officer and 30 men as a carrying party. This party will proceed from the Camp in advance of the Transport, and will move off at 4 p.m. Any details who have not proceeded with their Companies will go with this party & will report to the Officer in charge.

16. O.C. "B", "C", and "D" Companies will arrange each for a guide to report to the Adjutant at 6.30 p.m. tomorrow at Battalion Headquarters to accompany ration party, take over from his C.Q.M.S., and guide ration party to Company.

17. O.C. "B" and "C" Companies will please arrange to have a test S.O.S. each night in the trenches. A full report on each occasion should be forwarded to Battalion Headquarters by 9 a.m. the following morning stating the time taken from handing in the telephone message until the shell passes over the trench.

18. Company Commanders are requested to send in all returns punctually. Unpunctuality in this respect involves unnecessary correspondence.

                        (Sgd). A. C. Corfe, Lieut. Colonel,
Commanding 11th Bn. The Queen's Own (Royal West Kent) Rt. (Lewisham).

Copy No.
1. C.O.
2. Second in Command.
3. Adjutant.
4. War Diary.
5. O.C. "A" Coy.
6. O.C. "B" "
7. O.C. "C" "
8. O.C. "D" "
9. Asst. Adjt.
10. Lewis Gun Offr.
11. Quartermaster.
12. Transport Offr.
13. Intelligence Offr.
14. Signalling Offr.
15. R.S.M.
16. O.C., 11th "Queen's" R.W.S.R.
17. Medical Offr.
18. Office Copy.

S E C R E T.   OPERATION ORDER No.48.   Copy No...4.....
by Major J.C. Beadle,
Commanding 11th Bn. The Queen's Own (Royal
West Kent) Regt.

20th February, 1917.

1. The Battalion will be relieved by the 11th "Queen's" tomorrow, relief starting at 5.30 p.m.

2. Opposite numbers will take over in the order in which they relieve, and platoons will march off independently. Company Commanders will report to Battalion Headquarters as soon as relief is complete. Code word "THAW".

3. All movement will be by platoons at not less than 100 yards distance.

4. Maps, aeroplane photographs, trench stores, are to be handed over to incoming Unit, and a copy of receipts for Trench Stores handed in to Battalion Headquarters after relief. Periscopes and sniperscopes may be handed over to opposite number at the discretion of Company Commanders, a separate receipt in duplicate for these being obtained. (These must not be confounded with Trench Store Returns).

5. Officers trench bundles, mess boxes, blankets, (properly labelled) etc, will be sent to Battalion Headquarters by 4.30 p.m.. Each Company will detail a fatigue party for this, and also 4 men per Company, Headquarters included, to accompany Transport back to Camp in charge of their own Coy. property.

6. O.C. "A" Company will detail a fatigue party of 1 Officer and 20 men to report at Battalion Headquarters at 5.45 p.m. & will take all trench bundles, etc., down to VOORMEZEELE DUMP so as to reach there by 6.15 p.m. These men must report with full equipment ready for moving off.

7. Company cookers and Transport, under Company Quartermaster Sergeants, will meet the Battalion on the road behind DICKEBUSCH about H.27.d.8.2. there men will rest and have tea.

8. One cook per Company_____ will report to Battalion Headquarters at 5 o.c. to-day, and will proceed to ALBERTA CAMP.

9. Companies will occupy exactly the same accommodation as they left at ALBERTA CAMP.

10. Trenches must be left clean & in good order. A certificate to this effect signed by the Officer Commanding Company taking over to be obtained & handed in to the Orderly Room with the Trench Store Return on arrival at Rest Billet Fires will be left in the cook-houses, also tins of water.

11. The L.G.O. will arrange for one man from each Lewis Gun team to accompany the Transport & take over their Company guns on arrival at Camp, & the L.G.O. will detail one N.C.O. to be in charge of this party.

12. Company Commanders are responsible that all gum boots are handed over in as dry a condition as possible (in the manner in which they would like to receive them). On no account are any gum boots to be taken out of the trenches.

13. Immediately on return to Camp, O.C. Companies will render a return showing approximate number of all men available for fatigues in their Coys.

(Sgd) J.C. Beadle, Major,
Commanding 11th Bn. The Queen's Own (Royal West Kent) Rt.
(Lewisham).

Copy No. 1. C.O.   6. O.C. "A" Coy.   11. S.O.   O.C. 11th Queens.
        2. Second in Command. 7. O.C. "B" "   12. I.O.   17. M.O.
        3. Adjutant.   8. O.C. "C" "   13. Q.M.   18. Asst. Adjt.
        4. War Diary.   9. O.C. "D" "   14. T.O.
        5. Office Copy.   10. L.G.O.   15. R.S.M.

SECRET.   OPERATION ORDER No.47   Copy No. 3
by Major J.C. Beadle,
Commanding 11th Bn. The Queen's Own (Royal
West Kent) Regiment.

20th February, 1917.

1. The 47th Division is carrying out a raid on the enemy's Salient in in I.34.d. on the 20th February.(to-day).

2. The 41st Division will co-operate by means of:-
   (a) Artillery fire. Details arranged direct between the two Divisional Artilleries.
   (b) A smoke barrage, if wind is favourable, to obscure the high ground S. of the Canal about WHITE CHATEAU.

3. In the event of the wind being favourable O.C. "D" Company will arrange to form a smoke cloud by means of smoke candles from Trenches O.3.S. & C.4.1. The smoke cloud to commence at Zero hour and to be maintained for 50 minutes. The smoke cloud must on no account extend North of the line I.34.d.0.0. to I.35. central reference sheet 28 N.W. No. 4.

4. O.C. "D" Company will detail 1 Officer and 30 men to light the smoke candles.
   (1) 25 men will be actually required to light the smoke candles.
   (2) Each man will maintain two candles alight. These should be about 6 yards apart.
   (3) A candle burns for 4½ minutes. A second candle should be lit and thrown out after 4 minutes.
   (4) Each man will require 24 candles i.e. there will be 12 relays of 2 candles per man.
   (5) Arrangements must be made for proper supervision & issue of spare candles to any men having duds.
   (6) All men employed must be carefully rehearsed and must have plenty of matches and portfires if available.
   (7) The Commanding Officer will decide whether conditions are favourable for the barrage and will inform O.C. "D" Company 1 hour before ZERO using the following code.-
       THUNDER.- The barrage will take place.
       FROST.- The barrage will not take place.
   (8) A report on the success or otherwise of the barrage will be forwarded as soon as possible to Battalion Headquarters.

5. Zero hour will be 5 p.m.

6. Correct time will be communicated by telephone to O.C. "D" Company shortly after 2 p.m. on 20th instant.

7. All traffic will be stopped one hour before ZERO until one hour after. O.C. "B" Company will detail one Officer as O.C. traffic and arrange to police the communication Trenches.

8. As retaliation may be expected, the usual danger spots must be kept clear of men.

(Sgd) J. C. Beadle, Major,
Commanding 11th Bn. The Queen's Own (Royal West Kent) Regt.
(Lewisham).

Copy No. 1. C.O.
2. Second in Command.
3. War Diary.
4. Adjutant.
5. Signalling Offr.
6. O.C. "A" Coy.
7. O.C. "B" "
8. O.C. "C" "
9. O.C. "D" "
10. L.G.O.
11. I.O.
12. 122nd Machine Gun Coy.
13. 122nd Trench Mortar Battery.
14. 1st Canadian Tunnelling Coy.
15. Office Copy.
16. 228th Field Coy. R.E.
17. O.C. 20th London Regt.
18. Med. Offr.
19. R.S.M.

SECRET. OPERATION ORDER No. 49.   Copy No. M.5
by Lieut. Col. A.C. Corfe,
Commanding 11th Bn. The Queen's Own
(Royal West Kent) Regt. (Lewisham).

26th February, 1917.

1. The Battalion will relieve the 11th "Queen's" Royal West Surrey Regt tomorrow, and will take over trenches as hereunder, namely:-
   Right Front Company   "C" Company.
   Left Front Company.   "B" "
   Right Support Company.   "A" "
   Left Support Company.   "D" "

2. Reveille - 7.15 a.m.
3. Breakfasts - 7.45 a.m.

4. Order and time of march:-
   Signallers (Headquarters)........11.50 a.m.
   "B" Company......................11.55 a.m.
   "C" Company......................12.5 p.m.
   "D" Company......................12.20 p.m.
   Headquarters.....................12.30 p.m.
   "A" Company......................12.40 p.m.

   Lewis Gunners and Company Signallers will report to the O.C. Companies to which they are attached, and will march with their Companies.
   Snipers will move as a platoon of "B" Company.
   Platoon Commanders must not on any pretext halt their men in DICKEBUSCH.
   Platoons to march at 100 yards distance.
   Company Commanders will insist that these orders are observed. They are reminded that these are Divisional Orders.

5. The Battalion will halt and rest at H.27.d.8.2. The cookers will be sent on earlier and will have a hot meal ready for the men.
   O.C. Companies are responsible that all papers, tins, etc.; are buried.

6. The Companies will move off from here as follows.-
   Signallers (Headquarters)........2.15 p.m.
   "B" Company......................2.30 p.m.
   "C" Company......................2.40 p.m.
   "D" Company......................2.55 p.m.
   Headquarters.....................3.5 p.m.
   "A" Company......................3.15 p.m.

7. The Lewis Guns will be taken up by Transport this afternoon with 2 men per gun. The Lewis Gun Officer will detail 2 N.C.O.'s to be in charge of this party. The Transport Officer will please arrange for 2 limbers to be ready outside Battalion Headquarters at 4.30 p.m. They will arrange to change over the "Queen's" guns for our own during the course of tomorrow morning.

8. Officers Mess Boxes and Trench Bundles will be stacked in the Mess Room of the Details Hut. Officers Servants will remain behind with these and come up with the Transport in the evening, and they will also act as a loading party.

9. Each man will carry his pack and leave his surplus kit in a sandbag.
   Blankets in bundles of 10 & sandbags properly labelled will be stacked before moving off. O.C. Companies will see that Officers Valises are given over to their C.Q.M.S.'s and stacked in "D" Company's stores before moving off.

10. List of Trench Stores taken over will be forwarded to the Adjutant immediately after the relief is completed.

11. The relief will be carried out as quietly and carefully as possible, and completion reported to Battalion H.Q. by 'phone, Code Word, "RIGHT".

12. All waterbottles will be filled before moving off.

13. Company Commanders will be held responsible for the cleanliness of their Huts, Lines, Latrines, Wash-houses, Officers Mess Cook-houses, etc.

P.T.O.

-2-

14. Company Commanders will hand their Company Conduct Sheets into the Orderly Room this evening and obtain a receipt for same.

15. O.C. "A" Company will please detail a fatigue party of 1 Officer and 30 men as a carrying party. This party will proceed from the Camp in advance of the Transport, and will move off at 4 p.m. Any details who have not proceeded with their Companies will go with this party and will report to the Officer in charge.

16. O.C. "B", "C", and "D" Companies will arrange each for a guide to report to the Adjutant at 6.30 p.m. tomorrow at Battalion Headquarters to accompany ration party, take over from his C.Q.M.S., and guide ration party to Company.

17. O.C. "C" and "D" Companies will please arrange to have a test S.O.S. each night in the trenches. A full report on each occasion should be forwarded to Battalion Headquarters by 9 a.m. the following morning stating the time taken from handing in the telephone message until the shell passes over the trench.

18. Company Commanders are requested to send in all returns punctually. Unpunctuality in this respect involves unnecessary correspondence.

(Sgd) A. C. Corfe, Lieut. Colonel,
Commanding 11th Bn. The Queen's Own (Royal West Kent) Rt. (Lewisham).

Copy No. 1. C.O.
2. Second in Command.
3. Major Hickson.
4. Adjutant.
5. War Diary.
6. O.C. "A" Coy.
7. O.C. "B" Coy.
8. O.C. "C" Coy.
9. O.C. "D" Coy.
10. Asst. Adjt.
11. Lewis Gun Offr.
12. Quartermaster.
13. Transport Offr.
14. Intelligence Offr.
15. Signalling Offr.
16. R.S.M.
17. O.C. 11th "Queen's" R.W.S.R.
18. Medical Offr.
19. Office Copy.

S E C R E T.

C.O. & Second in Command.	S.O., M.O., & R.S.M.
Adjutant & File Copy.	Infantry Liaison Offr.
War Diary.	Artillery Liaison Offr.
O.C. "A" Coy.	122nd M.G. COY.
O.C. "B" "	228th Field Coy, R.E.
O.C. "C" "	Canadian Tun. Coy.
O.C. "D" "	122nd Trench Mortar Battery.
	Lewis Gun Offr.

Ref. O.O. 43.

Please send guides at 10.15 p.m.

(Sgd) A.C.Corfe, Lieut. Col.
Comndg. 11th Royal West Kent Rgt.

8/2/17.

S E C R E T.

C.O. & Second in Command.   Infantry Liaison Offr.
Adjutant and File Copy.   Artillery Liaison Offr.
War Diary.   122nd M.G. Coy.
O.C. "A" Coy.   228th Field Coy., R.E.
O.C. "B" "   Canadian Tun. Coy.
O.C. "C" "   122nd Trench Mortar Battery.
O.C. "D" "   Lewis Gun Offr.
S.O., M.O". & R.S.M.

Ref. O.O. 44. Sub-Sections 9 & 12.

    Extra train leaves POPERINGHE at 4.30 a.m.

    Tramway blocked, repairs in hand.

    ~~Truck "E" lost. Please endeavour to trace.~~

9/2/17.

                      (Sgd) A.C. Corfe, Lt. Colonel,
                      Commdg. 11th Royal West Kent Regt.

Dear Symonds,

I should like to write you about our show last night. The whole night's work was instructive to me. I was formerly under the impression that first raid would give no results, but that second, without barrage, would catch Bosch napping and working. The night's work proved again what so many of us Infantry Officers wont always admit, viz, that a barrage is absolutely essential.

Wire well cut, a good barrage and resolute Infantry, and the trick is accomplished. It seems to me therefore that there cannot be <u>too much</u> co-operation between Artillery and Infantry on these occasions.

No reasonable Infantry Officer, can expect his men to follow up a barrage and have no casualties - we know some of the difficulties you have to contend with - but I think it is here, that <u>the most careful liaison</u> between the two arms helps. For example - I was much struck with the care and attention given by Major Spain and all the Officers of his battery. Major Spain came to the front line himself on many occasions, to watch his registering. He frequently consulted with me, he knows and is known by the majority of my Officers, and in short, has established that feeling of confidence which is so desirable.

Captain Bray, as liaison Officer during night of 8/9th, was admirable, and was always in touch with the guns behind.

I should like to add a word on behalf of the Medium T.M's. For some days prior to the 8th, Lieut. Tilley has been working under great difficulties, and at one time it looked as though the Trench Mortars were not going to successfully accomplish their job of wire cutting. Lieut. Tilley however persevered, and his (the most important) part of the job was very well done.

Yours sincerely,

9/2/17.

Appendix B.

To
    O.C.,
        11th R.W.K.

      Beg to report that I went over with party this evening to enemy's trenches and blew two charges - roughly 16 lbs each - gun cotton in dugout. Dugout was square and timbered, with cover of about 3 - 4 feet of earth, entrance was revetted with Brushwood. I found the trenches were also revetted with this material and the section entered was plank floored and seemed to be well drained and deep cut with very little earthwork on parapet.

                                      (Sd) John Gray,
                                          2/Lieut. R.E.
                                          228th Field Coy.

February 8/17.

11th Bn. The Queen's Own (Royal West Kent) Regiment.

Report on Raids 8/9 Feby. 1917.

I have to report the following.- In accordance with Brigade Operation Order No. 83 a raid on the enemy trenches was carried out by my Battalion on the night of 8th February.

Intention. To enter enemy's trenches, destroy M.G. Emplacements or mine shafts - capture and kill the enemy.

Formation. The party was made up of 2 Officers (I Infantry and I R.E.) and 45 O.R.s distributed as follows - Left Bombing Squad, I N.C.O. and 8 men to which was attached an R.E. demolition party under an Officer (2/Lt. Gray, R.E.); Centre and Right Bombibg Squads, I N.C.O. and 8 men each.

O.C. Raid, 2/Lieut. FRENCH, with 4 Stretcher Bearers, moved with the Centre Party.

There was also a covering party of 10 men under an N.C.O. who remained outside our own wire. The Raiding Party was formed up and advanced in accordance with the Time Table detailed in O.O. 83.

A report by O.C. Raid - Appendix A is attached- which describes the results of the Centre Bombing Squad.

A report by the R.E. Officer - Appendix B- describes the condition of the trench, and destruction of the dugout in the portion entered by the Left Bombing Squad.

The Right Bombihg Party entered the enemy trench and bombed to the right, but encountered no opposition.

Results. The dugout mentioned in Appendix B. contained 9 men who came out willingly when ordered so to do, and 3 more were found cowering in the trench by the Centre Party and also came out when ordered.

The two outer parties extended outwards as far as time permitted but did not discover any more enemy.

Casualties. As mentioned in Appendix A. O.C. Raid was wounded before much progress had been made but he remained and advanced with the party. The total casualties to O.R.s were as follows.- 3 killed, 13 wounded, 2 missing. A large percentage of the casualties were apparently

-2-

caused by our own shells - this is to be regretted - but under such circumstances unavoidable.

Retaliation. The enemy did not retaliate to any great extent and his Machine Guns were practically silent.

A second Raid was carried out at 4.30 a.m. this morning in accordance with O.O.

Intention. As for the former operation.

Formation. This party was made up of two bombing squads under 2 Officers, Lieut. Gordon Smith, and 2/Lieut. W.O.C. Sewell and the two Sergeants who led left and centre parties of first Raid.

Result. The enemy had been very active with snipers since the conclusion of the first Raid and the party were detected immediately they left our own trench and were under heavy rifle fire. Notwithstanding, the two bombing squads advanced but when about 50 yards from the enemy wire were heavily bombed, the enemy also made a great row shouting, and the rifle fire was intense. Perceiving that further advance under these conditions was impossible O.C. Operations gave the signal to recall. It might be noted that on neither occasion were the enemy Machine Guns active.

Casualties. The whole party returned in safety. One man was, however, slightly wounded.

Retaliation. The enemy retaliated with slightly more vigour than on the occasion of the first operation but no material damage to our trenches was done.

During the retaliation for the second enterprise the enemy fired many golden lights - with no apparent result.

General. The barrage for the first operation was exceedingly good although naturally there were some "shorts". The failure of the second raid was in my opinion due entirely to the fact that there was no preliminary barrage.

In general the liaison arrangements between the Artillery and Infantry was all that could be asked for. The wire cutting by the Medium T.M.s though disappointing at the beginning of the week owing to misfortune from various causes, was exceedingly well done and the wire offered little or no obstacle.

The arrangements made by the Battalion Medical Officer were excellent, and all the wounded were evacuated in a most expeditious manner.

Appendix A.   -4-

STATEMENT BY 2/LIEUT. FRENCH NIGHT OF
8/9th February.1917.

We formed up in good order in "NO MAN'S LAND". The men were eager to get on and had to be restrained. We crawled out to about 50 yards from our own wire where the shells falling short kept our men back. Waited in shell-hole for H.E. to finish and shrapnel to begin. Then crawled forward to about 50 yards from enemy line where I saw several men knocked out. 3 I saw hit by H.E. and several when shrapnel was fired. Red lights went up on right and we rushed for it. The centre party suffered rather badly by our own fire and were no good as a fighting unit in the trench. The left party (Sergt. Cozens and R.E.s) got 8 or 9 prisoners

The Bosche was completely disorganised and offered no resistance. I saw two or three in a dugout opposite point. I jumped into trench; as they wouldn't come out I fired a revolver shot and then when they still remained I threw in two bombs.

The trench was revetted with wattlers and was in good condition. It was practically unhurt by shell-fire. I saw about 50 yards of it. There was a good firestep and the trench was quite 7 feet deep. The dugout I saw was a low one strutted with wood inside and had a low entrance with 4 - 5 feet of earth on top. I didn't see any duckboards.

There was a square black box of ammunition opposite the dugout packed in packets of five in what looked like waterproof material - probably paper.

Close to the ammunition was a box of ordinary German bombs hung on to the side of the trench (not let in like ours). The condition of the trench was very good.

I noticed a lot of "dud toffee apples" in enemy wire which was extremely well cut. There were 3 rifles with bayonets leaning against the trench and steel helmets resting on top of bayonets.

I was hit about 30 - 40 yards from our wire.

The right grenadier (rifle) a man with dark moustache stood up on enemy parapet and fired six grenades into support line shewing great courage in spite of the shrapnel bursting round him.

Sergt. Cozens conducted his party with great initiative and courage handling his men well

No retaliation from enemy and no sign of life in trench before we went over , except one Very Light.

I saw two of our men dead on my way back- one close to the German line.

I didn't notice yellow flares when whistle blew . A little man (bayonet man) was with me when we threw bombs into the dugout. He was a good fellow.

There were apparently big traverses and good in the trench.

The dugout is just to the right of the sap.

Army Form C. 2118.

WAR DIARY
or
INTELLIGENCE SUMMARY

(Erase heading not required.)

Instructions regarding War Diaries and Intelligence Summaries are contained in F. S. Regs., Part II. and the Staff Manual respectively. Title Pages will be prepared in manuscript.

Place	Date	Hour	Summary of Events and Information	Remarks and references to Appendices
ST.ELOI.	1/3/17.		Battalion in Trenches. 2/Lt. P.T.Cooksey rejoined from Base & taken on strength.	
	2/3/17.		do Battalion in Trenches.	
	3/3/17.		Strength of Battalion officers 41, Other Ranks 938.	
RENING-HELST.	4/3/17.		Battalion relieved in SPOIL BANK Sector by 11th Bn. "The Queen's" Royal West Surrey Regt.(vide O.O.50 attached), and marched back to ALBERTA CAMP arriving about 10 p.m. Casualties from 1-4th instant, O.R.s 1 killed, 2 wounded. 2/Lt.D.J.DEAN wounded.	
	5/3/17.		Battalion on R.E. fatigues.	
	6/3/17.		Two Companies practising organisation for attack. Remainder bathing, kit inspection, etc.	
	7/3/17.		Other two Companies practising organisation for attack. Remainder bathing, kit inspection, etc. Draft of 25 O.R.s joined Battn.	
	8/3/17.		Battalion at Company Training. 2/Lt. A.E.FENTON joined from Base & taken on strength.	
	9/3/17.		R.E. fatigues.	
ST.ELOI	10/3/17.		Battalion relieved 11th Bn. "The Queen's" Royal West Surrey Regt. in SPOIL BANK Sector (vide O.O.51 attached). Strength of Battalion Officers 42, O.R.s 966.	
	11/3/17.		Battalion in Trenches.	
	12/3/17.		do	
	13/3/17.		do	
	14/3/17.		do	
	15/3/17.		do Enemy particularly quiet.	
	16/3/17.		Battalion relieved in SPOIL BANK Sector by 11th Bn. "The Queen's" Royal West Surrey Regt. (vide O.O. 52 attached). Casualties 10-16th, Officers, 1 wounded, O.R.s 7 wounded.	
RENING-HELST.	17/3/17.		Draft of 12 O.R.s joined Battalion and taken on strength. R.E. fatigues. Strength of Battalion, Officers 41, O.R.s 981.	
	18/3/17.		Usual parade service and rest day.	

Army Form C. 2118.

WAR DIARY
or
INTELLIGENCE SUMMARY

(Erase heading not required.)

Instructions regarding War Diaries and Intelligence Summaries are contained in F. S. Regs., Part II. and the Staff Manual respectively. Title Pages will be prepared in manuscript.

Place	Date	Hour	Summary of Events and Information	Remarks and references to Appendices
RENING-HELST.	19/3/17.		Presentation of Medal Ribbons by Divisional Commander. Companies practise training in attack.	
	20/3/17.		Battalion bathing.	
	21/3/17.		Company training. Companies at Divisional Gas School for instruction in anti-gas shell measures.	
ST. ELOI.	22/3/17.		Battalion relieved 11th Bn. "The Queen's" Royal West Surrey Regt. in SPOIL BANK Sector (vide O.O. 53 attached). Draft of 25 O.R.s joined Battalion & taken on strength.	
	23/3/17. 24/3/17.		Battalion in Trenches. At 4.30 p.m. enemy intensely bombarded left of our line, chiefly with minethrowers, for two hours, effectually destroying it. Small raiding party came over at dusk but only succeeded in obtaining a wounded man's pay book. It is believed that this was part of a large raid, and that our artillery were successful in dispersing the greater number of the raiders. We suffered 21 casualties from the bombardment viz, 4 O.R.s killed, 1 Officer and 16 O.R.s wounded. Strength of Battalion Officers 41, O.R.s 998.	
	25/3/17.		Battalion in Trenches. Reclaiming left front line.	
	26/3/17.		do	
	27/3/17.		do	
	28/3/17.		do	
RENING-HELST.	29/3/17.		2/Lt. G.H.ARDILL joined the Battalion for duty from the Base. Battalion relieved in trenches by 11th Bn. "The Queen's" Royal West Surrey Regt. (vide O.O. 54 attached) and proceeded by route march to ALBERTA CAMP, RENINGHELST. Casualties from 22-29th instant O.R.s 4 killed, wounded 22, wounded at duty 18. 2/Lt.E.O.E. AYLETT wounded.	
	30/3/17.		R.E. fatigues.	
	31/3/17.		Company Training. Practice in attack. Strength of Battn.Offrs.39.O.R.s 973	

1/4/17. Commanding 11th Bn. The Queen's Own (Royal West Kent) Regt.

Lt.Colonel,
Commanding 11th Bn. The Queen's Own (Royal West Kent) Regt.

Army Form C. 2118.

WAR DIARY
or
INTELLIGENCE SUMMARY

(Erase heading not required.)

Instructions regarding War Diaries and Intelligence Summaries are contained in F. S. Regs., Part II and the Staff Manual respectively. Title Pages will be prepared in manuscript.

XI R W Kent Rgt
Vol 12

Place	Date	Hour	Summary of Events and Information	Remarks and references to Appendices
RENINGHELST. M.5.a.Sheet 28.	1.4.17.		Strength of Battalion :- Officers 39, Other Ranks 973. Battalion in ALBERTA CAMP, RENINGHELST, at rest.	
ST.ELOI. Sheet 28. S.W. O.2.	3.4.17 4.4.17		Captain A.W.Puttick, proceeded to England on Commanding Officer's Course. Battalion Relieved the 11th "Queen's" Royal West Surrey Regt., on the left Sector, ST. ELOI. O.3.c. & O.4.a. Sheet 28. S.W. Relief complete 8.50 p.m. O.O. 55 attached.	
	7.4.17		Raid by 47th Division, on our Left; Battalion to form Smoke Barrage. See O.O. 56 attached. Smoke could not be released owing to wind being in wrong direction. Very heavy retaliation by enemy, our casualties - 7 killed, 11 wounded, including Capt. T.C.WRIGHT, and 2/Lt. L.W.HUDSON., Trenches considerably damaged. Strength of Battalion :- Officers 39, O.R's 965.	
	8.4.17		Battalion in trenches, quiet day. Casualties for period ending 8th April, 1917, Officers, 2 wounded. Other Ranks, Killed 13, Wounded 13, Wounded at Duty, 9.	
	9.4.17		Battalion relieved by 7th Bn. London Regt. Proceeded by Route March to CHIPPEWA CAMP, RENINGHELST, vide O.O. 57 attached.	
RENING-HELST. M.5.a. Sheet 28.	10.4.17. 12.4.17		Arrived in Camp 5 a.m. Rest Day. Battalion moved to ALBERTA CAMP, by Route March, vide O.O.58 attached. 2/Lieuts. B.W.RODNEY, H.S.CARTER, R.H.W.F. BERNARD, joined the Battalion for duty, from G.H.Q. Cadet School. Captain & Adjutant A.J.Jimenez, rejoined the Battalion and resumed duties as Adjutant.	
	13.4.17		Battalion Training. 2/Lt. C.SAMS, joined Battalion for duty from G.H.Q. Cadet School.	
	14.4.17 16.4.17 18.4.17		Strength of Battalion :- Officers, 42, Other Ranks, 950. 2/Lieuts. P.D.BERTRAM, & O.P.BROWN, joined the Battalion for duty. Battalion relieved 32nd Bn. Royal Fusiliers, in the right sector ST.ELOI.	
ST.ELOI. Sheet 28.S.W. O.2.	20.4.17.		O.7.b. to O.2.c. Sheet 28.S.W. Vide O.O.59 attached. Battalion in trenches. Day quiet until 7.30 p.m., when enemy opened an intense bombardment of our left front with heavy artillery and Minenwerfers obliterating our front line, and portions of the Reserve and communication trenches, lasting for 1½ hours. Enemy raiding party followed, and succeeded in entering the front line. Our troops prevented him reaching his object-ive - the Mine Shaft in the support line, by rifle and Lewis Gun fire. The Garrison of the Crater in front of our line were missing. In addition	

WAR DIARY or INTELLIGENCE SUMMARY

Army Form C. 2118.

Place	Date	Hour	Summary of Events and Information	Remarks and references to Appendices
ST. ELOI.	20.4.17	Cont.	we suffered the following casualties. 1 Officer, 2/Lt.B.W.RODNEY, Killed. Other Ranks, Killed 4, Wounded 13.	
	21.4.17.		Strength of Battalion :- Officers 43, Other Ranks 921.	
	22.4.17.		Captain C.F.STALLARD, joined the Battalion for duty.	
RENING-HELST.	23.4.17.		Battalion relieved by 32nd Bn. Royal Fusiliers, and marched to ALBERTA CAMP RENINGHELST, vide O.O.60 attached. Relief complete 2.30 p.m. Casualties for tour in trenches 18th - 23rd April.= Officers. Killed 1. Other Ranks, Killed 4, Missing 8, Wounded 13.	
STEENVOORDE. (Ref. Hazebrouck 5a.)	25.4.17.		Battalion marched to STEENVOORDE en route for RECQUES Training Area. vide O.O. 61 attached, and occupied billets in close proximity to the town.	
BROXEELE.	27.4.17.		Battalion continued its march to RECQUES Training Area, stopping at BROXEELE and ROUBROUCK in billets for the night. Vide O.O.62 attached.	
ZOUAFQUES.	28.4.17.		Battalion continued its march, arriving at its destination and billeting at ZOUAFQUES. Vide O.O.63 attached. Strength of Battalion :- Officers 43, Other Ranks 927. 2/Lt. G.D.GODDEN, joined the Battalion for duty from Base.	
	29.4.17.		Battalion starts training for the Offensive.	
	30.4.17.		Strength of Battalion :- Officers 43, Other Ranks 929.	

A. J. Jimenez Capt
for
Lt. Colonel.
Commanding 11th Battalion "The Queen's Own"
Royal West Kent Regiment. (Lewisham).

S E C R E T.   OPERATION ORDER NO. 50.   Copy No........
                by Lieut. Col. A.C. Corfe,
              Commanding 11th Bn. The Queen's Own
                (Royal West Kent) Regt. (Lewisham).

                                              3rd March, 1917.

1. The Battalion will be relieved by the 11th "Queen's" tomorrow, relief starting at 5.30 p.m.

2. Opposite numbers will take over in the order in which they relieve, and platoons will march off independently. Company Commanders will report to Battalion Headquarters as soon as relief is complete. Code word "MIST".

3. All movement will be by platoons at not less than 100 yards distance.

4. Maps, aeroplane photographs, trench stores, are to be handed over to incoming unit, and a copy of receipts for Trench Stores handed in to Battalion Headquarters after relief. Periscopes and sniperscopes may be handed over to opposite number at the discretion of Company Commanders, a separate receipt in duplicate for these being obtained. (These must not be confounded with Trench Store Returns).

5. Officers trench bundles, mess boxes, blankets, (properly labelled) etc., will be sent to Battalion Headquarters by 4.30 p.m. Each Company will detail a fatigue party for this, and also 4 men per Company, Headquarters included, to accompany Transport back to Camp in charge of their own Company property.

6. O.C. "C" Company will detail a fatigue party of 1 Officer and 20 men to report at Battalion Headquarters at 5.45 p.m. & will take all trench bundles, etc., down to VOORMEZEELE DUMP so as to reach there by 6.15 p.m. These men must report with full equipment ready for moving off.

7. Company cookers and Transport, under Company Quartermaster Sergeants, will meet the Battalion on the road behind DICKEBUSCH about H.27.d.8.2. there men will rest and have tea.

8. One cook per Company, under Corpl. Alderton, will report to Battalion Headquarters at 3.30 to-day, and will proceed to ALBERTA CAMP.

9. Companies will occupy exactly the same accommodation as they left at ALBERTA CAMP.

10. Trenches must be left clean & in good order. A certificate to this effect signed by the Officer Commanding Company taking over to be obtained and handed in to the Orderly Room with the Trench Store Return on arrival at Rest Billet. Fires will be left in the cook-houses, also tins of water.

11. The L.G.O. will arrange for one man from each Lewis Gun team to accompany the Transport & take over their Company guns on arrival at Camp, & the L.G.O. will detail one N.C.O. to be in charge of this party.

12. Company Commanders are responsible that all gum boots are handed over in as dry a condition as possible (in the manner in which they would like to receive them). On no account are any gum boots to be taken out of the trenches.

13. Immediately on return to Camp, O.C. Companies will render a return showing approximate number of all men available for fatigues in their Coys.

                    (Sgd) A. C. Corfe,
        Commanding 11th Bn. The Queen's Own (Royal West Kent) Regiment.
                                              (Lewisham).

Copy No.1. C.O.   8. O.C. "A" Coy.   14. I.O.
        2. Sec. in Command. 9. O.C. "B" "   15. Q.M.
        3. Major Hickson.   10. O.C. "C" "   16. T.O.
        4. Adjutant.   11. O.C. "D" "   17. R.S.M.
        5. Asst. Adjt.   12. L.G.O.   18. O.C. 11th Queen's.
        6. War Diary.   13. S.O.   19. M.O.
        7. Office Copy.

S E C R E T.   OPERATION ORDER NO. 25.   Copy No....4

by Lieut. Col. A. C. Corfe,
Commanding 11th Bn. "The Queen's Own"
5th April, 1917.   Royal West Kent Regiment. (Lewisham).

1. A Raid will be carried out by 47th Division on enemy trenches in I.34.b & d., on April 7th, 1917.

2. 41st Divisional Artillery will co-operate by a bombardment of ST. ELOI CRATERS, and other places on April 7th, commencing 6 a.m. as under :-

    6 a.m. - 9 a.m.
    10.20 a.m. - 11.20 a.m.
    2 p.m. - 2.30 p.m.
    During the raid.

3. O.C. "C" Coy., will arrange to completely evacuate trenches O.33 and O.34 not later than 7.30 a.m. on the 7th., until completion of operations, and until he is satisfied that it is safe to return.

O.C's 122 Machine Gun Company, and Trench Mortar Battery, will cover the unoccupied portion of trenches with Machine Gun and Stokes Gun Fire.

4. If wind is favourable (from W.N.W. to W.S.W.) O.C. "B" Coy., will arrange to form a Smoke Barrage from trenches O.38 and O.41, from Zero to Zero plus 60.

This smoke cloud must not extend N. of a line from I.34.c.9.1. to I.35.c.1.2.   O.C. "B" Coy., will be responsible that the wind is suitable for the discharge.

For this purpose, 3000 smoke candles and 60 boxes fuzes will be sent up; O.C. "B" Coy., will station 30 men at regular intervals along trenches O.38 and O.41, who will each let off 2 candles per minute.

5. O.C's "B" & "C" Companies will make any arrangements for the dispositions of their front line garrison they think fit, only the minimum number required to hold the line being retained.

6. Zero hour will be notified later, and correct time communicated to all concerned.

7. O.C's "B" & "C" Companies will send a report by 6 p.m. April 6th, as to their dispositions for holding the line in detail.

    (Sgd) A. C. Corfe, Lt. Colonel.
    Commanding 11th Bn. ,"The Queen's Own"
    Royal West Kent Regiment. (Lewisham).

Copy No.1. C.O.
  2. 2nd in Command.
  3. Adjutant.
  4. War Diary.
  5 Office Copy.
  6. O.C. "A" Coy.
  7. O.C. "B" "
  8. O.C. "C" "
  9. O.C. "D" "
  10. L. G. O.
  11. Int. Officer.
  12. B. B. O.

x Reference paragraph No.4 above, only 2550 S moke Candles
will be issued, and each man is to light 2 Candles per
10 yards per 2 minutes.

S E C R E T.   OPERATION ORDER NO.57.   Copy.No. 4
by Lieut.Col. A.C.Corfe,
Commanding 11th Bn. "The Queen's Own"
Royal West Kent Regiment, (Lewisham).

8th April, 1917.

1. The Battalion will be relieved by the 7th London Regiment tomorrow, relief starting about 9.30 p.m. Front Line Companies will arrange to have only the minimum garrison in the line at time of relief to avoid congestion.

2. Company Commanders will hand over all the Line held, also SEPTEMBER POST. For this purpose O.C. "C" Company will detail one section under a Sergeant to take over SEPTEMBER POST. This section will rendezvous at junction of OLD FRENCH TRENCH and CONVENT LANE at 9 a.m. tomorrow, where guides from HAMLET will conduct them to SEPTEMBER POST which they will take over.

3. O.C. Companies will detail 1 man per Platoon with 2 men from Headquarters, and 1 man from SEPTEMBER POST, to meet Lieut. Gordon-Smith, at SPOIL BANK at 6.30 p.m. tomorrow. They will proceed to KRUISSTRAATHOEK, by 8 p.m., and guide the relieving Units in to their respective positions.
"A" Coy. will be relieved by "A" Coy. 7th London Regt.
"B" "   "   "   "   " "D" "   "   "   "   "
"C" "   "   "   "   " "C" "   "   "   "   "
"D" "   "   "   "   " "B" "   "   "   "   "

4. On relief each platoon will march off independently. O.C. Coys. will report by wire in CODE to Battalion Headquarters as soon as relief is complete.

5. All movement must be by platoons at not less than 100 yards distance. CONVENT LANE and OLD FRENCH TRENCH will be reserved for the relieving unit only. Maps, Aeroplane Photos, Trench Stores, Local Dumps of Ammunition, Bombs, Water and Rations, will be handed over to incoming unit. Periscopes, Sniperscopes, and all Battalion property will be taken away.

6. Officers Trench Bundles, Mess Boxes, Blankets properly labelled, etc., will be sent to Battalion Headquarters by 7 p.m. Each Company will detail a fatigue party for this, also 4 men per Company and Headquarters to accompany Transport to Camp in charge of their own Company property.

7. O.C. "C" Coy., will detail a fatigue party of 1 Officer & 20 men, to report at Battalion Headquarters at 9 p.m., and will take Trench Bundles etc down to VOORMEZEELE DUMP to reach there by 10 p.m. These men must report with full equipment ready for moving off. The Officer in Charge will be responsible for the safe delivery of all stores under his charge.

8. The Lewis Gun Officer will arrange for 1 man from each Lewis Gun Team to accompany the Transport and take over his gun on arrival at RENINGHELST; 1 N.C.O. will be in charge of this party.

9. O.C. Companies must make a special effort to hand over trenches especially those in rear, scrupulously clean. A Certificate to this effect, signed by O.C. relieving company, will be obtained, and handed into the Orderly Room with the Trench Store Return on arrival at RENINGHELST. Fires and tins of water will be left in Cookhouses. O.C. Companies will do everything in their power to assist the relieving Officer in taking over.

10. O.C. Companies will be responsible that all Gum Boots and Trench Stores are handed over in the manner in which they would like to receive them. No Gum Boots will be taken from the Trenches.

11. The Battalion will proceed to CHIPPEWA CAMP, RENINGHELST,

P.T.O.

- 2 -

12. Platoons will proceed to CHIPPEWA via DICKEBUSCH, HALLEBAST CORNER, LA CLYTTE, then to the right along the RENINGHELST ROAD to the CAMP. Guides will be outside the Camp, under arrangements made by the Transport Officer, to conduct platoons to their quarters. A Hot meal will be provided on arrival in Camp, and O.C. Companies will report arrival accompanied by a return of Fatigue Strength.

13. Rum will be issued on the way between DICKEBUSCH and HALLEBAST CORNER at H.33.c.4.8. Platoons must only halt for the shortest (Road junction).
    possible time, to avoid congestion on the road.

14. The Relieving Lewis Guns will be brought up tonight. The Lewis Gun Officer will arrange to relieve his guns tomorrow. The incoming teams will come up early and our teams will march off under their Sergeants on relief.

15. Two Cooks per Company under L/C. Alderton, will report at Battn. Headquarters tomorrow mid-day, and will proceed back to Camp where they will receive orders from the R.Q.M.S.

                  (Sgd) A. C. Corfe. Lt. Colonel.
                  Commanding 11th Bn. "The Queen's Own"
                  Royal West Kent Regiment. (Lewisham).

Copy No. 1. C.O.
      2. Second in Command.
      3. Adjutant.
      4. War Diary.
      5. Office Copy.
      6. O.C. "A" COY.
      7. O.C. "B" "
      8. O.C. "C" "
      9. O.C. "D" "
     10. Lewis Gun Officer.
     11. Intelligence Officer.
     12. Bombing Officer.
     13. Signalling Sgt.
     14. Transport Officer.
     15. Medical Officer.
     16. R.S.M.
     17. R.Q.M.S.
     18. O.C. 7th London Regt.
     19. O.C. 1st Canadian Tun. Coy.

SECRET.

OPERATION ORDER No.55.   Copy No.........
by Lieut. Col. A.C. Corfe,
Commanding 11th Bn. The Queen's Own
(Royal West Kent) Rgt.

3rd April, 1917.

1. The Battalion will relieve the 11th "Queen's" Royal West Surrey Rgt. tomorrow, and will take over trenches as hereunder, namely:-
    Right Front Company.   "C" Company.
    Left Front Company.   "B"   "
    Right Support Company.   "A"   "
    Left Support Company.   "D"   "

2. Reveille   7.15 a.m.
3. Breakfasts   8 a.m.
4. Dinners.   12 noon.

5. Order and time of march:-
    Signallers (Headquarters).......1.30 p.m.
    "D" Company.....................1.40 p.m.
    "A" Company.....................1.55 p.m.
    Headquarters...................2.5 p.m.
    "B" Company.....................2.15 p.m.
    "C" Company.....................2.25 p.m.
   Lewis Gunners and Company Signallers will report to the O.C. Companies to which they are attached, & will march with their Companies.
   Snipers will move as a platoon of "A" Company.
   Platoon Commanders must not on any pretext halt their men in DICKEBUSCH.
   Platoons to march at 100 yards distance.
   Company Commanders will insist that these orders are observed. They are reminded that these are Divisional orders.

6. The Battalion will halt and rest at N.26.b.Central. The cookers will be sent on earlier and have tea ready for the men.
   O.C. Companies are responsible that all papers, tins, etc., are buried.

7. The Companies will move off from here as follows:-
    Signallers (Headquarters).......4 p.m.
    "D" Company....................4.10 p.m.
    "A" Company....................4.25 p.m.
    Headquarters...................4.35 p.m.
    "B" Company....................4.45 p.m.
    "C" Company....................4.55 p.m.

8. The Lewis Guns will be taken up by transport this afternoon with 2 men per gun. The Lewis Gun Officer will detail 2 N.C.O.'s to be in charge of this party. The Transport Officer will please arrange for 2 limbers to be ready outside Battalion H.Q. at 6 p.m. They will arrange to change over the "Queen's" guns for our own during the course of tomorrow morning.

9. Officers mess boxes, and trench bundles will be stacked in the Sergeants' Mess. Officers servants will remain behind with these & come up with the Transport in the evening, & they will also act as a loading party.

10. Each man will carry his pack & leave his surplus kit in a sandbag. Blankets in bundles of 10 & sandbags properly labelled will be stacked before moving off. O.C. Companies will see that Officers valises are given over to their C.Q.M.S.'s & stacked in "D" Company's stores before moving off.

11. List of trench stores taken over will be forwarded to the Adjutant immediately after the relief is completed.

12. The relief will be carried out as quietly & carefully as possible, and completion reported to Battalion H.Q. by 'phone, "BAB" Code being used.

13. All waterbottles will be filled before moving off.

14. Coy. Commanders will be held responsible for the cleanliness of their Huts, Lines, Latrines, Wash-houses, Officers mess Cook-houses, etc..

P.T.O.

15. Company Commanders will hand their Company Conduct Sheets into the Orderly Room this evening & obtain a receipt for same.

16. O.C. "A" Company will please detail a fatigue party of 1 Officer & 30 men as a carrying party. This party will proceed from the camp in advance of the transport, and will move off at 4 p.m. Any details who have not proceeded with their Companies will go with this party and will report to the Officer in charge.

17. O.C. "B", "C", and "D" Companies will arrange each for a guide to report to the Adjutant at 6.30 p.m. tomorrow at Battalion H.Q. to meet ration party, take over from his C.Q.M.S., & guide ration party to Company.

18. O.C. Right and Left Front Companies will please arrange to have a Test S.O.S. each night in the trenches. A full report on each occasion should be forwarded to Battalion H.Q. <u>by 6.30 a.m.</u> the following morning stating the time taken from handing in the telephone message until the shell passes over the trench.

19. Company Commanders are requested to send in all returns punctually. Unpunctuality in this respect involves unnecessary correspondence.

20. A nominal roll of men remaining behind (stating cause) will be handed in to the Orderly Room before Companies move off.

(sgd.) A. C. Corfe, Lieut. Colonel,
Commanding 11th Bn. The Queen's Own
(Royal West Kent) Regt. (Lewisham).

Copy No. 1. C.O.
2. Second in Command.
3. Adjutant.
4. War Diary.
5. Office Copy.
6. O.C. "A" Coy.
7. O.C. "B" Coy.
8. O.C. "C" Coy.
9. O.C. "D" Coy.
10. Lewis Gun Officer.
11. Quartermaster.
12. Transport Officer.
13. Signalling Sergt.
14. Intelligence Officer.
15. Bombing Officer.
16. R.S.M.
17. O.C. MUSCLE.
18. Medical Officer.

SECRET.   OPERATION ORDER No. 51.   Copy No...

by Lt. Col. A.C. Corfe,
Commanding 11th Bn. The Queen's Own
(Royal West Kent) Rt. (Lewisham).

9th March, 1917.

1. The Battalion will relieve the 11th "Queen's" Royal West Surrey Regt. tomorrow, and will take over trenches as hereunder, namely:-
   Right Front Coy.   "A" Coy.
   Left Front Coy.   "D" Coy.
   Right Support Coy.   "C" Coy.
   Left Support Coy.   "B" Coy.

2. Reveille 7.15 a.m.
3. Breakfasts 8 a.m.

4. Order and time of march:-
   Signallers (Headquarters)......12.20 p.m.
   "D" Coy.........................12.25 p.m.
   "A" Coy.........................12.35 p.m.
   "B" Coy.........................12.50 p.m.
   Headquarters....................1 p.m.
   "C" Coy.........................1.10 p.m.

   Lewis Gunners and Company Signallers will report to the O.C. Companies to which they are attached, and will march with their Companies.
   Snipers will move as a Platoon of "D" Company.
   Platoon Commanders must not on any pretext halt their men in DICKLBUSCH.
   Platoons to march at 100 yards distance.
   Company Commanders will insist that these orders are observed. They are reminded that these are Divisional Orders.

5. The Battalion will halt and rest at H.27.d.8.2. The cookers will be sent on earlier and will have a hot meal ready for the men.
   O.C. Companies are responsible that all papers, tins, etc, are buried.

6. The Companies will move off from here as follows:-
   Signallers (Headquarters)......2.45 p.m.
   "D" Coy.........................3 p.m.
   "A" Coy.........................3.10 p.m.
   "B" Coy.........................3.25 p.m.
   Headquarters....................3.35 p.m.
   "C" Coy.........................3.45 p.m.

7. The Lewis Guns will be taken up by Transport this afternoon with 2 men per gun. The Lewis Gun Officer will detail 2 N.C.O.'s to be in charge of this party. The Transport Officer will please arrange for 2 limbers to be ready outside Battalion Headquarters at 5 p.m. They will arrange to change over the "Queen's" guns for our own during the course of tomorrow morning.

8. Officers mess boxes and trench bundles will be stacked in the Mess Room of the Details Hut. Officers servants will remain behind with these and come up with the Transport in the evening, and they will also act as a loading party.

9. Each man will carry his pack and leave his surplus kit in a sandbag. Blankets in bundles of 10 and sandbags properly labelled will be stacked before moving off. O.C. Companies will see that Officers valises are given over to their C.Q.M.S.'s and stacked in "D" Company's stores before moving off.

10. List of trench stores taken over will be forwarded to the Adjutant immediately after the relief is completed.

11. The relief will be carried out as quietly and carefully as possible, & completion reported to Battalion H.Q. by 'phone, Code Word, "COLD."

12. All waterbottles will be filled before moving off.

13. Coy. Commanders will be held responsible for the cleanliness of their Huts, Lines, Latrines, Wash-houses, Officers Mess Cook-houses, etc.

P.T.O.

-2-.

14. Company Commanders will hand their Company Conduct Sheets into the Orderly Room this evening and obtain a receipt for same.

15. O.C. "C" Company will please detail a fatigue party of 1 Officer and 50 men as a carrying party. This party will proceed from the camp in advance of the Transport, and will move off at 4 p.m. Any details who have not proceeded with their Companies will go with this party and will report to the Officer in charge.

16. O.C. "A", "B", and "D" Companies will arrange each for a guide to report to the Adjutant at 7.30 p.m. tomorrow at Battalion Headquarters to accompany ration party, take over from his C.Q.M.S., and guide ration party to Company.

17. O.C. "A" and "D" Companies will please arrange to have a Test S.O.S. each night in the trenches. A full report on each occasion should be forwarded to Battalion Headquarters by 7 a.m. the following morning stating the time taken from handing in the telephone message until the shell passes over the trench.

18. Company Commanders are requested to send in all returns punctually. Unpunctuality in this respect involves unnecessary correspondence.

(Sgd). A.C. Corfe, Lieut. Colonel,
Commanding 11th Bn. The Queen's Own (Royal West Kent) Rt.(Lewisham).

Copy No. 1. C.O.
2. Second in Command.
3. Major Hickson.
4. Adjutant.
5. Asst. Adjutant.
6. War Diary.
7. Office Copy.
8. O.C. "A" Coy.
9. O.C. "B" Coy.
10. O.C. "C" Coy.
11. O.C. "D" Coy.
12. Lewis Gun Officer.
13. Quartermaster.
14. Transport Officer.
15. Signalling Officer.
16. Intelligence Officer.
17. Bombing Officer.
18. R.S.M.
19. O.C. MUSCLE.
20. Medical Officer.

Adjutant

S E C R E T. OPERATION ORDER NO.58   Copy No. 4
by Lieut. Col. A. C. Corfe,
Commanding 11th Bn. "The Queen's Own"
Royal West Kent Regt. (Lewisham).

11th April, 1917.

1. The Battalion will move to its old quarters at ALBERTA CAMP tomorrow. Each Company will occupy exactly the same quarters as formerly.

2. Packs of all men recently inoculated, properly labelled will be dumped at the end of the Duckboards by the Sergeants Mess by 1.30 p.m. Officers Valises, Mess Boxes, Medical Officer's and Orderly Room Boxes will be at the same place by 2 p.m.

3. Each Company and Headquarters will detail 1 N.C.O. and 3 men to superintend the loading of these stores, and will accompany Transport back to Camp. Each N.C.O. will be responsible for his Company property.

4. The Transport Officer will arrange for 1 Limber per Company, 2 for Packs and 2 G.S. Wagons for Headquarter Stores etc, and horses for the Cookers, to be at CHIPPAWA CAMP by 2.30 p.m.

5. Companies will march off by Platoons as under:-
    "B" Company   2 p.m.
    "A"   "   2.15 p.m.
    "C"   "   2.30 p.m.
    "D"   "   2.45 p.m.
    Headquarters.   3 p.m.
The Route taken is left to the discretion of O.C. Companies.

6. All men except those recently inoculated will carry full equipment, packs and blankets.

7. The Guard will remain at CHIPPAWA CAMP until the incoming Unit arrives. On arrival at ALBERTA CAMP, O.C. "B" Company will detail a Guard of 1 N.C.O. and 4 men to mount at once.

8. Before leaving CHIPPAWA CAMP, O.C. Companies will be satisfied that their huts and lines are scrupulously clean.

(Sgd) A. C. CORFE. Lieut. Colonel.
Commanding 11th Bn "The Queen's Own"
Royal West Kent Regiment. (Lewisham).

Copy No.1. C.O.   No.9. O.C. "D" Coy.
      2. Second in Command.   10. L.G.O.
      3. Adjutant.   11. I.O.
      4. War Diary.   12. B.B.O.
      5. Office Copy.   13. M.O.
      6. O.C. "A" Coy.   14. T.O.
      7. O.C. "B" "   15. R.S.M.
      8. O.C. "C" "   16. R.Q.M.S.

S E C R E T.   OPERATION ORDER No.60   Copy No.....
by Lieut.Col. A.C.Corfe,
Commanding 11th Bn "The Queen's Own"
Royal West Kent Regiment.(Lewisham).

1. The Battalion will be relieved by KNUCKLE tomorrow, relief starting about 10 a.m. Front Line Companies will please arrange to have only the garrison in the line at time of relief, so as to avoid congestion. On relief, the Battalion will proceed to ALBERTA CAMP, RENINGHELST. The Quartermaster will take over the Camp tomorrow morning, and C.Q.M.S's will meet their Companies at the Camp.

2. Opposite numbers will take over in the order in which they relieve and platoons will march off independently. Company Commanders will report by wire to Battalion Headquarters as soon as relief is completed. Private code to be used.

3. All movement will be by platoons at ¼ of an hour intervals.

4. Maps, Aeroplane photographs, trench stores, local dumps of S.A.A. bombs, water, rations, and Defense Schemes are to be handed over to incoming unit, and a copy of the receipt for trench stores must be sent to the Adjutant after relief.

5. Periscopes and Very Pistols must be handed over and <u>separate receipts taken.</u>

6. Officers Trench Bundles, blankets properly labelled, etc will be sent to the BRASSERIE by 9.30 p.m. tonight. Each Company will detail a fatigue party for this, also 4 men per Company and Headquarters to accompany transport to Camp in charge of their own Company property.

7. Lewis Gunners and Company Signallers will be relieved at the same time as their Companies. Snipers will march off under their Sergt when relieved.

8. The Transport Sergeant will arrange for 1 limber per Company for Lewis Guns to be at Y.M.C.A. Hut, DICKEBUSCH, tomorrow, as follows:-
   - 1st Limber   10.45 a.m.
   - 2nd.   "   11.45 a.m.
   - 3rd.   "   12.45 p.m.
   - 4th.   "   1.45 p.m.

9. Lewis Guns will be taken by their platoons as far as DICKEBUSCH where they will be loaded on the Company Limber, the Lewis Gun Team being responsible for same. O.C. Companies will detail one N.C.O. and one man per Lewis Gun Team to march with each limber.

10. O.C. Companies must make a special effort to hand over trenches, especially those in rear, scrupulously clean. A Certificate to this effect signed by O.C. relieving Company will be obtained and handed to the Adjutant with the trench store return. Fires and tins of water will be left in cookhouses. O.C. Companies will do everything in their power to assist the relieving Officer in taking over.

11. O.C. Companies will be responsible that all gum boots and trench stores are handed over in the manner in which they would like to receive them. No gum boots will be taken from trenches.

12. O.C. Companies will detail 2 Cooks per Company to report at Battalion Headquarters at 6 a.m. They will proceed to ALBERTA CAMP in charge of Sergt. Alderton, and report to the R.Q.M.S.

P.T.O.

- 2 -

13. A hot meal will be provided on arrival in Camp.

14. O.C. Companies will report arrival in Camp, accompanied by a return of fatigue strength.

15. Companies will occupy same accommodation as they left in ALBERTA CAMP.

                (Sgd) A.C.Corfe, Lieut.Colonel.
                Commanding 11th Bn "The Queen's Own"
                Royal West Kent Regiment. (Lewisham).

Copy No.			
1	C.O.	10.	Intelligence Offr.
2	Adjutant.	11.	Bombing Offr.
3	War Diary.	12.	Medical Offr.
4	Office Copy.	13.	Signalling Offr.
5	O.C. "A" Coy.	14.	Lieut. Kerr.
6	O.C. "B" "	15.	R.S.M.
7	O.C. "C" "	16.	A/Quartermaster.
8	O.C. "D" "	17.	Transport Sergt.
9	Lewis Gun Offr.	18.	O.C. KNUCKLE.

SECRET.   OPERATION ORDER No. 52.   Copy No........
                                 by Lt. Col. A.C. Corfe,
                             Commanding 11th Bn. The Queen's Own
                                (Royal West Kent) Rt. (Lewisham).

                                                      15th March, 1917.

1. The Battalion will be relieved by the 11th "Queen's" tomorrow, relief starting at 6.30 p.m.

2. Opposite numbers will take over in the order in which they relieve, and platoons will march off independently. Company Commanders will report by wire to Battalion Headquarters as soon as relief is complete. Code word "WET".

3. All movement will be by platoons at not less than 100 yards distance.

4. Maps, aeroplane photographs, trench stores are to be handed over to incoming unit, & a copy of receipts for Trench Stores handed in to Battalion H.Q. after relief. Periscopes and sniperscopes may be handed over to opposite number at the Discretion of Coy. Commanders, a separate receipt in duplicate for these being obtained. (These must not be confounded with Trench Store Returns.).

5. Officers trench bundles, mess boxes, blankets, (properly labelled) etc., will be sent to Battalion H.Q. by 4.30 p.m. Each Coy. will detail a fatigue party for this, & also 4 men per Coy., Headquarters included, to accompany Transport back to Camp in charge of their own Coy. property.

6. O.C. "A" Coy. will detail a fatigue party of 1 Officer & 20 men to report at Battalion H.Q. at 6.15 p.m., & will take all trench bundles etc, down to VOORMEZEELE DUMP so as to reach there by 7 p.m. These men must report with full equipment ready for moving off.

7. Coy. cookers & Transport, under Coy. Quartermaster Sergeants, will meet the Battalion on the road behind DICKEBUSCH about H.27.d.8.2. There men will rest and have tea.

8. One cook per Coy. under Cpl. Alderton, will report to Battalion H.Q. at 3.30 to-day, and will proceed to ALBERTA CAMP.

9. Companies will occupy exactly the same accommodation as they left at ALBERTA CAMP.

10. Trenches must be left clean & in good order. A certificate to this effect signed by the Officer Commanding Coy. taking over to be obtained & handed in to the Orderly Room with the Trench Store Return on arrival at Rest Billet. Fires will be left in the cook-houses, also tins of water.

11. The L.G.O. will arrange for 1 man from each Lewis Gun team to accompany the Transport & take over their Coy. guns on arrival at Camp, and the L.G.O will detail one N.C.O. to be in charge of this party.

12. Coy. Commanders are responsible that all gum boots are handed over in as dry a condition as possible (in the manner in which they would like to receive them). On no account are any gum boots to be taken out of the trenches.

13. Immediately on return to camp O.C. Companies will render a return showing approximate number of all men available for fatigues in their Companies.

                            (Sgd) A. C. Corfe, Lt. Colonel,
              Commanding 11th Bn. The Queen's Own (Royal West Kent) Regt.
                                                      (Lewisham).

Copy No.1. C.O.   8. O.C. "A" coy.   15. Q.M.
        2. Second in Com.   9. O.C. "B" "   16. T.O.
        3. Major Hickson.   10. O.C. "C" "   17. R.S.M.
        4. Adjt.   11. O.C. "D" "   18. O.C. "MUSCLE.
        5. Asst. Adjt.   12. L.G.O.   19. M.O.
        6. War Diary.   13. S.O.   20. B.B.O.
        7. Office Copy.   14. I.O.

War Diary

S E C R E T.   OPERATION ORDER NO.59   Copy No...4..
by Lieut.Col.A.C.Corfe,
Commanding 11th Bn "The Queen's Own"
Royal West Kent Regiment. (Lewisham).

17th April, 1917.

1. The Battalion will relieve KNUCKLE tomorrow, and will take over trenches as under:-
   Right Front Company   "A" Coy.
   Left Front Company.   "D" "
   Reserve XXXXXXXXXXXX Coy.   "C" " (in McGEE Trench).
   XXXX Support Coy.   "B" " (in R.Line).

2. Reveille 6.30 a.m.
   Breakfasts 7 a.m.

3. Order and Time of march:-
   Signallers (H.Qrs.)   7.30 a.m.
   "D" Company.   7.45 a.m.
   "A" "   8.45 a.m.
   "B" "   9.45 a.m.
   "C" "   10.45 a.m.
   Headquarters.   11.45 a.m.

4. Lewis Gunners and Company Signallers will report to O.C. Companies to which they are attached, and will march with their companies.
   Snipers will move off as a platoon of "D" Company.
   Platoon Commanders must not on any pretext halt their men in DICKEBUSCH. Platoons to march at 15 minute intervals.
   Company Commanders will insist that these orders are observed.

5. The Lewis Guns will be taken up by Transport as far as DICKEBUSCH. The Transport Officer will arrange for 1 limber per company.
   O.C. Companies will detail 1 Sergt. per company and 1 man per Lewis Gun Team to march with each limber. Each platoon will carry their Lewis Guns from DICKEBUSCH, the Lewis Gun Teams being responsible for same.

6. Officers Mess boxes and trench bundles will be stacked in the Sergeants Mess. Officers Servants will remain behind with these and come up with the Transport in the evening, and they will also act as a loading party.

7. Each man will carry his pack, and leave his surplus kit in a sandbag. Blankets <u>in bundles of ten</u>, and sandbags <u>properly labelled</u>, will be stacked before moving off. O.C. Companies will see that Officers Valises are given over to their C.Q.M.S's and stacked in the Quartermaster's Stores, before moving off.

8. List of Trench Stores taken over will be forwarded to the Adjutant immediately after the relief is completed.

9. The relief will be carried out as quietly and carefully as possible, and completion reported to Battalion H.Q. by phone, "B A B" Code being used.

10. All Waterbottles will be filled before moving off.

11. Rations for the whole day must be carried by all ranks.

12. Company Commanders will be held responsible for the cleanliness of their huts, lines, latrines, wash-houses, Officers'Mess Cookhouses etc.

P.T.O.

- 2 -

13. Company Commanders will hand their Company Conduct Sheets into the Orderly Room this evening and obtain a receipt for same.

14. O.C. Companies will arrange each for 1 guide per Company to report to the Adjutant at 8.30 p.m. tomorrow, at Battalion Headquarters, to meet ration party, take over from his C.Q.M.S., and guide ration party to Company.

15. O.C. Right and Left front Companies will please arrange to have a test S.O.S. each night in the trenches. A full report on each occasion should be forwarded to Battalion Headquarters by 6.30 a.m. the following morning, stating the time taken from handing in the telephone message until the shell passes over the trench.

16. Company Commanders are requested to send in all returns punctually. Unpunctuality in this respect involves unnecessary correspondence.

17. A nominal roll of men remaining behind (stating cause) will be handed into the Orderly Room before Companies move off.

18. Platoons will meet guides from KNUCKLE at DICKEBUSCH Y.M.C.A. Hut.

    (Sgd) A.C.Corfe. Lieut. Colonel.
    Commanding 11th Bn. "The Queen's Own"
    Royal West Kent Regiment. (Lewisham).

Copy No. 1. C.O.
      2. Second in Command.
      3. Adjutant.
      4. War Diary.
      5. Office Copy.
      6. O.C. "A" Coy.
      7. O.C. "B" "
      8. O.C. "C" "
      9. O.C. "D" "
     10. Lewis Gun Officer.
     11. Intelligence Officer.
     12. Signalling Officer.
     13. Bombing Officer.
     14. Medical Officer.
     15. Transport Officer.
     16. R.S.M.
     17. Quartermaster.
     18. O.C. KNUCKLE.
     19. O.C. DAGGER.

SECRET.   OPERATION ORDER No.53.   Copy No. 6
                           by Lieut. Col. A.C. Corfe,
                              Commanding 11th Bn. The Queen's Own
                              (Royal West Kent) Rt. (Lewisham).

                                                    21st March, 1917.

1. The Battalion will relieve the 11th "Queen's" Royal West Surrey Regt. tomorrow, and will take over trenches as hereunder, namely:-
                Right Front Company   "C" Coy.
                Left Front Company.   "B" Coy.
                Right Support Coy.   "A" Coy.
                Left Support Coy.   "D" Coy.

2. Reveille   7.15 a.m.
3. Breakfasts   8 a.m.

4. Order and time of march.-
                Signallers (Headquarters)..............12.20 p.m.
                "B" Company...........................12.25 p.m.
                "C" Company...........................12.35 p.m.
                "D" Company...........................12.50 p.m.
                Headquarters..........................1 p.m.
                "A" Company...........................1.10 p.m.
   Lewis Gunners and Company Signallers will report to the O.C. Companies to
   which they are attached, & will march with their Companies.
   Snipers will move as a platoon of "B" Company.
   Platoon Commanders must not on any pretext halt their men in DICKEBUSCH.
   Platoons to march at 100 yards distance.
   Company Commanders will insist that these orders are observed. They are
   reminded that these are Divisional Orders.

5. The Battalion will halt and rest at H.27.d.8.2. The cookers will be sent
   on earlier and have a hot meal ready for the men.
   O.C. Companies are responsible that all papers, tins, etc., are buried.

6. The Companies will move off from here as follows:-
                Signallers (Headquarters).........2.45 p.m.
                "B" Company......................3 p.m.
                "C" Company......................3.10 p.m.
                "D" Company......................3.25 p.m.
                Headquarters.....................3.35 p.m.
                "A" Company......................3.45 p.m.

7. The Lewis Guns will be taken up by Transport this afternoon with 2 men per
   gun. The Lewis Gun Officer will detail 2 N.C.O.'s to be in charge of this
   party. The Transport Officer will please arrange for 2 limbers to be ready
   outside Battalion H.Q. at 5.30 p.m. They will arrange to change over the
   "Queen's guns for our own during the course of tomorrow morning.

8. Officers mess boxes, and trench bundles will be stacked in the Sergeants
   Mess. Officers servants will remain behind with these and come up with the
   Transport in the evening, & they will also act as a loading party.

9. Each man will carry his pack & leave his surplus kit in a sandbag. Blankets
   in bundles of 10 & sandbags properly labelled will be stacked before moving
   off. O.C. Companies will see that Officers valises are given over to their
   C.Q.M.S.'s & stacked in "D" Company's stores before moving off.

10. List of trench stores taken over will be forwarded to the Adjutant
    immediately after the relief is completed

11. The relief will be carried out as quietly and carefully as possible, and
    completion reported to Battalion H.Q. by 'phone, "Bab" Code being used.

12. All water bottles will be filled before moving off.

13. Coy. Commanders will be held responsible for the cleanliness of their Huts,
    Lines, Latrines, Wash-houses, Officers mess cook-houses, etc.

14. Company Commanders will hand their Coy. Conduct Sheets into the Orderly
    Room this evening & obtain a receipt for same.

                                                            P.T.O.

15. O.C. "A" Company will please detail a fatigue party of 1 Officer & 30 men as a carrying party. This party will proceed from the Camp in advance of the Transport, & will move off at 3 p.m. Any details who have not proceeded with their Companies will go with this party & will report to the Officer in Charge.

16. O.C. "B", "C", and "D" Companies will arrange each for a guide to report to the Adjutant at 7.30 p.m. tomorrow at Battalion H.Q. to accompany ration party, take over from his C.Q.M.S., & guide ration party to Coy.

17. O.C. "B" and "C" Companies will please arrange to have a Test S.O.S. each night in the trenches. A full report on each occasion should be forwarded to Battalion H.Q. by 6.30 a.m. the following morning stating the time taken from handing in the telephone message until the shell passes over the trench.

18. Company Commanders are requested to send in all returns punctually. Unpunctuality in this respect involves unnecessary correspondence.

19. A nominal roll of men remaining behind (stating cause) will be handed into the Orderly Room before Companies move off.

      (Sgd) A. C. Corfe, Lieut. Colonel,
 Commanding 11th Bn. The Queen's Own (Royal West Kent) Rt. (Lewisham).

Copy No. 1. C.O.
   2. Second in Command.
   3. Adjutant.
   4. Asst. Adjutant.
   5. War Diary.
   6. Office Copy.
   7. O.C. "A" Coy.
   8. O.C. "B" Coy.
   9. O.C. "C" Coy.
  10. O.C. "D" Coy.
  11. Lewis Gun Officer.
  12. Quartermaster.
  13. Transport Officer.
  14. Signalling Officer.
  15. Intelligence Officer.
  16. Bombing Officer.
  17. R.S.M.
  18. O.C. MUSCLE.
  19. Medical Officer.

War Diary

S E C R E T.   OPERATION ORDER NO.61   Copy No. 3
                by Lieut.Col. A.C.Corfe,
                Commanding 11th Bn "The Queen's Own"
                Royal West Kent Regt. (Lewisham).

                                                24th April, 1917.

1. The Brigade will march tomorrow to STEENVOORDE en route for RECQUES Training Area. Starting Point road junction N.W. of Z in ZEVECOTEN.

2. Order of March :- 122nd Bde. Trench Mortar Battery., 12th East Surrey Regt., 11th Royal West Kent Regt., 15th Hampshire Regt., 18th K.R.R.C., 122nd Machine Gun Company.

3. The usual clock hour halts will be observed.

4. The march will be continued on the 27th and 28th under orders to be issued later.

5. The Battalion will parade tomorrow at 9.30 a.m. on road outside Bn. Headquarters, head of column facing RENINGHELST. Order of March:-
   Band, A, B, C, D, Headquarters and Transport.

6. Dress. Fighting Order with waterproof sheets under flap of haversack. Steel helmets to be strapped on haversack. Haversack to be worn on the back.

7. Transport will march in rear of the Battalion.

8. A Billeting Party of 1 N.C.O. per Company and Headquarters, will report to Lieut. Gordon-Smith, at 7.30 a.m. tomorrow. This party must have full particulars of the requirements of their Companies and must have bicycles.

9. Immediately on arrival in billets O.C. Companies must report the exact position of their Company Headquarters, to the Adjutant.

10. Two Motor Lorries are being sent to the Battalion to transport blankets and packs.

11. Blankets in bundles of 10, and packs, will be stacked outside the Quartermaster's Stores by 7.30 a.m. These must be stacked separately and by companies, and must be properly labelled. Every pack must have the name of the man and his Company clearly marked on it. O.C. Companies will each detail one man to proceed with lorries. These men must report to the Adjutant for instructions.

12. Officers Kits must be stacked outside the Quartermaster's Stores by 7.30 a.m. to be loaded on the G.S.Wagons.

13. Mess Cart will be loaded by 9 a.m.

14. Lewis Guns, Mobile Reserve of S.A.A. and Grenades, must be loaded on limbers at 6 p.m. tonight.

15. The Medical Officer's Cart will be loaded at 6 p.m.

16. The Transport Sergeant will see that the G.S.Wagons, Limbers, M.O's Cart and Mess Cart, are on the road outside Battalion Headquarters to be loaded at above times.

                                                    P.T.O.

-2-

17. O.C. "C" Coy., will detail 1 Officer & 20 Men to load the Motor Lorries tomorrow morning. The same party will unload the lorries on arrival at STEENVOORDE.

18. Sick Parade will be at 7 a.m.

19. Particular attention to be paid on the march to "March Discipline" No men will be allowed to ride on any wagons. Company Commanders will be responsible for taking the names of any men who fall out on the march. No man will fall out without permission from an Officer.

20. Dinner will be had on arrival at STEENVOORDE.

                                 (Sgd) A.C.Corfe. Lieut. Colonel.
                                      11th Bn "The Queen's Own"
                              Royal West Kent Regiment (Lewisham).

Copy No.			
1.	O.C.	10.	Intelligence Offr.
2.	Adjutant.	11.	Signalling Offr.
3.	War Diary.	12.	Bombing Offr.
4.	Office Copy.	13.	Lt. Kerr.
5.	O.C. "A" Coy.	14.	Medical Offr.
6.	O.C. "B" "	15.	R. S. M.
7.	O.C. "C" "	16.	A/Quartermaster.
8.	O.C. "D" "	17.	Transport Sergt.
9.	L. G. O.		

SECRET.   OPERATION ORDER NO. 62.   Copy No. 2.
by Lieut.Col. A.C.Corfe,
Commanding 11th Bn. "The Queen's Own"
Royal West Kent Regt. (Lewisham).

26th April, 1917.

1. The Brigade will march tomorrow to ROUBROUCK in column of three's

2. In addition to clock hour halts there will be a two hour halt when head of column reaches LE TOM about 12 noon.

3. The Transport will be Brigaded (except Cookers, watercarts, and Mess Cart), and head of transport must pass the starting point (Bandstand) STEENVOORDE) at 9.1 a.m.

4. The Battalion will parade in column of three's (not column of 4's) at 8.50 a.m. on road outside "C" Company's Headquarters, facing STEENVOORDE, tail of column at "C" Company's Headquarters.
 Order of March. "D" Coy, Headquarters, Band, "A", "B", "C" Coys., Lewis Gun Handcarts, remainder of transport. Dress - Fighting Order.

5. O.C. Companies must see that their companies are told off in 3 lines; the leading and rear platoons× must have their magazines charged in case of attack by hostile aircraft. × of the Battalion

6. Immediately on arrival in billets, companies must send 3 runners per company to Battalion Headquarters to report the exact position of their company Headquarters.

7. Blankets in bundles of 10 will be stacked outside their respective Headquarters at 6.30 a.m., to be loaded on Motor Lorries. O.C. Companies will each detail 2 men to proceed with lorries.

8. Officers Kits must be stacked outside their respective Company Headquarters at 7 a.m., the G.S. Wagons calling for same. The Quartermaster will detail a representative to supervise the packing and he must report to the Transport Officer at ~~7 a.m.~~ 6.30 a.m.

9. Mess Cart will call at each Company Headquarters at 7.30 a.m., to pick up the one Mess box allowed per company on the Mess Cart.

10. G.S. Wagon and Mess Cart must on no account be delayed at Company Headquarters.

11. Breakfasts will be had before moving off.

12. Dinners will be had on the march at mid-day halt.

13. Sick parade at 6.0 ~~7.30~~ a.m. at Battalion Headquarters. N.C.O's and men reporting sick will rejoin their companies at the starting point, and will be marched there under the senior N.C.O.

(Sgd) A. C. Corfe, Lieut.Colonel.
Comndg. 11th Bn. "The Queen's Own"
Royal West Kent Regiment (Lewisham).

Copy No. 1 C.O.
2. Adjutant.
3. War Diary.
4. Office Copy.
5. O.C. "A" Coy.
6. O.C. "B" "
7. O.C. "C" "
8. O.C. "D" "
9. L."G."O."
10. Intelligence Offr.
11. Bombing Offr.
12. Signalling Offr.
13. Transport Offr.
14. Medical Offr.
15. R.S.M.
16. Quartermaster.

War Diary

OPERATION ORDERS No 63
by Lieut. Col. A.C. Corfe
Comdg. 11th R.W.K. Regt
27th April 1917

1. The Brigade will continue its march tomorrow to the RECQUES Training Area.
2. The Battn. will be billetted at ZOUAFQUES.
3. The Battn. will parade in column of three's at 9. am on road outside Battn. H.Q. at church BROXEELE, head of column facing West. Order of March "C" H-Qrs. Band "D" "B" "A" Coys, Handcarts, Transport.
4. Blankets in bundles of 10 & packs will be stacked outside their Coy. H.Q. by 6.30 am. The Lorries will make 2 journeys. O/C Coys will detail 3 men per Coy. to proceed with lorries on first journey, & leave 2 men per coy. behind to come with lorries on second journey. One man per Coy. must return with the lorries after the first journey to guide lorries to their respective Coys. The men must be given written instruction.
5. The Meco Cart will report at Battn. H.Q. at 8.30 am.
6. Breakfasts will be had before moving off.
7. Dinner will be had on the march.
8. Sick parade at 6. am at the School (Battn H.Q.)
9. Billetting parties will parade at Battn. H.Q. at 4.30 am and will report to Lt. G. Gordon Smith.

(Sgd) A.C. Corfe. Lieut. Col.
Comdg. 11th Bn. R.W.Kent. Regt.

SECRET.   OPERATION ORDER NO.54.   Copy No. 4.
by Lieut. Col. A.C. Corfe,
Commanding 11th Bn. The Queen's Own
(Royal West Kent) Rt. (Lewisham).

28th March, 1917.

1. The Battalion will be relieved by the 11th "Queen's" tomorrow, relief starting at 7 p.m. Front Line Companies will please arrange to have only the garrison in the line at the time of relief, so as to avoid congestion.

2. Opposite numbers will take over in the order in which they relieve, and platoons will march off independently. Coy. Commanders will report by wire to Battalion H.Q. as soon as relief is complete. Code to be used.

3. All movement will be by platoons at not less than 100 yards distance.

4. Maps, aeroplane photographs, trench stores are to be handed over to incoming unit, & a copy of receipts for Trench Stores handed in to Battalion H.Q. after relief. Periscopes & sniperscopes may be handed over to opposite number at the discretion of Coy. Commanders, a separate receipt in duplicate for these being obtained. (These must not be confounded with Trench Store Returns.).

5. Officers trench bundles, mess boxes, blankets (properly labelled) etc, will be sent to Battalion H.Q. by 5 p.m. Each Coy. will detail a fatigue party for this, & also 4 men per Coy., Headquarters included, to accompany Transport back to Camp in charge of their own Coy. property. Officers servants & cooks who are returning to camp in advance, must report at Battalion H.Q. at 3 p.m. & be marched down under the senior soldier.

6. O.C. "C" Coy. will detail a fatigue party of 1 Officer & 20 men to report at Battalion H.Q. at 7.45 p.m. & will take all trench bundles, etc., down to VOORMEZEELE DUMP so as to reach there by 8.15 p.m. These men must report with full equipment ready for moving off.

7. Coy. cookers and Transport under Coy. Q/M. Sergts. will meet the Battalion on the road behind DICKEBUSCH about H.26.b.Central. There men will rest & have tea.

8. One cook per Coy., under Col. Alderton, will report to Battalion H.Q. at 3.30 to-day, & will proceed to ALBERTA CAMP.

9. Companies will occupy exactly the same accommodation as they left at ALBERTA CAMP.

10. Trenches must be left clean & in good order. A certificate to this effect signed by the Officer Commanding Coy. taking over to be obtained and handed in to the Orderly Room with the Trench Store Return on arrival at Rest Billet. Fires will be left in the cookhouses, also tins of water.

11. The L.G.O. will arrange for 1 man from each Lewis Gun Team to accompany the Transport & take over their Coy. guns on arrival at camp, & the L.G.O. will detail one N.C.O. to be in charge of this party.

12. Coy. Commanders are responsible that all gum boots are handed over in as dry a condition as possible (in the manner in which they would like to receive them.). On no account are any gum boots to be taken out of trenches.

13. Immediately on return to camp O.C. Coys. will render a return showing approximate number of all men available for fatigues in their Companies.

(sgd) A.C. Corfe, Lt. Colonel,
Commanding 11th Bn. The Queen's Own (Royal West Kent) Rt. (Lewisham).

Copy No.1. C.O.   7. O.C. "B" Coy.   13. B.B.O.
     2. Adjt.   8. O.C. "C" Coy.   14. T.O.
     3. Asst.Adjt.   9. O.C. "D" Coy.   15. M.O.
     4. War Diary.   10. L.G.O.   16. Q.M.
     5. Office Copy.   11. S.O.   17. O.C. MUSCLE.
     6. O.C. "A" Coy. 12. I.O.   18. R.S.M.

CODE OF SIGNALS FOR OFFENSIVE OPERATIONS ONLY

By Signal	Meaning
A.	No signs of enemy ahead
B.	Enemy are retiring at . . . .
C.	Held up by barrage at . . . .
D.	Held up by Strong Point at . . . . .
F.	Enemy offering strong resistance at . . . . . .
G.	Further bombardment required
H.	Lengthen range
I.	Am in touch with Battalion on my right.
J.	Raise barrage
K.	Lower barrage
L.	Have passed . . . . (Map Square)
M.	Enemy apparently preparing to attack
N.	Short of Ammunition
O.	Barrage wanted at . . . .
P.	Reinforcements wanted at . . . . . .
Q.	Am in touch with Battalion on my left
R.	Am still advancing
S.	Artillery Target at . . . .
T.	Tank disabled at . . . .
U.	Tanks have reached . . . .
V.	Tanks required at . . . .
W.	Short of Water
X.	Held up by Machine Gun Fire . . . . .
Y.	Short of Grenades
Z.	Held up by wire at . . . .
O.K	We are all right

The Map location of the point of the line to which reference is made will be given, if necessary, by the clock code, the position of the sender being considered as the centre of the clock face and the hour 12 being always taken as pointing due North. The distance in yards from the point it is desired to describe will be given by a letter of the alphabet. "A" representing 50 yards B 100 yards; C 200; D 300 and so on. The direction will be given by the hour on the Imaginary clock face, e.g. If it were necessary to ask for the range to be lengthened at a point 400 yds North West of Battalion H.Q the message would be H.H.H. E10; H.H.H being acknowledged by T and the whole message by the code letters of the sender followed by R.D. Distances of 150, 250 &c will be given by a two letter signal, e.g B.A - 150, C.A - 250.

XXVI   SIGNAL COMMUNICATIONS

1. When Battalions are moving from OLD FRENCH TRENCH into position behind the DAMSTRASSE, they can make use of the following:-

    1. Divisional Communication Post established by 123rd Infantry Brigade at C.2.b.3½.3½
    2. 123rd Infantry Brigade Forward Station at RUINED FARM
    3. 123rd Infantry Brigade Forward Station in the DAMSTRASSE at or near the end of OAR STREET.

2. As soon as possible after the attack on the BLACK LINE begins the 123rd Infantry Brigade Forward Station in the DAMSTRASSE will be taken over by 122nd Infantry Brigade Signals, and 122nd Infantry Brigade "A" and "B" detachments will follow the last wave of the attacking troops.

    Battalions can then make use of:-

    1. Station in DAMSTRASSE at or near the end of OAR STREET.
    2. Station established by "A" detachment in or near Dugouts at Eastern corner of PHEASANT WOOD.
    3. Station established by "B" detachment at or near junction of OBSCURE TRENCH and OBOE TRENCH at O.10.c.1.9.

3. During Offensive Operations, Brigade Headquarters and Battalion Headquarters
    a. will adopt the code calls used in connection with aeroplane signalling for all forms of signalling.
    b. These code calls will be used in conjunction with single letters representing sentences as shown in the attached list. The message will, for example, take the following form:-
        "C.O. WUB COY. 10.20 am" meaning "To 123rd Infantry Brigade. We are short of ammunition. From 11 the Royal West Kent Reg. 10.20 a.m."
    c. Responsibility for coding and decoding is on sender and receiver of messages, and not on the signallers.

4. Arrangements for communication between advanced troops and aeroplanes will be as follows:-
    a. 2 Contact aeroplanes will be up from Zero to half an hour till 6 hours after Zero. One will work North of the Canal and one South of it. Contact aeroplanes will be distinguished by 3 broad white bands on the fuselage (body) and by the blowing of a Klaxon horn by means of

plane

b. Contact aeroplanes will call for flares by firing a White Light and sounding a Klaxon Horn.

Leading Infantry will light Flares approximately at the following times:-
Zero plus 4 hours and 30 minutes
Zero plus 5 hours and 30 minutes

Infantry must however, ensure that the aeroplane is calling for flares, before lighting up. The colour of these flares will be GREEN.

c. A wireless aeroplane will be up throughout the day from 1 hour after Zero for the purpose of looking out for counter attacks. In the event of a counter attack, this machine will warn the Infantry by means of flares. A RED flare will signify that the attack is North of the Canal, and a GREEN flare, South of the Canal. This machine will also transmit Infantry messages calling for Barrage.

d. The Ground Signal Sheet and call letters at Battalion Headquarters should be kept rolled up and only exposed when the aeroplane calls.

XXXI. CARRYING PARTIES and MATERIAL

1. 15 men from each Battalion to act as Carriers for 122nd Trench Mortar Battery. To report to O.C. 122nd Trench Mortar Battery at MICMAC CAMP at 9a.m. on "Y" day.

2. O.C. 18 Kings Royal Rifle Corps will detail a Company to be at disposal of Assaulting Troops 122nd Infantry Brigade for carrying material forward, after the objective has been gained. This Company will be situated in OAK SUPPORT. Assaulting Units will send guides back to this point. One platoon 18th Kings Royal Rifle Corps being at the disposal of each Assaulting Battalion, & one at the disposal of 122nd Machine Gun Company and 122nd Trench Mortar Battery.

3. A Dump of Barbed wire and stakes will be situated at SHELLEY FARM. O.C 18th Kings Royal Rifle Corps will arrange to get this forward to OAK SUPPORT as early as possible on "Z" day for subsequent carrying forward to new Front Line gained.

XXV. GAS AND SMOKE

1. Two Sub-Sections of No. 2 Special Company R.E. with 8 mortars will be allotted to the 41st Division.

2. During the preliminary bombardment, they will form gas and smoke barrages in front of the DAMMSTRASSE and MARTEN'S FARM. On "Z" Day they will form a similar barrage with smoke alone, from ZERO till ZERO + 20 minutes. The position for the mortars will be approximately O.2.6.5.1.

3. From ZERO + 1 hour till ZERO + 3 hours 30 minutes, the Divisional Artillery will form a smoke barrage on a line from O.11.b.05.60. to OASIS DRIVE near NUTTVEN FARM.

4. "Z" Special Co. R.E. will be attached to the 41st Division. Prior to "Z" Day it will be employed for projector discharges against the LINE of the DAMMSTRASSE.

5. The execution of the above operations depends on the suitability of the wind. The decision as to this lies with the Commanders of the Special Companies.

APPENDIX "D"

MARKING OF GRAVES AND EFFECTS.

1. Graves will be marked with a disc hung on a wire rod which will be stuck in the ground at the head of the grave :-

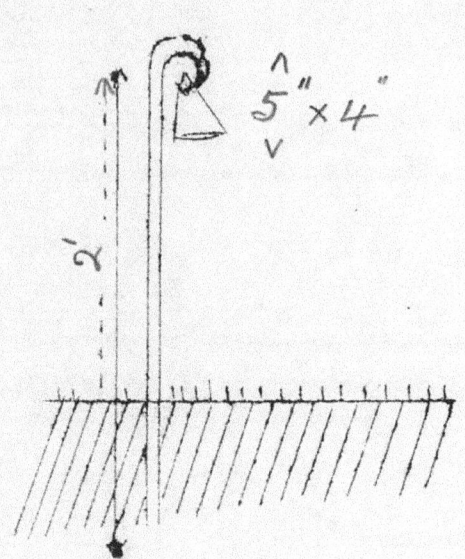
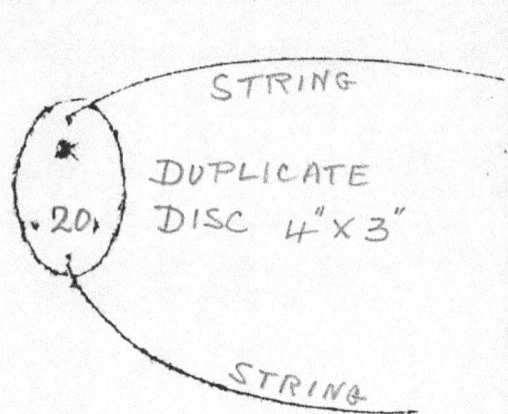

2. A duplicate disc bearing the same number as the disc over the grave will be tied to each :-
   (a). Packet of effects (if only one body is buried in the grave).
   (b) Sandbag of packets of effects (if more bodies than one are buried in the grave.).

3. A number of these rods and discs (in duplicate) will be issued to the Divisional Burial Officers, who will be held responsible that every disc not returned is accounted for on a roll vide pro forma below.
   Discs and rods will be supplied by Corps Burial Officer.

SYSTEM OF BURIAL.

1. (i). Remove boots, greatcoat and equipment, and place them on one side for salvage.
   (ii). Collect all personal effects and the RED identity disc and place them in a ration bag or packet and tie it up. The GREEN identity disc will be left on the man's body and buried with it.
   (iii). Sort ration bags into sandbags.
   (iv). Lower body into grave.

2. Burying parties must observe the following routine :-
   (a). Remove clothing from the dead till ready to place in the grave.
   (b). Bury British, French and German separately.
   (c). Bury Officers with men, except General Officers, whose bodies will be disposed of as directed by the Senior Staff Officer on the ground.
   (d). Sandbag parties (See system of burial 2 b.).
   (e). Mark each grave (whether containing one or more bodies) with a wire rod and disc; the duplicate disc will be tied to the single packet of effects or to the sandbag of packets of effects (according to whether one or more bodies are buried in the same grave).
   (f). Retain sandbags containing effects of British and dispose of them as in 5.a.

P.T.O.

SYSTEM OF BURIAL (CONTINUED).

(g). Mark sandbags containing effects of French "C.S.O." and send to Corps Salvage Officer.

(h). Mark sandbags containing effects of Germans "Xth Corps "G" " and send it at once to Xth Corps G.S. "I".

5. The Officer in charge of a burial party on completion of his work will make a nominal roll in the following form :-

Xth Corps Graves Map Reference.	No.	Regtl. Number.	Rank.	Name.	Regiment.	Religion.
X H.36.d.4.2.	/20.	100.	Pte.	T. Jones.	1st D. L. I.	C. of E.

He will sign and date the roll and <u>print</u> his own name and regiment.
He will send the sandbags and rolls to his Battalion Headquarters.

ROUTES and COMMUNICATION TRENCHES

XXVII

1. It is proposed to extend existing Routes and Communication Trenches to join up with the German system as far as the BLUE LINE.

2. Beyond the BLUE LINE Communication Trenches will be continued to the BLACK LINE, Brigades on the BLACK LINE digging back and Brigades on the BLUE LINE digging forward.

3. The following Communication Trench will be dug by this Battalion:-
O.C. "B" Coy will detail a party to dig back a Communication Trench from OBOE TRENCH to OAR ALLEY

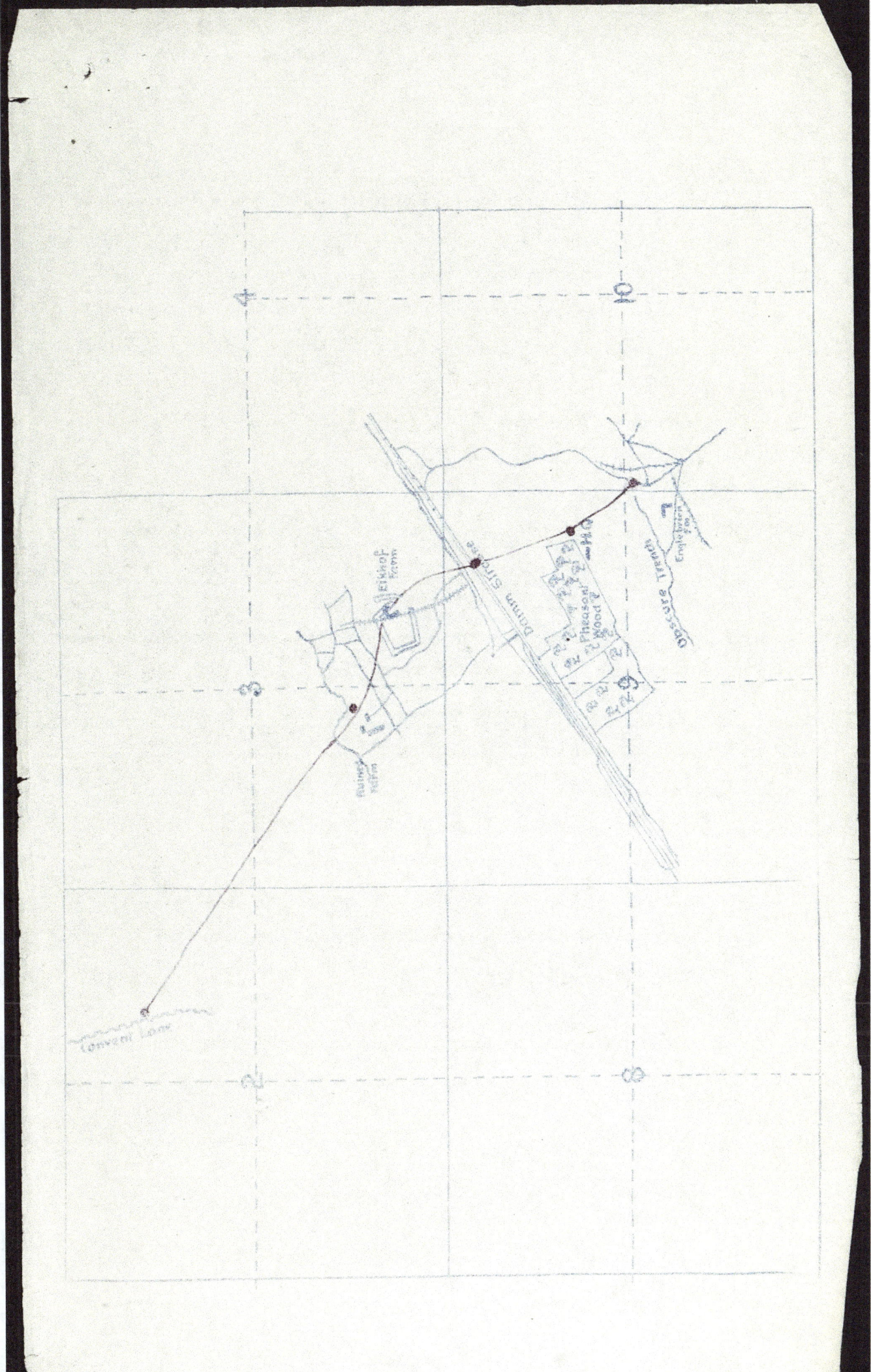

XXVIII. ARTILLERY

1. The probable length of the Bombardment will be 5 days during which the enemy's trench system, headquarters, signal exchanges, etc. will be attacked, and wire cut in the back system by howitzer fire with 106 fuse.

2. Certain areas and Communications will be subjected to frequent intermittent bombardment by heavy howitzers and 60 pounders until Zero. This will "train" the enemy to use certain communications and areas left unshelled. These will then be subjected to concentrated fire when supports or supplies are likely to be coming up.

3. The Barrage in support of the attack will consist of a creeping barrage of 18-pdrs preceding the Infantry in lifts of 25 yards per minute, and a standing barrage on definite trenches and defensive systems of 18-pdrs, and all natures of howitzers.

   Field Artillery will be distributed so that the fire of three 18 pdrs and one 4.5" Howr. Batteries can be taken off the barrage to deal with any special task allotted to it or any portion of it as the Divisional Commander directs.

   Consolidation during its earlier stages will be covered by a protective barrage. This barrage will not be stationary but will search and sweep at intervals.

   The attached table shows the distribution of the barrage in depth and the danger area to our own troops when Fuze 106 is being used.

4. In the event of BLACK LINE line being successfully captured, all heavy artillery of the Right Double Group (as reinforced) will be directed on ODYSSEY TRENCH which forms the objective of 24th Division. Rate of fire "moderate". Half an hour after report of capture of BLACK LINE the protective barrage will be lifted forward to a distance of about 500 yards from the BLACK LINE throughout the front to admit of Infantry patrols proceeding to reconnoitre. Orders for this lift will be issued by Corps.

XXIV. MACHINE GUN AND TRENCH MORTAR ARRANGEMENTS.

1. A Machine Gun Barrage co-ordinated by the Corps Machine Gun Officer is to be maintained in stages :-
   1. In front of the 1st Objective - RED LINE.
   2. In front of the 2nd Objective - BLUE LINE.
   3. In front of the 3rd Objective - BLACK LINE.

   The barrage will open in the case of each objective, at the time the Infantry commence their advance, and be continued for half an hour after they are timed to reach it. During the intervening periods of the barrage, the guns will answer an S.O.S. Signal by curtain fire.

2. Two Sections 122nd Machine Gun Company will be detailed for barrage work, and the remaining two sections will co-operate with Assaulting Infantry, 122nd Infantry Brigade, on attack of BLACK LINE.

3. The two sections 122nd Machine Gun Company detailed to co-operate in advance on the BLACK LINE, will closely follow the Assaulting Infantry from position of Assembly about OLD FRENCH TRENCH, between CONVENT LANE and Divisional Left Boundary, as far as a general line O.9.c.8.8. - forward edge of PHEASANT WOOD - O.10.a.1.6½ - O.10.a.3½.7½.
   Both sections will select positions on this line covering front & flanks to repel counter attacks or deal with enemy machine guns.

4. One section will be previously detailed to move forward to system of trenches immediately behind the BLACK LINE, as soon as they are in the hands of the Assaulting Infantry. The O.C. Section will use his own discretion as to the time to move the guns forward. He will detail one sub-section to frontage gained by 12th East Surrey Regt., and one sub-section to frontage gained by 11th Royal West Kent Regt. One gun of the latter sub-section to be allotted to strong point at O.10.a.2.4.
   The O.C. Section remaining on line mentioned in para. 3 will have his guns in such a position as to cover front and flanks of the Brigade, before the other section moves forward.

5. O.C., 122nd Trench Mortar Battery will detail one mortar to accompany each of the Assaulting Battalions, to assist during the attack should a strong point hold it up, and to take up positions covering the line gained.
   One gun with the 11th Royal West Kent Regt. to be prepared to enfilade OBOE TRENCH and deal with strong point at O.10.a.2.4. & to move forward to junction of OBOE TRENCH and OBSCURE TRENCH when the objective has been gained.

ADMINISTRATIVE INSTRUCTIONS IN CONNECTION WITH FORTHCOMING OPERATIONS.

SECRET.

Ref. Sheet 28. 1/40,000.

NOTE.

The attack will take place on Zero Day, and will be referred to as "Z" day. The preceding 5 days as "Y", "X", "W", "V", "U" day. Days after Zero - as "A", "B", "C" days.

I. PERSONNEL. *These instructions will be issued later.*

(i) The following Officers will take part in the attack:-
(These will be notified later.)

(ii) The following personnel will be left behind:-
(a) All remaining Officers.
(b) Two Company Sergeant Majors.
(c) Each Company - 1 Sgt., 1 Corpl., 1 L/Cpl.,
(d) Each Platoon - 3 Privates.
(e) 33% Lewis Gunners, Snipers, Signallers, Runners.

II. REINFORCEMENT CAMP.

A Divisional Reinforcement Camp will be formed at Brigade School at N.4.b.4.4., at which all details left behind will be accommodated. *and reinforcements*

III. PRISONERS OF WAR.

Prisoners of War will be sent to Brigade Headquarters under escort (usual strength 10% of the number of prisoners). Receipt will be obtained for same.

IV. BATTLE STRAGGLERS.

If any portion of the Battalion is East of the BOLLAR BEEK the Regimental Police, will be posted along the line of the BEEK to prevent straggling.

V. RATIONS.

By system explained in Table A it will be unnecessary to send up any food or water by road from after U/V night until Z/A night for any troops East of DICKEBUSCH.
Every man to be in possession of a serviceable ration on Z day, for possible consumption on A day.
All Iron Rations of all casualties must be collected in case of emergency reserve.
Chewing Gum will be issued for consumption on Zero day.
Supply of rations to Transport Lines and troops West of DICKEBUSCH will be under normal conditions. ~~(This Brigade will not draw rations from Dump on Y day as will not be in the area).~~

VI. WATER.

(i) 120 petrol tins have been allotted to this Battalion for consumption on W and Z day, in case the existing supplies fail, at the following points :-
For W day - Lt Battn. I.31.d.4.6.   40 tins.
          do.   I.32.c.5.2.   80 "

For Z day - . Points to be notified later.

(ii) The sources of water supply are as follows:-
(a) Stand Pipes (1) N.6.b.4.9.
               (2) O.1.a.1.6.
               (3) I.31.d.25 & 2/160 gal. tanks & Barrel.
               (4) I.31.d.5.9. 4/100 gal. tanks & Barrels.

P.T.O.

- 2 -

  (b) Wells in VOORMEZEELE.
    (1) I.31.c.3½. 5½.
    (2) I.31.c.6.4.
  Both these supplies are plentiful, 2 scoops of Chlorinated Lime required.

  (c) Spring.   OLD FRENCH TRENCH, I.32.d.7½.2½.

  In the event of all above supplies failing, water will be brought up in petrol tins in normal way on 1st.Line Transport, empty tins being exchanged for full at unloading point.

3. Xth Corps are running a 4" main from DICKEBUSCH LAKE via MIDDLESEX LANE to MOATED GRANGE.
   As soon as circumstances permit the 4" main will be pushed forward to DOME HOUSE, O.6.d.9½.6½., and tanks established under the DAMMSTRASSE near this point.

4. WASHING WATER.
   The BOLLART BEEK - not fit for drinking, as it is liable to contamination from a branch stream which runs into it from the German Lines.

5. Companies will arrange for all ground gained by them to be searched for wells or other source of water supply, and for the discovery of such to be reported at once to Battalion Headquarters in order that arrangements may be made to test water, which must on no account be used until declared fit to drink by Medical Authorities.

6. Water in Back Area.
   Watercarts may be filled at
   (1) G.34.c.5½.1.
   (2) G.29.d.75.50 (in 47th Div. Area).
   (3) G.35.c.2.0.   (not yet completed. 20/5/17).
   (4) M.6.d.7.6.   -   do. -
   (5) H.28.d.2.1½.
   (6) M.0.a.2.0½.

   Horse Waterpoints:-
   (1) M.4.a.6.0.
   (2) M.6.b.4.0.
   (3) G.36.b.4.2.
   (4) N.1.a.6.8½.
   (5) H.31.b.5½.3.
   (6) M.6.a.6.2.   (not yet completed. 20/5/17).
   (7) H.5.b.6.3½.   -   do -
   Watering programmes for animals will be issued later.

VII. MEDICAL.

1. Regimental Aid Posts.
   No.1. I.32.d.1.1½)
      II. I.32.c.5.½) For 123rd Infantry Bde.

     III. O.1.b.5.9.)
      IV. O.1.b.2.6.) For 124th Infantry Bde.

   As soon as the situation permits these R.A.P's will be pushed forward.
   ~~R.A.P. of this Battalion will be in rear of the 4th.~~

2. Divisional Collecting Post. - VOORMEZEELE. I.31.c.4.7½.

3. Advanced Dressing Station   - DICKEBUSCH. H.27.d.4.1.

continued:-

VII. MEDICAL CONTINUED:-

Walking wounded by down communication trenches to Collecting Post (VOORMEZEELE) thence to DICKEBUSCH Advanced Dressing Station.

Captain J.La T.Lander, R.A.M.C., D.S.O., M.C., will be in charge of Advance bearers. His Headquarters will be at Collecting Station, VOORMEZEELE.

Requests for assistance will be addressed to him. If he is unable to furnish assistance, Divisional H.Q. "A", should be communicated with.

Note. M.O. to read attached Xth Corps letter - Appendix A attached.

VIII. ORDNANCE.

(1) Divisional Ordnance Store remains as at present G.34.d.6.5.
(2) Normal procedure to continue.
(3) All captured war material will be sent back at once to Divisional Ordnance.

IX. AMMUNITION.

(1) Divisional Dump - S.A.A., GRENADES, VERY LIGHTS, ETC. G.24.d.6.7. - on OUDERDOM - VLAMERTINGHE ROAD.

(2) Advanced Brigade Dumps.
(i) Right Brigade. I.31.d.2.5.
    Left Brigade. I.31.d.5.9.
                  I.32.d.2.8.

If necessary the Reserve Brigade will draw from these Brigade Dumps.

(3) Amounts of various natures of ammunition kept at above dumps, is shewn on Appendix B.

(4) The supply of ammunition from the Divisional Dump to Brigade Dumps will be by 1st Line Transport of Units to VOORMEZEELE, thence by tramway to dumps.

(5) On and after the first day of the bombardment, the present Brigade Dump at DICKEBUSCH, H.34.a.7.6., can be drawn on by either of the Brigades, in front line, to replenish their forward Brigade Dumps and to provide the extra ammunition to be carried by every man on going into action.

(6) Ammunition now distributed in Strong Points & Front Line system under the Divisional Defence Scheme, will be left in sites until further orders as to salvage are received.

X BURIALS.

(1) The Xth Corps Burial scheme is attached, vide Appendix D.

(2) Companies will be issued with a small supply of the discs and wire rods to enable them to bury any of their own dead. They must account for every disc received by them, and forward rolls, discs, and packets of effects to Battalion H.Q. Any discs not used must be returned to Battalion H.Q. It will probably be some time before the Corps Burial Parties will arrive on the spot, therefore, companies must set to work to bury their own dead as soon as possible after attack, though in every case the instructions laid down in Appendix D must be strictly adhered to.

P.T.O.

X BURIALS CONTINUED:-

(3) Sites selected for Burial Grounds must be used as far as possible.
Position of Sites will be notified later.

XI. VETERINARY.

(1) The Mobile Veterinary Section will remain at its present position at G.33.c.C.l9.

(2) An advanced Veterinary Dressing Station for reception of all sick and wounded animals will be established in the stable of the farm at H.6.b.l9.0., from the first day of the bombardment (V day).

(3) Evacuation from the Advanced Veterinary Dressing Station to the Mobile Veterinary Section will be carried out under arrangements to be made by A.D.V.S.

XII. COMMUNICATIONS.

(1) Trench Tramways.
   (a) CAFE BELGE to VOORMEZEELE, at disposal of Tunnelling Coys. only.
   (b) Continuation of (a)
     (i) to SHELLEY DUMP, I.32.d.2.5.
     (ii) to OXFORD STREET, O.1.b.9.5.
   These lines will be at the disposal of Left & Right Bde. respectively.
   (c) A branch from (b) (ii) to MOATED GRANGE O.1.b.2.5. for conveyance of R.E. material, and evacuation of wounded from R.A.P., to A.D.S., at VOORMEZEELE.

(2) Road Communication.
To avoid the use of the CAFE BELGE - VOORMEZEELE- ST.ELOI road, and to avoid VOORMEZEELE in the event of the latter being heavily shelled, an Overland Track fit for wheels (lightly loaded wagons) is being prepared from the neighbourhood of BELLEGOED FARM H.30.d.9.8., to SHELLEY DUMP I.32.d.2.5., and passing to the East of VOORMEZEELE.
This track will normally be at disposal of the Left Brigade in the Line. As soon as possible after Zero, this track will be extended via SHELLEY FARM to German Front Line System in the vicinity of RUINED FARM.

(3) In dry weather all return traffic from VOORMEZEELE will use the track N.6.a.5.8. - GORDON FARM - S.W. corner of DICKEBUSCH LAKE.
In wet weather however, the track must only be used by pack Transport, and all return traffic from VOORMEZEELE will then use the circuit VOORMEZEELE - KRUISSTRAATHOEK - N.E. up the YPRES - VIERSTRAAT road and then N.W. by the new switch road running to the East of SWAN CHATEAU (I.19.c.) and home by YPRES - DICKEBUSCH road.

(4) Back Area. The Overland Tracks in the back area are shewn on Map B. (T.O. only)

XIII. TRAFFIC CONTROL. (T.O. only)

(1) The battle traffic circuit affecting this Division is shewn on the attached sketch (Map "B") by arrows.
Traffic on all other roads will follow the Second Army Traffic Map, issued herewith (Map "C").

continued:-

XIII TRAFFIC CONTROL CONTINUED:-

(2). (a) Troops and traffic may use the roads most convenient to them provided the above circuits and traffic routes are adhered to.
  (b) Infantry on the march may use any road in either direction, but the Transport must follow the circuit routes.
  (c) Motor and Ambulance cars have right of way in either direction on all roads, but must follow traffic circuits as much as possible.
  (d) When the cross country tracks are passable the following classes of traffic must make use of them :-

  Civilian Carts.

  Empty Horse Transport.

  Small parties of pedestrians and mounted men.

  Infantry whenever possible.

(3) When the road is dry enough, Ammunition Wagons and Infantry Transport from Camps in Square M.4 proceeding to the Divisional Dump at OUDERDOM will use the track N.5.a.5.2. - G.35.c.7.5. - G.35.a.5.8. in the direction named, i.e. Northwards, to avoid congestion at the road junction at ZEEVECOTEN.

(4) The Traffic circuit for vehicles going to VOORMEZEELE will be CAFE BELGE - KRUISSTRAATHOEK - VOORMEZEELE - South Westwards to Point N.36.d.5.8. - ELZENWALLE - KRUISSTRAATHOEK - North East to WITHUIS CABARET - and then by the new switch road running North East round SWANN CHATEAU to the main road.

(5) In dry weather, all traffic returning from VOORMEZEELE will proceed by the new overland track via the North end of RIDGE WOOD and the South end of DICKEBUSCH LAKE.

(6) The overland track to DICKEBUSCH is shewn on Map "B" by dotted black line.

XIV. TRENCH TRAMWAY TRAFFIC.

(N.B. These instructions will take effect from mid-day on May 26th 1917).

(1) Rolling Stock.
Trucks are distributed as required to Units who are entirely responsible for their care and upkeep.

(2) Any truck requiring repairs which cannot be carried out by the unit, must be returned to the Traffic Superintendent at the Tramway Depot at VOORMEZEELE, when a new truck will be given in exchange.

(3) There is a great shortage of trucks, and it is therefore imperative that units should return to the Traffic Superintendent any trucks not required for immediate use. On no account must trucks, even though damaged, be left thrown about.

(4) A reserve of trucks will be kept at the Tramway Depot at VOORMEZEELE.

(5) It is imperative that any damage done to the track by shell fire, or otherwise, should be reported at once to the ~~Maintenance Officer,~~ Headquarters at VOORMEZEELE, to enable him to affect repairs without delay, and thus ensure traffic being interfered with as little as possible.

P. T. O.

XV. FIRST LINE TRANSPORT.

(1) First Line Transport will remain in its positions ready to move at 2 hours notice.

XVI. SANITATION.

(1) The greatest care must be paid to Sanitation.
All troops whether situated in the firing line or in rear must invariably make provision for latrines, no matter how short their stay in a particular site may be.

(2) The indiscriminate fouling of the ground by using shell holes as latrines, as was done on the captured area last year on the SOMME, must be carefully guarded against. Regimental Police must be used to prevent this practice.

(3) All manure in horse lines must be disposed of by burning, or, where this cannot be done by building it into compact heaps <u>well away from camps</u>, and covering it with earth.

(4) In view of the lack of water in the district it is of the utmost importance that all sources of water should be carefully conserved. Special care must be taken to prevent soapy water from ablution benches filtering into streams.

(5) In every unit special steps must be taken to protect all food from flies and rats.

XVII. SALVAGE.

(1) All parties and individual men returning from the Front Line must carry back some salvaged article with them.

(2) Salvaged articles will first be collected by units in numerous small dumps distributed throughout the trench area, whence they will be cleared by means of the Trench Tramway to Brigade Salvage Dumps at the loading sidings in VOORMEZEELE.

XVIII. BATHS AND LAUNDRY.

Baths and Laundry will be carried on during operations as usual.

XIX. R. E. STORES.

(1) Up to "Z" Day arrangements for the supply of R.E. Stores will continue as at present.

(2) <u>Hutting Dump.</u>

OURDERDOM, G.29.d.8.3. R.E. Workshops and dump of material to be dealt with in the workshops. Material for back area, hutting material etc and special stores, such as pumps, trench stores etc, .

<u>Divisional Dumps.</u>

DICKEBUSCH, H.27.d.0.3.   Divisional Dump for Forward Area.
CAFE BELGE, H.24.c.3.0.   Advanced Divisional Dump. Junction of Light Railway with Trench Tramway.

<u>Advanced Dumps. (for troops in Line).</u>
VOORMEZEELE, I.31.a.3.0., Field Coy. Dump for Support Battalion
MOATED GRANGE, C.1.b.25.45. Field Coy. Dump for Right Bn. Sector.
SHELLEY LANE. I.32.d.2.3. Field Coy. Dump. for Left Bn. Sector.

continued:-

XX. R.E. STORES CONTINUED.

(4). **Method of Indenting for stores.**

Units in the Line may draw stores on an indent countersigned by a R.E. Officer of the Field Coy. working in their area, from that Field Coy's Forward Dump.
(OUDERDOM, DICKEBUSCH, and CAFE BELGE Dumps, are under the immediate control of the C.R.E. Field Coys. may draw from these dumps on their own authority, except for certain stores.)
(The 10th Middlesex Pioneers may draw their own authority certain stores from DICKEBUSCH DUMP.)
All other units must obtain the authorisation of the C.R.E., before drawing stores from any R.E. Dump.
Hutting Material is an exception to the foregoing remarks. All indents for this must be countersigned by the Officer in charge Hutting, before issue is made from OUDERDOM DUMP, where all hutting material is kept.

(5) Prior to "Z" day, all dumps will be stocked up to the establishments necessary for the commencement of offensive operations.
From "Z" day inclusive:-
(i) DICKEBUSCH Dump will continue to be the main Divisional dump.
(ii) CAFE BELGE Dump will cease to exist.
(iii) VOORMEZEELE will be the Advanced Divisional Dump.
(iv) Forward Dumps will be as now, MOATED GRANGE Dump, and SHELLEY LANE Dump, with probably 2 dumps within the present German Lines situated 1 on each of the two main pack routes.
(vi) From "Z" day inclusive;-Stores may be drawn from all dumps by any unit, and no indent or authority will be necessary. Storemen i/c Dumps may however receive orders to reserve certain stores for certain units, but subject to this provision, stores will be issued on demand if available.

XXI. REPORTS AND RETURNS.

(4) O.C. Coys., will report any localities where it is known there are dead or wounded left on the Field, or large quantities of salvage.

XXII. PACKS AND SURPLUS BAGGAGE.

Packs and surplus baggage will be stored at RENINGHELST in Barn at G.34.d.6.8.
Surplus clothing and equipment of each man will be tied up in the pack, which will be stacked at the Q.M.Stores. Packs should be labelled with the man's name and Number.

----------o----------

TABLE "A"

For consump-tion on.	Rations sent up.	Water dumped in 2 gall. petrol tins.	Remarks.
U Day.	Normal.	Normal supply.	
V "	U/V night.	do.	
W "	do.	120 tins dumped.	
X "	nil.	nil.	Bn. out of line.
Y "	nil.	nil.	do.
Z "	Y/Z night on the man	120 tins dumped.	
A "	do.	-	

APPENDIX "B".

	Divisional Dump.	Each Brigade Dump.
S. A. A.	1,000,000.	250,000.
Grenades Mills No. 5.	30,000	7,500.
Grenades Rifle.	5,000.	2,000.
Blank S.A.A.		
Stokes Shells.	5,000.	2,000.
Stokes Cartridges Red.	5,000.)	2,000.)
" " Green.	5,000.)	2,000.)
Very Lights White 1"	4,000.	1,000.
" " " 1½"	1,500.	500.
Webley Pistol S.A.A.	10,000.	1,000.
"P" Grenades.	2,000.	250.

S.C.S. Signals.
Flares.   } As available from Army.
Rockets.   } quantities depend largely
Coloured Very Lights.   } on tactical considerations.
Smoke Candles.   }

Majority of T.M. ammunition required to be dumped at or near guns before operations commence.

Or equivalent number all green with "Rings".

WAR DIARY
or
INTELLIGENCE SUMMARY

(Erase heading not required.)

Army Form C. 2118.

XI RW Kent Rᵗ
WO/13

Place	Date	Hour	Summary of Events and Information	Remarks and references to Appendices
ZOUAFQUES. Ref. Hazebrouck 5a, & Sheet 27 N.E.	1/5/17. 5/5/17. 12/5/17.		Battalion in Training for the offensive. 2/Lt. H.A.QUARTERMAIN joined the Battalion and taken on strength. Strength of Battalion 44 Officers, 912 Other Ranks. Strength of Battalion 44 Officers, 899 Other Ranks.	
BROXEELE. Ref. Hazebrouck 5.A. STEENVOORDE.	15/5/17. 16/5/17.		Battalion began march back to 41st Divisional Area billeting for the night at BROXEELE and ROUBROUCK, vide O.O. No.64 (attached). Battalion continued march to Divisional Area billeting for the night near STEENVOORDE. Vide O.O. No.65 (attached).	
RENINGHELST Ref. M.5.a. Sheet 28.	17/5/17.		Battalion completed its march to the 41st Divisional Area. Vide O.O. No.66 (attached), and took over ALBERTA CAMP from the 21st Battalion K.R.R.C. Strength of Battalion 44 Officers, 885 Other Ranks.	
DICKEBUSCH. H.28. Sheet 28.	20/5/17.		The Battalion took over billets from the 23rd Battn. The Middlesex Regt. in Brigade Reserve, near DICKEBUSCH LAKE. Vide O.O.No.67 (attached). 2/Lieut. C.P. WEBB joined the Battalion for duty. Strength of Battalion 45 Officers, 939 Other Ranks.	
ST. ELOI. Sheet 28. S.W.	31/5/17. 0.2.		The Battalion was relieved in Brigade Reserve by the 18th K.R.R.C., and relieved 23rd Battalion The Middlesex Regt. in the Right Sub-Sector of the Divisional Front. Vide O.O. 68 (attached). Casualties from 20-31st May - Officers, Wounded 1. Other Ranks, Killed 5, Wounded 24. Strength of Battalion 44 Officers, 915 Other Ranks.	
	1/6/17.			

Lieut. Colonel,
Commanding 11th Bn. "THE QUEEN'S" OWN"
(Royal West Kent) Regt. (Lewisham).

S E C R E T.   OPERATION ORDER NO. 67   Copy No. 5.
by Lieut. Col. A.C. Corie,
Commanding 11th Bn. Royal West Kent Regt.
(Lewisham).

18th May, 1917.

1. The Battalion will relieve OAR in Brigade Reserve in DICKEBUSCH tomorrow, and will take over from their opposite numbers.

2. Order and time of march:-
   "C" Coy.   9 a.m.   )
   "A" "   10.15 a.m.   )
   "D" "   13.30 a.m.   ) To DICKEBUSCH.
   Headqrs.   12.45 p.m.   )
   "B" Company under Company arrangement to MICMAC CAMP.

3. Route:- OVERLAND TRACK. *Transport by usual route.*

4. Lewis Gunners and Company Signallers will report to their respective Companies.

5. Platoon Commanders must not halt their platoons in DICKEBUSCH. Platoons to march at 15 minutes interval.

6. Lewis Guns will be taken up by Transport as far as DICKEBUSCH. The Transport Officer will detail one limber per company to report to the Lewis Gun Officer at 8 a.m. tomorrow. ~~These limbers will proceed with the first platoon of each company.~~
   O.C. Companies will each detail 1 N.C.O. per Coy. and 1 man per Lewis Gun Team, to march with each limber. Platoons will carry their guns from DICKEBUSCH.

7. Officers Mess Boxes and Valises must be stacked outside Battalion Headquarters by 9 a.m. The Transport Officer will detail Mess Cart and 1 G.S. Wagon to proceed to DICKEBUSCH ~~and will act as a loading party~~ with the above.
   Officers Servants will accompany Officers Mess Cart and G.S. Wagon to DICKEBUSCH, and will act as a loading party.
   Mess Boxes and Valises will be unloaded at DICKEBUSCH and carried to their respective Headquarters.

8. Officers surplus kits will be stacked in their respective Store Huts.
   Headquarter Officers Surplus Kits will be stacked outside Battn. Headqrs., and will be taken to the Quartermaster's Stores by Transport.

9. Each man will carry his pack and leave his surplus kit in a sandbag. Blankets in bundles of ten and sandbags properly labelled will be stacked in Company Store Huts.
   Headquarter blankets will be stacked outside Bn. Headqrs., and taken to the Quartermaster's Stores by transport.

10. List of Trench Stores taken over will be forwarded to the Adjutant after relief is complete.

11. Relief will be reported to Battn. Headqrs., by BAB Code.
12. Waterbottles must be filled before moving off.
13. Breakfasts will be had before leaving.
14. The unconsumed portion of the day's rations will be carried by all ranks.
15. The Transport Officer will detail one limber to carry dixies. Dixies must be loaded up by 9 a.m.
16. Nominal rolls of all men left behind (stating cause) will be handed in to the Orderly Room before moving off.
17. 2/Lieut. H. Roughley, and 1 N.C.O. & 3 men of "C" Coy. (preferably Bombers), will proceed to G.H.Q. Line and report to 2/Lieut. Newman 23rd Middlesex Regt., at 11.30 a.m. tomorrow and take over the Bomb and Ammunition Dumps.

(Sgd) A. C. Corie.   Lieut. Colonel.
Commanding 11th Bn. Royal West Kent Regt.

P.T.O.

Copy No.	1.	C.O.	Copy No. 10.	L.G.O.
	2.	2nd in Command.	11.	I.O.
	3.	Adjutant.	12.	S.O.
	4.	Office Copy.	13.	B.B.O.
	5.	War Diary.	14.	M.O.
	6.	O.C. "A" Coy.	15.	T.O.
	7.	O.C. "B" Coy.	16.	R.S.M.
	8.	O.C. "C" Coy.	17.	Q.M.
	9.	O.C. "D" Coy.	18.	OAR.

S E C R E T.   OPERATION ORDER No.64.   Copy No. 4.

by Lieut.Col. A.C.Corfe,
Commanding 11th Bn. "The Queen's Own"
Royal West Kent Regiment.(Lewisham)

14th May, 1917.

1. The 122nd Infantry Brigade will march tomorrow to RUKROUCH AREA, en route for the 41st Divisional Area.

2. There will be a halt and water for ¾ of an hour at top of WATTEN HILL.

3. The march will be continued on the 16th & 17th instant.

4. The Battalion will parade at 4 a.m. on main village road facing N.E. Head of the column at Northern entrance to village.
   Order of March.
   Band, Runners, A, B, C, & D Coys., Headquarters, & Transport.

5. Dress. Fighting Order, with waterproof sheet under flap of haversack. Steel Helmets to be strapped on haversack.

6. Immediately on arrival in billets, O.C. Companies will report the exact position of their Company Headquarters to the Adjutant.

7. 2 Motor Lorries will be sent to the Battalion to transport blankets and packs. O.C. Coys., and Headquarters must each detail 2 men to proceed with the lorries on the first journey, and 2 men for the second journey. These men will load the lorries.

8. Blankets in bundles of 10 and packs, will be stacked outside the Quartermaster's Stores by 8.30 p.m. tonight. These must be stacked separately and by Companies, and must be properly labelled.

9. Officers Kits must be stacked outside the Quartermaster's Stores by 3.30 a.m. tomorrow, to be loaded on the G.S. Wagon.

10. Mess Cart must be loaded by 3.30 a.m. tomorrow.

11. All remaining transport must be loaded tonight.

12. Particular attention must be paid to march discipline. No men are allowed to ride in wagons. Company Commanders will be responsible for taking the names of all men who fall out on the march. No man to fall out without permission of an officer.

13. Breakfasts will be had on the march. Dinners will be had on arrival in the new area.

(Sgd) A. C. Corfe, Lieut.Colonel.
Commanding 11th Battalion "The Queen's Own"
Royal West Kent Regiment.   (Lewisham).

Copy No. 1. C.O.   10. I.O.
        2. 2nd In Command.   11. T.C.
        3. Adjutant.   12. S.O.
        4. War Diary.   13. M.O.
        5. Office Copy.   14. R.B.O.
        6. O.C. "A" Coy.   15. R.S.M.
        7. O.C. "B" "   16. Qr.Mr.
        8. O.C. "C" "
        9. O.C. "D" "

SECRET Copy No 1

OPERATION Order No 65

Ref: Hazebrouck 5A   by Lieut Col. A.C. Corfe
     1/100000   Commdg 11" Battn Royal West Kent Regt

15" May 1917

The Brigade will march tomorrow to STEENVOORDE

The Battalion will parade at Cross Roads 1/4 mile S.W. of ROUBROUCK on BROXEELE – ROUBROUCK Road at 4.30 am facing N.E.

ORDER of MARCH. Signallers, Runners, "D" Coy, Band, "B", "C", "A", Headquarters, Transport.

Halt for Breakfast at LE MENEGAT.

There will be another halt for water near BAVINCHOVE for 1½ hours.

Officers kits and Mess Boxes to be ready outside their respective Company Headquarters by 3.30 am.

Blankets to be stacked at Company Headquarters before leaving.

O/C Companies will detail same men as to-day to proceed with the Lorries.

Billeting party to report to Lieut G. Gordon Smith at ROUBROUCK at 7 a.m.

Dinners on arrival in new area

           (Sd) Lieut Col. A.C. Corfe
           Commdg 11" Battn Royal West Kent Regt

Copy No 1. C O
2. Adjutant
3. War Diary
4. O/C A
5. " B
6. " C
7. " D
8. R.S.M.
9. Quartermaster

OPERATION ORDER No 66 Copy No 3.
By Lt Col. A.C. Corfe
Commd̄ 11th Battn R. West Kent Regt

Ref Hazebrouck 5A 16th May 1917
1/100000

— x —

1. The Battalion will proceed tomorrow to RENINCHELST - Alberta Camp.
2. The Battalion will parade with head of the column facing N. at crossroads on Belgian Boundary 400 yards S.E. of second E in BEAUVOORDE at 6.50 am.
3. <u>Order of March</u> H.Q. B. Band, C. A. D. Transport.
4. Breakfasts will be had before leaving.
5. Dinners will be had on arrival at Camp.
6. Blankets will be stacked at Company H.Q. before leaving.
7. O/C Companies will detail same men as to-day to proceed with Lorries
8. Lorries and Officers kits to be unloaded and stacked on parade ground on arrival at ALBERTA CAMP.

(sd) A.C. Corfe Lieut Col
Commdg 11th Battn Royal West Kent Regt

Copy No 1 C.O.
     2 Adjt
     3 War Diary
     4 O/C A Co
     5   " B "
     6   " C "
     7   " D "
     8 R.S.M
     9 Q.M.

SECRET.

OPERATION ORDER No. 68.   Copy No. 4.
by Lieut. Col. A.C. Corfe,
Commanding 11th Bn. "THE QUEEN'S OWN"
(Royal West Kent) Regt. (Lewisham).

30th May, 1917.

1. The Battalion will relieve the 23rd Middlesex in the line tomorrow and take over trenches in the Right Sub-Sector.-
    Right Front Coy.   "A" Coy.
    Left Front Coy.   "D" Coy.
    Support Coy.   "B" Coy. (in R. line).
    Reserve Coy.   "C" Coy. (in McGee trench).

2. The 18th K.R.R.C. will take over the present disposition of the Companies. Sufficient personnel will be left behind to hand over.

3. Order and time of march:-
    Signallers...........8 a.m.
    "D" Coy..............8.15 a.m.
    "B" Coy..............9.15 a.m. (1st Platoon to arrive at DICKEBUSCH).
    "A" Coy..............10.15 a.m.
    Headquarters.........11.15 a.m.
    "C" Coy..............11 a.m.

4. Platoons will march at an interval of 15 minutes.

5. Lewis Guns will be taken up by hand by Platoons. The Transport Officer will detail one limber to carry "B" Coy. guns as far as DICKEBUSCH. This limber will also carry "B" Coy. mess-boxes and trench bundles

6. Mess-boxes, and Officers trench bundles will be taken up by hand.

7. Surplus Officers kits will be stacked in house next to water cart in DICKEBUSCH by 10 a.m. One man per Coy. will be detailed to look after these kits which will be loaded up and taken to Quartermaster's Stores.

8. List of trench stores taken over will be forwarded to the Adjutant.

9. Relief to be carried out as quietly and carefully as possible, and completion reported to Battalion Headquarters by runner.

10. All water bottles will be filled before moving off.

11. Rations must be carried on the man for the whole day.

12. Dixies will be carried up by hand.

13. Secret documents and maps referring to the forthcoming operations must not be taken beyond the R. line.

14. Rations for the 1st June will be brought up at midnight. 31/1. and will be dumped at the BRASSERIE. (N.6.a.2.5.).

15. Usual returns must be sent punctually.

16. Front companies will arrange to have a Test S.O.S. each night in the trenches. A full report on each occasion should be forwarded to Battn Headquarters by 6.30 a.m. the following morning stating the time taken from handing in the 'phone message until the shell passes over the trenches.

P.T.O.

-2-.

17. Lewis Gunners and Bombers under instructions at Transport Lines will rejoin their Companies in the line and will march up under the Bombing Officer with "B" Coy.

18. Telephones are not to be used except in cases of extreme emergency.

         (sgd). A. C. Corfe, Lieut. Col.,
         Commanding 11th Bn. "The Queen's Own"
         (Royal West Kent) Regt. (Lewisham).

```
Copy No. 1. C.O.            7.  O.C. "A" Coy.    13. R.S.M.
         2. Adjt.           8.  O.C. "B"  "      14. L.G.O.
         3. Sec. in Con.    9.  O.C. "C"  "      15. B.B.O.
         4. War Diary.     10.  O.C. "D"  "      16. O.C. CAR.
         5. Office Copy.   11.  T.O.              17. M.O.
         6. S.O.           12.  Q.M.
```

On His Majesty's Service.

42/4

11th R.W. Kent

War Diaries

June 1917

Secret

XI R W Reid Esq
95/14

War Diary. May 1917
(to be attached to)

11th (SERVICE) BATTALION
ROYAL WEST KENT REGT.
JUN 1 1917
Ref..............................

11th R.W. Kent
June 1917

Army Form C. 2118.

WAR DIARY
or
INTELLIGENCE SUMMARY
(Erase heading not required.)

Instructions regarding War Diaries and Intelligence Summaries are contained in F. S. Regs., Part II. and the Staff Manual respectively. Title Pages will be prepared in manuscript.

Place	Date	Hour	Summary of Events and Information	Remarks and references to Appendices
ST. ELOI.	1/6/17.		Strength of Battalion 43 Officers, 920 Other Ranks. Battalion in trenches in front of ST. ELOI. Preliminary bombardment for offensive, little retaliation on our trenches.	
MICMAC NORTH.	5/6/17.		Battalion relieved by 124th Infantry Brigade and proceeded by route march to MICMAC (North) CAMP, vide O.O. 70 attached. Casualties for period June 1 - 5th, 1 O.R. killed, 15 O.R. wounded.	
ST. ELOI.	6/6/17.		Battalion moved up to ASSEMBLY AREA for attack into OLD FRENCH TRENCH, vide O.O. 71 attached.	
	7/6/17.		Battalion took part in successful attack on the WYTSCHAETE-MESSINES Ridge, vide O.O. 69, also copy of report on attack attached.	
	8/6/17.		Battalion was relieved by 73rd Infantry Brigade at 5 a.m., vide report on operations attached, and proceeded to OLD FRENCH TRENCH in reserve.	
	9/6/17.		Battalion in OLD FRENCH TRENCH.	
			Strength of Battalion 36 Officers, 792 Other Ranks.	
	10/6/17 & 11/6/17.		Battalion in reserve in OLD FRENCH TRENCH. 2/Lieut. L.E.HALE joined for duty, as Transport Officer, and taken on strength.	
	12/6/17.		Battalion relieved 8th and 17th Battn. London Regt. in the line immediately south of YPRES-COMINES CANAL. Relief complete 12 m.n. Headquarters WHITE CHATEAU. O.O. 72 attached.	
	13/6/17.		Battalion in trenches.	
	14/6/17.		Battalion attacked OBLIQUE ROW and OPTIC TRENCH in conjunction with 15th K.R.R.C. on right, and 24th Div. on left. Operation entirely successful, vide O.O. 73 and report on attack attached. 4.45 p.m. enemy counterattacked, but was repulsed, only a few succeeded in entering our trenches. (Report attached). 15th Hnts. Regt. relieved our right front line Company which moved into support in OPAL TRENCH O.O. 74 attached.	
	15/6/17.		Battalion relieved in front line system by 18th East Surrey Regt. and moved by platoons into support in old German front line, see O.O. 75 attached.	
	17-16/6/17.		Strength of Battalion 33 Officers, 742 Other Ranks. Battalion in support, rest and bathing.	

WAR DIARY
or
INTELLIGENCE SUMMARY

(Erase heading not required.)

Army Form C. 2118.

Place	Date	Hour	Summary of Events and Information	Remarks and references to Appendices
ELZEN-WALLE	19/6/17		Battallion relieved by 10th R.W.Kent Regt. and moved by route march to bivouacs near ELZENWALLE, vide O.O.76 attached. Casualties from 7 – 19th inclusive, Killed – 3 Officers. Capt. T.G. Fraser. 2/Lt. A.E. Fenton. 2/Lt. C. Goas. 37 Other Ranks. Wounded. 7 Officers. 1 O.R. Missing. Capt. C.F. Stallard. " R. Maltby. Lt. G.Gordon-Smith. 2/Lt. R.H.W.F. Bernadd. " H.S. Carter. " H.A. Quartermain. " J.H. Greenwood. 290 Other Ranks.	
	20-21/6/17		Battalion resting and refitting.	
	22/6/17		Lieut. Col. A.G. COPPH left to take temporary command of Brigade. Major J.C. Beadle assumed command of Battalion in his absence. Q.M. and Hon. Lt. E. GOULDS reported for duty. Capt. J.S.DOYLE reported as M.O. vice Lieut. D.I. CONNOLLY, on leave to Ireland, and Lieut. R.G. ROGERS rejoined the Battalion.	
	23-27/6/17		Battalion in rest at ELZENWALLE. Strength of Battalion 35 officers. 686 Other Ranks.	
ROUKLOS-NILLE	28/6/17		Battalion was relieved by the 21st Battn. London Regt. and proceeded by route march to billets in ROUKLOSHILLE area for rest and training.	
	29/6/17		Rest and refitting.	
	30/6/17		Strength of Battalion 35 Officers. 677 Other Ranks.	

1/7/17.

[signed] John Beadle
Major,
Commanding 14th Bn. "THE QUEEN'S OWN"
(Royal West Kent) Regt. (Lewisham).

S E C R E T.   OPERATION ORDER No. 69.   Copy No......
by Lieut. Col. A.C. Corfe,
Commanding 11th Bn. "THE QUEEN'S OWN"
(Royal West Kent) Regt. (Lewisham).

4th June, 1917.

Ref. Map 1/20000.
WYTSCHAETE. and Map E.

1. The 41st Division in conjunction with 19th Division on its Right, and 47th Division on its Left is to attack the enemy's position on ZERO Day.

2. The Objectives of the 41st Division are shown on Map E.
   - 1st Objective.   RED LINE.
   - 2nd   "   BLUE LINE.
   - 3rd   "   BLACK LINE.

3. The first two Objectives will be taken by the 124th Infantry Brigade on the Right, and the 123 Infantry Brigade on the Left.
   The 140th Infantry Brigade will be on the Left of the 123rd Infantry Brigade.

4. The 122nd Infantry Brigade in conjunction with 3 Battalions of the 124th Infantry Brigade on the Right, and 2 Battalions 140th Infantry Brigade on the Left, will capture the BLACK LINE from Southern Corner of DENYS WOOD, C.15.b.3.9. to junction of OBLONG SUPPORT with trench in continuation of Sunken Road, C.10.a.8½.3½.

5. The attack will be carried out by
   - 12th East Surrey Regt.   on the Right.
   - 15th Hampshire Regt.   in the Centre.
   - 11th R.West Kent Regt.   on the Left.

   The 15th Battalion London Regt. will be on the Left of the 11th Royal West Kent Regt.

6. Two Sections Machine Gun Company will co-operate with Assaulting Infantry in attack of the BLACK LINE.

7. One Light Trench Mortar with 60 rounds will accompany each of the Assaulting Battalions.

8. The Battalion frontage will be divided equally between Companies. Order of Companies from Right to Left -
   A, B, C, D.

9. Time Table and plan of Attack:-

   ZERO minus 2 hours.   All Units will be in their assembly areas as shown on Map E.

   ZERO plus 2 hours.   Assaulting Battalions will advance from their Assembly Areas in Artillery formation. As soon as they are clear of OLD FRENCH TRENCH 2 Sections of 122nd Machine Gun Company will move Eastward along line of OLD FRENCH TRENCH until in rear of Assaulting Battalions, and then will advance behind them.

   ZERO plus 3 hours.   12th East Surrey Regt., 15th Hants, and 11th R.W.Kent Regt. will each be formed up in two waves behind the DAMMSTRASSE as shown on Map E., the Right Flank of the 12th East Surrey Regt. resting on OASIS ROW and the Left of the 11th R.W.Kent Regt. on OAR LANE.

   ZERO plus 3 hours and 20 minutes.   Waves will move forward over the DAMMSTRASSE to get formed up close under the barrage, which will be beyond the DAMMSTRASSE.

P.T.O.

9. (Contd.).

  ZERO plus 3 hours & 40 mins. The Creeping Barrage will move forward and the Assaulting Troops with it for the attack on the BLACK LINE.
The Leap Frog method will be employed for the attack. Each Battalion will be in two waves, with Companies on a two platoon frontage. Companies will detail their own "Moppers Up", the first wave being responsible for "Mopping Up" forward, after the second wave has passed through it.

  ZERO plus 4 hours & 15 mins. Capture of BLACK LINE.

  ZERO plus 5 hours & 30 mins. 47th Division are going to attack DELBSKE FARM. 11th R.W.Kent Regt. will capture and hold ride running from this farm through RAVINE WOOD. RIDE runs about 100 yards in front of and parallel to OBLONG RESERVE.

10. After capture of BLACK LINE a front line will be organised in its vicinity.
The 122nd Infantry Brigade will hold their portion as a Divisional FRONT LINE; LEFT SECTOR.

11. Communication Trenches will be dug back from OBOE TRENCH to OAR ALLEY.
O.C. "B" Company will detail party for this.

12. The Vickers Machine Gun defence of the line will be co-ordinated by O.C. 122nd Machine Gun Company with 4 guns on a general line along forward edge of PHEASANT WOOD to O.10.a,3½.7¾. A number of guns of the 123rd Infantry Brigade will also be in a position to cover the front.
 One Sub-section will be detailed to front held by 11th R.W.Kent Regt. One gun of this Section will be allotted to STRONG POINT at O.10.a.2.4.
 The attack on the BLACK LINE will be covered by a Machine Gun barrage.

13. The Light Trench Mortar with the Battalion will assist during the attack should a strong point hold it up, and will subsequently take up positions covering line gained.

14. The barrage in support of the attack will consist of a creeping barrage of 18 pounders, preceding the Infantry in lifts of 25 yards per minute, and a standing barrage on definite trenches and defensive systems, of 18 pounders, and all natures of Howitzers.

15. The Artillery barrage after lifting off the BLACK LINE will creep forward to a line 300 yards in advance of the BLACK LINE in order to admit of patrols moving out.

16. At ZERO plus 5 hours & 30 minutes, when 11th R.W.Kent Regt. secure line Ride running from DELBSKE FARM through RAVINE WOOD, the barrage will lift back a further 100 yards on this front.

17. Strong patrols will be pushed forward to clear the ground towards ODYSSEY and OLIVE TRENCHES, as the attack will be continued at ZERO plus 10 hours by troops of the 24th Division against these trenches.

18. Two Sections of TANKS will accompany the advance.

19. A MINE will be exploded at ZERO under Nos. 2 and 3 CRATERS.

                  Continued.

-3-

20. Gas and Smoke Barrages will be employed according to suitability of the wind.

21. A Contact Patrol will be up from ZERO (if light enough) till 6 hours after ZERO.
Leading Infantry will light Flares approximately at the following times :-
    ZERO plus 4 hours, 30 minutes.
      "   "   5 hours, 30 minutes.
Infantry must however, ensure that the aeroplane is calling for Flares before lighting up.

22. A Wireless Aeroplane, which will be up throughout the day, will warn the Infantry of impending counter-attacks by means of Flares.
A RED Flare will signify that attack is NORTH of the Canal.
A GREEN Flare - SOUTH of the Canal.
This machine will also transmit Infantry messages calling for barrage.

23. Brigade Report Centre at BOLLART BEEK Dug-outs, I.31.d.3.6.
Battalion Report Centre -

24. Personnel for the attack will be as laid down in S.S.135, as far as possible.

25. Carrying Party. A Carrying Party of 15 Other Ranks will be told off to report to the Trench Mortar Battery at a time to be notified later. Companies will provide men as under:-
    "A" Coy.   4 men.
    "B" Coy.   2 men.
    "C" Coy.   5 men.
    "D" Coy.   4 men.

26. General direction of attack is 157 degrees true bearing.

27. O.C. "B" Company will tell off a small garrison to hold Strong Point C.10.a.2.5. - at Trench Junction.

28. The situation will be reported to Battalion Headquarters as frequently as circumstances permit.

                        (sgd.) A. C. Corfe, Lieut. Col.,
                        Commanding 11th Bn. "THE QUEEN'S OWN"
                        (Royal West Kent) Regt. (Lewisham).

Copy No. 1. C.O.   9. L.G.O.
       2. Adjutant.   10. B.O.
       3. Sig. Offr.   11. T.O.
       4. O.C. "A" Coy. 12. M.O.
       5. O.C. "B" Coy. 13. R.S.M.
       6. O.C. "C" Coy. 14. I. Sgt.
       7. O.C. "D" Coy. 15. War Diary.
       8. Q.M.   16. Office Copy.

<u>S E C R E T.</u> OPERATION ORDERS NO.70.   Copy No. 4
by Lieut. Col. A.C. Corfe,
Commanding 11th Bn. "THE QUEEN'S OWN"
(Royal West Kent) Regt. (Lewisham).

5th June, 1917.

1. The Battalion will be relieved to-day by Units of the 124th Infantry Brigade.

2. Relief will be completed by 2 p.m. in accordance with attached March Table.

3. Relief will be reported to Battalion Headquarters by new Second Army Trench Code issued yesterday.

4. All movement will be by platoon at 200 yards interval.

5. Trench Stores will be handed over to the incoming Unit, a copy of same will be sent to the Adjutant after relief.

6. Lewis Gunners and Company Signallers will be relieved same time as Companies.

7. Snipers, if not relieved by 9.30 a.m. will report to Battalion Headquarters and the Intelligence Sergeant.

8. Lewis Gun limbers will be at "Salmon's Place" at DICKEBUSCH at 10 a.m. for two Companies and at 11 a.m. for the remaining two Companies (one limber per two Companies).

9. Company Commanders' horses have been ordered to be at "Salmon's Place", DICKEBUSCH as follows:-
"A" Coy. at 10 a.m.
"B", "C", and "D" Companies 11 a.m.

10. The Transport Officer has arranged for guides to be at the Battalion Quartermaster's Stores, MICMAC, to guide Companies to MICMAC NORTH CAMP.

11. Companies will report their arrival at MICMAC to the Adjutant.

(sgd.) A.C. Corfe, Lieut. Col.,
Commanding 11th Bn. "THE QUEEN'S OWN"
(Royal West Kent) Regt. (Lewisham).

Copy No. 1. Adjutant.
2. War Diary.
3. O.C. "A" Coy.
4. O.C. "B" "
5. O.C. "C" "
6. O.C. "D" "
7. R.S.M.
8. Int. Sergt.

SECRET.

Ref. Map :— 28/4 ???
Map E.

OPERATION ORDERS No. 71.   Copy No. 3
by Lieut. Col. A.C. Corfe, D.S.O.,
Commanding 11th Bn. "THE QUEEN'S OWN"
(Royal West Kent) Regt. (Lewisham).

6th June, 1917.

1. The Brigade will march to the Assembly Area on Y/Z night.

2. Starting Point - Junction of OUDERDOM - HALLEBAST Road, and H.32.a.5.2.
   Head of Battalion to pass Starting Point at 9 p.m.

3. The Battalion will parade at 6.30 p.m. in Full Fighting Order on Football Ground.
   Order of march - Headquarters, "D", "C", "B", "A". Companies.

4. Companies must be concentrated in the Assembly Area by ZERO minus 3 hours.

5. All movements will be by Platoons at 50 yards interval. If Troops or Transport are met at points where Overland Track crosses road, Platoons will double across through the intervals.

6. Normal clock hour halts will not be observed. There will be a five minutes halt at every clock half hour, from the half hour till 25 minutes to the hour, and again from the hour till 5 minutes past.

7. Route.- Overland Route to ENGLISH WOOD - CHATEAU SEGARD - TRAMWAY TRACK - OLD FRENCH TRENCH.

8. Lewis Guns will be carried on pack ponies as far forward as possible. They will be unloaded during a five minute halt so as to cause no delay to Troops in rear.
   The Transport Officer will arrange for one pack animal to accompany each Platoon.

9. The Starting Point, H.32.a.5.2. will be marked by a red lamp. The Provost Sergeant will detail 3 men to report to an Officer of the Brigade Staff at the Starting Point at 8.45 p.m. for instructions.

10. There will be no smoking after passing the Starting Point till daylight.

11. Bombs, Rifle Grenades and Lewis Gun magazines to be issued from the Battalion Dump in OLD FRENCH TRENCH, must be drawn at once on arrival.

12. All waterbottles must be filled before leaving.

13. Companies will report to Battalion Headquarters when they are in position in the Assembly Area.

14. Battalion Report Centre at the Assembly Area will be I.33.c.1½.3.

15. The R.A.P. will be at SHELLY Dump before the Battalion moves forward to the DAMMSTRASSE.
    The R.A.P. will then push forward to the DAMMSTRASSE.

16. Rations - One day's rations and iron rations will be carried by all ranks.

17. Watches will be synchronised at 2.30 p.m. and 8.30 p.m.

(sgd.) A.C. Corfe, Lieut. Col., D.S.O.,
Commanding 11th Bn. "THE QUEEN'S OWN" Royal West Kent Regt.

Copy No.1. C.O. 2. Adjt. 3. War Diary. 4. Office Copy. 5. O.C. "A",
6. O.C. "B". 7. O.C. "C". 8. O.C. "D". 9. L.G.O. 10. T.O.
11. M.O. 12. S.O. 13. B.B.O. 14. Q.M. 15. A/R.S.M. 16. I.Sgt.

REPORT ON ATTACK 7th JUNE, 1917.

Ref: WYTSCHAETE 28. S.W. 2. 1/10,000. & 41st. Div. Map.

ASSEMBLY. The Battalion was in position in the ASSEMBLY AREA, OLD FRENCH TRENCH, at 1 a.m. 7th instant.

ORDER OF BATTLE. The Battalion in 2 waves with Companies on a two platoon front. Order of Companies from Right to Left, A,B,C,D.

ZERO. 3.10 a.m. First phase of attack started.

ADVANCED ASSEMBLY POSITION. At 5.10 a.m. the Battalion moved forward in Artillery Formation to advanced position of assembly behind the DAMMSTRASSE.
The Battalion was in position in 2 waves at 5.40 a.m. having passed through very slight enemy barrage with very few casualties.

ASSEMBLY UNDER BARRAGE. At 6.30 a.m. the waves moved forward over the DAMMSTRASSE under our own barrage preparatory to the attack.
The Battalion had to extend slightly to the left on the front of the 140th Infantry Brigade so as to keep in touch with them. A hostile machine gun on our left flank enfiladed our two waves inflicting several casualties. A TANK moved forward and put the machine gun out of action.
Battalion H.Q. were established at O.10.a.6.6.

ATTACK. At 6.50 a.m. the barrage lifted and waves moved forward. Practically no enemy barrage.
A hostile machine gun at N.E. corner of PHEASANT WOOD held up the advance for a short time.
A party under Captain R. Maltby, and 2/Lieut. J. H. Greenwood rushed forward and captured the gun killing three of the team.
The Battalion then pushed forward to OBLONG TRENCH which was captured at 7.5 a.m. after slight opposition by enemy.
The second wave reinforced the first wave and the whole line pushed forward to OBLONG RESERVE.
In this trench there were 40 to 50 of the enemy who showed some fight until our line got close up to them when some of them ran back, and the remainder gave themselves up.
The BLACK LINE was captured at 7.30 a.m.
At this point the barrage was falling very short and we had several casualties from our own shells.
The line, however, pushed forward as far as the road leading from DELBSKE FARM to ENGLEBRIER FARM.
Several dug-outs were cleared on this road.
As we were having several casualties from our own barrage, which had not lifted far enough forward the line had to fall back about 20 yards this side of OBLONG RESERVE.
At this point the Battalion dug in and consolidated their position.
At 3.10 p.m. troops of the 24th Division passed through us.
The Battalion was relieved at 5 a.m. on the 8th instant by a Company of the 73rd Infantry Brigade.

Lieut. Colonel,
Commanding 11th Bn. "THE QUEEN'S OWN"
(Royal West Kent) Regt. (Lewisham).

11/6/17.

SECRET. OPERATION ORDERS No. 72   Copy No. 6
by Lieut. Col. A.C. Corfe, D.S.O.,
Commanding 11th Bn. "THE QUEEN'S OWN"
Ref: Map WYTSCHAETE (Royal West Kent) Regt. (Lewisham).
5.a. 28 S.W.2.

1. The 122nd Infantry Brigade will relieve the 140th Infantry Brigade South of the YPRES-COMMINES Canal on the night 12-13th June, 1917. Relief to be complete by 8 a.m. June 13th.

2. The Battalion will take over from the 8th and 17th Battalions London Regts. in the left Sub-Sector with the 18th K.R.R.C. on its right, to-night.

3. Companies will be distributed as under:-

   Left Front Company.   "D" Company.
   Right Front Company.   "C" Company.
   Support Company.   "B" Company.
   Reserve Company.   "A" Company.

4. Companies will relieve in the order above stated, Headquarters will bring up the rear. The leading platoon of "D" Company will be at junction NORFOLK ROAD and Old Front Line at 9.30 p.m.

5. Lewis Gun teams will march with their platoons.

6. Four guides from Front Company of 17th London Regt. will meet "D" Company at 9.30 p.m. at junction of NORFOLK ROAD and late Front Line, and 4 from Front Line Company of 8th London will meet "C" Company at same point at 9.40 p.m.

7. Interval. Companies will march off in order named at 10 minutes interval. "D" Company will lead off at 9 p.m.
   Platoons must keep a distance of at least 100 yards.

8. Trench Stores, maps, aeroplane photographs, etc., will be taken over, and receipts for same sent to Battalion Headquarters on relief.

9. Completion of relief will be notified by new code to Battalion Headquarters.

10. Surplus Officers kits and mess-boxes, blankets, etc., will be stacked by Companies near Orderly Room. All personnel not going up to the line will parade at 8.30 p.m. on road near Orderly Room.

11. The Transport Officer will send up for cookers and 2 limbers to take back surplus Officers kits and mess-boxes. These can be supplied from the ration limbers.
    One water cart will remain at Battalion Dump.

12. All available shovels will be taken up to the line.

13. All water bottles will be full on moving off, and each man will carry rations for tomorrow.

(sgd). A. C. CORFE, Lt. Col.,
Commanding 11th Bn. "THE QUEEN'S OWN"
(Royal West Kent) Regt. (Lewisham).

Copy No. 1. C.O.   10. T.O.
        2. Sec. in Command.   11. Q.M.
        3. Adjutant.   12. M.O.
        4. Asst. Adjt.   13. O.C. "A" Coy.
        5. Office Copy.   14. O.C. "B" "
        6. War Diary.   15. O.C. "C" "
        7. Sig. Offr.   16. O.C. "D" "
        8. B.O.   17. R.S.M.
        9. Int. Sergt.   18. O.C. 8th Ldn. Regt.
                                   19. O.C. 17th Ldn. Regt.

SECRET   No. 73.

OPERATION ORDERS by Lt. Col. A.C. Corfe, D.S.O.
Commanding 11th (S) Battn. "The Queen's Own"
(Royal West Kent) Regt. (Lewisham).

June 13th. 1916.

Ref. Map. - WYTSCHAETE (28 S.W.) Edition 5A.

1. A combined operation will be carried out by 122nd Inf. Brigade on right of CANAL and by 24th Division on left of CANAL tomorrow 14th inst; Zero hour will be notified later.

2. Objective of 122nd Inf. Brigade will be that portion of OLIVE TRENCH not held by us, from O 10 d 7.8½, OPTIC TRENCH to its junction with OBLIQUE ROW, thence northwards along same to its junction with CANAL.

3. The 18th K.R.R.C. will carry out the operation with 2 Companys on the right and the 11th R.W.Kent Regt. with 3 Companys on the left.
   The frontage of Battalion is from O 5 c 2.2 along OPAL RESERVE to CANAL.

4. Companies will be disposed for the attack as follows:- "C" Coy on the right, "B" Coy in centre and "D" Coy on left, in present front line with "A" Coy in support.

5. "B" Company will move from its present position tomorrow at 1 p.m. by sections at 300 yards distance, all movement to be by trench, to front line.
   "A" Company will take over "B" Company's position on vacation by the latter, moving there by trench. At Zero they will occupy the front line when the assaulting Companies have left it.

6. At Zero "B" and "C" Companies will advance in one wave behind barrage and will occupy and mop up OPTIC TRENCH from O 11 a 45.55 to O 5 d 4.5.
   After assaulting Companies have gone forward "D" Company will clear OBLIQUE ROW and occupy it up to the CANAL.
   They will establish a block and bombing post at O 5 d 6.6. Eight men will be detailed for this.

7. "B" and "C" Companies after arrival in OPTIC TRENCH will each detail 12 men with one Lewis Gun team to push forward at Zero plus 25 minutes as soon as the barrage permits to raid OPTIC SUPPORT. Each party will be under an Officer.
   When the raiders return the Lewis Gun teams will take up positions 300 yards in front of OPTIC TRENCH to cover consolidation of the latter - the final objective.

8. ARTILLERY.
   The creeping barrage will move forward at the rate of 100 yards in 4 minutes. It will pause for 15 minutes 150 yards in front of OPTIC TRENCH and will move forward to its final position 150 yards beyond OPTIC SUPPORT. Vide map Appendix.
   The standing barrage will cover the left flank and shell all enemy points in the vicinity of GREEN WOOD and HOLLEBEKE and Square O.6, the Canal crossing between Locks and OBLIQUE TRENCH.

9. MACHINE GUNS.
   The 122nd M.G. Company will move forward 4 guns behind assaulting Infantry to positions between OPAL Reserve and OPTIC TRENCH to be ready to deal with a hostile counter attack. M.G's barrage will also co-operate in barrage on points in rear of enemy lines.

10. 122nd T.M.B. will detail guns for defence of the following points.

   O 5 c 0.9)
   O 11 a 3.5½) To be put into position when object has been
   O 5 d 2.8) gained
   O 5 d 4.5½)

11. Each Company will carry at least 30 shovels and every available man will help to consolidate the final objective.

12. The 12th E. Surrey Regt. will move up One Company to OAK RESERVE, One Company to OAK CRESCENT and SWITCH and Two Companies to OPAL TRENCH and OPAL SUPPORT as soon after Zero as possible.

13. There will be a contact aeroplane. B, C and D Companies will send to Battalion Headquarters by 10 a.m. tomorrow for 100 flares which will be distributed. Times at which flares will be lit will be notified later.

14. REPORTS
    Frequent messages will be sent back during the operations.
    All messages will be sent to the present "C" Company Headquarters from whence they will be transmitted to Battalion Headquarters by phone - or runner if the line is broken.

15. All prisoners captured will be sent back to O.C. "A" Company who will pass them under escort to Bn. Headquarters.

16. DRESS. 2 Bombs will be carried by each man, also 5 sandbags in belt

17. A communication trench will be dug back by "B" Company from OPTIC TRENCH about O 5 d 2.4 to OPAL RESERVE at O 5 c 6.7.

18. DUMPS.
    226th Field Company R.E. will form a dump at ~~a 4~~ O 10 d 6.8.
    O.C. "D" Company will dump at O 5 c 1.9. 500 sandbags, 20 picks and 50 shovels for the attack.

19. Sgt. Nightingale will be in charge of a carrying party of 8 men to be detailed by O.C. "A" Company to take Lewis Gun ammunition to OPTIC TRENCH when the latter is captured.

(signed) A.C.CORFE

Lt. Colonel.

S E C R E T

    O.C.,
        A. B. C.& D.

        Further to O.O.73 dated yesterday.

1. ZERO HOUR will be at 7.30 p.m. today.

2. Bombardment will continue today but will slacken at 3 p.m. and after.

3. Each Company will send Officer at 4 p.m. to Battalion Headquarters to synchronise watches.

4. Contact aeroplane will call for flares about 8 p.m.

5. The house at O.11.a.1½.0 will be taken and held by 18th K.R.R.C.

6. 18th K.R.R.C. will establish a signal office in concrete dugout on extreme right of our present front line.

7. RATIONS. Previous instructions are cancelled. Each Company will detail a guide to report to R.S.M. at Battalion Headquarters at 2.45 p.m. today. These men will guide ration party of 12th E. Surreys up tonight about 11.30 p.m.

8. As soon as objective in OPTIC TRENCH has been gained White VERY Lights will be fired back towards OPAL RESERVE.

                (sd) R. KERR
                                Lieut.
                A/ Adjt.
14/6/17.   for Lieut. Col. Commanding 11th R.W.K.

To:-
   Headquarters,
      122nd Infantry Brigade.

   I beg to submit the following report on attempted enemy counter attack this evening.

   The enemy bombarded the front line from 4.45 p.m. to 4.50 p.m. with 5.9 shells. When the barrage lifted and the enemy started to come over S.O.S. was sent up but no reply was received from our artillery.

   A few enemy bombers came over the first block in bombing post down OBLIQUE TRENCH but were speedily driven back. The enemy apparently came up OBLIQUE TRENCH threw over some bombs, and while this was going on, a few men came over the parapet of OPTIC SUPPORT towards our front line. These were subjected to heavy fire from our M.Gs. and our Lewis Guns. Enemy was beaten back by 5.5. p.m.

   Enemy barrage was put up between OPTIC TRENCH and OPAL Reserve and WHITE CHATEAU and other points in rear were also shelled by 5.9s.

   Our barrage when it came was very regular and effective.

   Our casualties are few. At beginning of attack enemy machine guns barraged our front line from direction of I 32 d.

115/6/17   (sgd) A. C. Corfe.
                                    Lieut. Col.
                              Commanding 11th R.W. Kent.

S E C R E T

OPERATION ORDER No. 74

By Lt. Col. Corfe, Commanding 11th R.W. Kent Regt.

15th June 1917.

1. The 15th Hants are moving into the line tonight and will take over our front line in OPTIC TRENCH from the right to O 5 c 9½.0.

2. Our Battalion frontage will therefore be from O 5 c 9½.0 along OPTIC TRENCH via OBLIQUE ROW to CANAL. Only "C" Company is affected by the change.

3. Companies will be distributed as follows:-
"B" Coy. O 5 c 9½.0 to junction OPTIC TRENCH and OBLIQUE ROW exclusive.
"D" Coy from latter point inclusive to Canal.
"A" Coy as at present.
"C" In OPAL RESERVE from Wood at D 5 c 2½.1½ to join up with "A" Coy.

4. O.C. "C" Coy will detail 4 guides to report Battalion Headquarters at 8.30 p.m. to guide Company of 15th Hants taking over their front.

5. On relief "C" Coy will take up position as detailed in para. 3.

6. The wire sent up to O.C. "A" Coy to be put out tonight will be sent by hi. to "B" and "D" Coys only and will be put out by them.

7. O.C. "C" Coy will report when relief is complete.

(sd) A.C. Corfe   Lt. Col.
Commanding 11th R. W. Kent Regt.

S E C R E T   OPERATION ORDER. No. 75

By Lt. Col. A.C. Corfe, D.S.O. Commanding
11th. Bn. Royal West Kent Regt.

16th June 1917.

1. The Battalion will be relieved by 12th East Surrey Regt. tonight.

2. Four Guides per Company will report to 2/Lt. LINDSAY at Battalion Headquarters before 8 p.m. He will be given instructions at Battalion Headquarters re meeting East Surreys and guiding them up. O.C. Companies willbe responsible that these guides know the way: they must be best men in Platoon.

3. A, B, C & D Companies will be relieved by A. B. C & D Companies 12th East Surreys respectively.

4. Relief will be reported to Battalion Headquarters by wire or runner by Group "999".

5. Each Company will detail 1 officer and 4 guides per Company to report to Battalion Headquarters at 12 noon. These will go and find out dispositions of 12th E. Surreys, return to their Coys and guide their platoon back on relief. Officers detailed will receive full instructions at Battalion Headquarters.

6. On relief the Battalion will move back in support to OAK TRENCH and OAK SUPPORT.

7. All trench stores, photogrpahs, 2 1" Very Pistols per Company will be handed over (the pistols on loan) and receipts taken for same.

8. Relieving Companies will arrive in order, D. B. A. C. with 5 minutes interval between platoons.

(sgd) A. C. CORFE
Lt. Col.
Commanding 11th R.W.Kent Regt.

To:-
    Headquarters,
      122nd Infantry Brigade.

Report on Operations, evening of 14th June 1917.

Ref:- WYTSCHAETE 28. S.W. 2.

At 7.30 p.m. (ZERO), three Companies went over in one wave, their objective being OPTIC TRENCH, from 0 11 a 45.55 to junction with OBLIQUE TRENCH, and thence along OBLIQUE ROW to CANAL at 0 5 b 2.2½.

The objective was gained by the two right Companies at 7.45 p.m. The left Company also gained its objective quickly, slightly over running, thus coming under severe enemy machine gun fire.

Bombing squads and LEWIS GUN teams were pushed forward by the two right Companies to mop up OPTIC SUPPORT, where little opposition was encountered.

These parties returned at about 8.15 p.m. to help in consolidating, the L.G. teams remaining in front post to cover Companies were in touch with each other, and with Battalion on right by 8.30 p.m.

The left Company established a block and bombing post in OBLIQUE TRENCH at 0 5 d 5.5½.

A communication trench was started from 0.5 d 2.1½ joining our old front line (OPAL RESERVE) at 0 5 c 4.5 . This was dug through by daybreak to an average depth of 3' 6".

228th Field Coy, R.E. put out barbed wire in front of objective. By daybreak the trench was opened up all along our front.

<u>Barrage.</u> Our own was very good. Very few shells were short, and the men kept close up in consequence.

The enemy put a fairly heavy barrage in rear of OPAL RESERVE, and bombarded indiscriminately WHITE CHATEAU and back areas.

<u>Opposition.</u> Objectives appeared to be held lightly by posts who offered stubborn resistance.

<u>Prisoners.</u> Fifteen in all were taken, of whom 4 were wounded, and three subsequently killed by enemy barrage.

<u>Casualties.</u>
2 officers, 6 O.Rs, killed.
1 Officer, 24 O.Rs. wounded.

Enemy casualties believed heavy; he was seen retiring from OPTIC TRENCH whilst the attack was being pushed home. Our LEWIS GUNNERS dealt effectively with all exposures.

                    (sgd) A.C.CORFE
            Lieut Col. Commanding 11th R.W.Kent

16/6/17.

SECRET.   OPERATION ORDERS No.76.   Copy No. 5

by Lieut. Col. A.C.Corfe, D.S.O.,
Commanding 11th Bn. "THE QUEEN'S OWN"
(Royal West Kent) Regt. (Lewisham).

Ref: 28 S.W.

19th June, 1917.

1. The Battalion will be relieved by the 10th Battn. Royal West Kent Regt. to-day, relief starting about 6 p.m.
 On relief the Battalion will proceed to bivouacs in H.35.d. (between Scottish Wood and Ridge Wood).
 Companies will be relieved by their opposite numbers.

2. Platoons will march off independently on relief under direction of guides. O.C. Companies will report relief by runner.

3. Movement will be by platoons at 300 yards interval.

4. Trench stores, any aeroplane photographs, dumps of S.A.A., bombs, if any, will be handed over to relieving Unit and a receipt taken.

5. O.C. Companies will detail one guide per platoon to be at Blighty Bridge, SPOIL BANK, at 5.30 p.m. under an Officer to be detailed by O.C. "D" Company.

6. Lewis Guns will be relieved at 4 p.m. Guns and magazines will be taken to Battalion Dump at OLD FRENCH TRENCH to be loaded in the limbers.

7. Signallers will be relieved at same time as their Companies.

8. Officers trench bundles, mess-boxes, dixies, etc., must be stacked at Battalion Dump by 6 p.m.

9. The Transport Officer will arrange for one limber per Company, 2 for Headquarters, and Officers mess-cart to be at Battalion Dump, OLD FRENCH TRENCH, at 6 p.m. O.C. Companies must see that their limbers are loaded as soon as possible, so as to allow the Transport to get away.

10. O.C. Companies must make a special effort to hand over trenches scrupulously clean. A certificate to this effect signed by O.C. relieving Company will be obtained and handed over to the Adjutant with Trench Store Returns.

11. O.C. Companies will detail 2 men per platoon to report to 2/Lieut. FREEMAN at Battalion Headquarters at 2 p.m.
 This party will proceed to the new camp as an advance party.
 One man per platoon will return to his platoon by 6 p.m. to act as a guide to the new camp.

12. Arrival in camp will be reported to the Adjutant, and attached Strength Return forwarded at the same time.

(sgd.). A. C. Corfe, Lieut. Col.,
Commanding 11th Bn. "THE QUEEN'S OWN"
(Royal West Kent) Regt. (Lewisham).

Copy No. 1. O.C.
2. Adjt.
3. Asst. Adjt.
4. Sec. in Com.
5. War Diary.
6. Office Copy.
7. S.O.
8. M.O.
9. T.O.
10. Q.M.
11. O.C. "A" Coy.
12. O.C. "B" Coy.
13. O.C. "C" Coy.
14. O.C. "D" Coy.
15. R.S.M.
16. O.C. 10th Bn.R.W.K.rgt.
17. L.G. Sergt.

Map Ref:-
Sheet 28/40000

27 SE/20000

OPERATION ORDERS No.77.
by Major J. C. Beadle,
Commanding 11th Bn. "THE QUEEN'S OWN"
(Royal West Kent) Regt. (Lewisham).

Copy No...5....

27th June, 1917.

1. The 132nd Infantry Brigade will be relieved by the 142nd Infantry Brigade tomorrow, 20th instant, and will proceed by route march to ROUKLOSHILLE AREA.

2. The Battalion after being relieved will march in column of 3's to the Transport Lines (Rozenhill Camp) by half Companies at 200 yards interval. Order of March - "A", "B", "C", "D", Coys., & Headquarters. Usual clock hour halts.

3. The Battalion will have dinner at the Transport Lines, and will resume the march at time to be notified later. All transport will be ready to move off after dinner.

4. Dress - Fighting Order with waterproof sheets under flap of haversack. Steel Helmets to be worn as far as Transport Lines. They will then be strapped on the haversack. - Haversack to be worn on the back.

5. The Transport Officer will arrange for 4 Lewis Gun Limbers, tool Cart, M.O.'s cart, Mess Cart, and 1 G.S. Wagon for Officers kits, signalling equipment, etc., to be left at the camp by 6 a.m. These will be loaded up by 9.30 a.m. and return to the Transport Lines.

6. Officers kits and mess boxes must be stacked by 9 a.m.

7. The Transport Officer will also send up horses for cookers and watercarts. Cookers will proceed to Transport Lines behind their respective Company.

8. O.C. "D" Coy., will detail 1 N.C.O. and 20 men to report to the Orderly Officer at 8 a.m. as a loading party.
The Orderly Officer will supervise the loading of all the limbers and lorries, and will report to the Adjutant when all transport is loaded up and ready to move off.

9. Two motor lorries are being sent to the Battalion to transport packs. Packs must be stacked by 7.30 a.m.
All packs will be stacked by Companies and must be properly labelled. Every pack must have the name of the man and his Company clearly marked on it. Great care must be taken in loading the lorry so as to prevent the packs of the Companies being mixed up.
O.C. Companies will detail 1 man per Company to proceed with each lorry.

10. Particular attention to be paid on the march to march discipline. -No man will be allowed to ride on any wagon.
Company Commanders will be responsible for taking the name of any man who falls out.
No man will fall out without permission from an Officer.

11. Immediately on arrival in new area O.C. Companies will at once report the exact position of their Company Headquarters to the Adjutant.

12. Sick parade 8.30 a.m.

13. All waterbottles must be filled before moving off.

(sgd) J. C. Beadle, Major,
Commanding 11th Bn. "THE QUEEN'S OWN"
(Royal West Kent) Regt. (Lewisham).

1. A/C.O.
2. Adjt.
3. Asst Adjt.
4. Office Copy.
5. War Diary.
6. O.C. "A" Coy.
7. O.C. "B" Coy.
8. O.C. "C" Coy.
9. O.C. "D" Coy.

10. S.O.
11. M.O.
12. B.O.
13. R.Q.Q.M.
14. T.O.
15. R.S.M.

MARCH TABLE TO ACCOMPANY OPERATION ORDER NO. 70.

11th Royal West Kent Regiment.

RELIEVING UNITS.	"IN" ROUTE.	"OUT ROUTE".	Head of Relieving Unit to reach.	REMARKS.
H.Q. 10th "QUEENS" R.W. SURREY REGT. & two Companies.	Victoria Deep Dug-outs. Trenches O.1.1. O.1.2. & O.2.1. R.Line P.& O. to Middlesex Lane-Middlesex Lane.	Overland Track Victoria Street. Middlesex Lane to MIC-G.H.Q. 2nd Line - MAC. Gordon Farm - Nth. Duckboards H.32.d. & 2f. Hallebast-Ouderdom Road to H.31.b.&.3.	Front Line 8 a.m.	P.& O.Trench not to be used.
H.Q. 21st K.R.R.C. & two Companies.	Victoria Deep Dug-outs. Trenches O.2.2. O.2.3. & O.2.4. R.Line Middlesex Lane to Crater Lane, McGEE Trench.	-do-	Front Line 6.30 a.m.	
Party 26th Royal Fusiliers.	R.Line Crater Lane Victoria to BUS HOUSE ROAD. Street.	-do-	Front Line 5.30 a.m.	

Army Form C. 2118.

WAR DIARY
or
INTELLIGENCE SUMMARY

(Erase heading not required.)

11 R.W. Kent Regt.

Place	Date	Hour	Summary of Events and Information	Remarks and references to Appendices
ROCKLOSHILLE	1.7.17.		Strength of Battalion Officers 35, Other Ranks. 677. Battalion resting and training at LE ROCKLOSHILLE.	
	2.7.17.		Captain A.W. PUTTICK rejoined from C.O.'s Course, Aldershot.	
	3.7.17.		Two Companies under 2/Lt. C.E.MALPASS moved to Ridge Wood for work in forward area as working parties.	
	4-6.7.17.		Battalion and Specialist Training and rest. Draft of 176 other ranks arrived and taken on strength.	
	7.7.17.		Draft of 90 other ranks arrived and taken on strength. Strength of Battalion Officers 32, Other Ranks 941.	
	8-10.7.17.		Battalion and Specialist Training. 2/Lt. A. ROYLE arrived and taken on strength.	
	10-14.7.17.		Battalion and Specialist training. Strength of Battalion Officers 32, Other Ranks 916. 2/LTS. R.O. RUSSELL and J. LINDSAY promoted to rank of Lieut.	
	14-17.7.17.		Battalion and Specialist Training. Lt. Col. A.C. CORFE, D.S.O., rejoined Battalion from leave.	
	18.7.17.		Captain A.W. PUTTICK assumed duties of A/2nd in Command of 12th East Surrey Regt.	
	18-19.7.17.		Battalion and Specialist Training.	
	20.7.17.		Battalion marched to WESTOUTRE and carried out a practice attack for impending operations, vide O.O.78 attached which gives the scheme for the attack proper.	

Army Form C. 2118.

WAR DIARY
or
INTELLIGENCE SUMMARY

(Erase heading not required.)

Instructions regarding War Diaries and Intelligence Summaries are contained in F. S. Regs., Part II. and the Staff Manual respectively. Title Pages will be prepared in manuscript.

Place	Date	Hour	Summary of Events and Information	Remarks and references to Appendices
BOIS KLOSHILLE	21.7.17.		Battalion Sports. 2/LT. A.D. DENTON joined the Battalion for duty, and 2/LTS. H.A. QUARTERMAIN and P.T. COOKSEY rejoined from Base, wounded 7.6.17. Strength of Battalion officers 32, Other Ranks 968.	
	22.7.17		Major C. MURDOCH arrived for attachment as supernumerary 2nd in Command. Draft of 60 Other Ranks arrived & taken on strength.	
WESTOUTRE.	23.7.17.		Battalion moved by route march to camp in the WESTOUTRE area vide O.O. 79 attached.	
SPOIL BANK.	24.7.17.		Battalion relieved the 6th Battalion London Regt. in the line(vide O.O. 80 attached) behind HOLLEBEKE. Transport and Details moved to MURRUMBRIDGEE and WOOD CAMPS respectively. Trench strength of Battalion officers 18 Other Ranks 530.	
	24-28.7.17.		Battalion in trenches, weather good; heavy German shelling and a good many casualties. Strength of Battalion Officers 30. Other Ranks 964.	
	29-30.7.17.		Holding the trenches. Casualties up to 30th instant. Offrs. 2/LT.C.P. WEBB killed, 2/Lt. A.D. DENTON wounded. Other Ranks. 13 killed. 58 wounded.	
	31.7.17		Battalion attacked HOLLEBEKE with 123rd Brigade on the left, and 18th K.R.R.C. on right, vide O.O. 78 and Administrative Orders attached. Objective gained with heavy casualties owing to the fact that the Battalions on the flanks could not attain their objectives.(Report on attack attached.) Casualties for tour of duty 24.7.17 to 5.8.17. Officers killed 4, wounded 8, Other Ranks Killed 32, wounded 241, Missing 54. On HOLLEBEKE on 31.7.17.	

Army Form C. 2118.

WAR DIARY
or
INTELLIGENCE SUMMARY

(Erase heading not required.)

Place	Date	Hour	Summary of Events and Information	Remarks and references to Appendices
SPOIL BANK (Contd.).	1.8.17.		The following Officers became casualties during the tour of duty :- Killed - CAPT. F. SQUIRE, 2/LT. C.P. WEBB, 2/LT.F.C. WESTMACOTT; died of wounds, 2/LT. O.P. BROWN; wounded, 2/LTS. G.H. ARDILL, B.W. ASHWORTH, T.G. PLATT, C.C. BERGER, A. ROYLE, D.G. GODDEN, H.A. QUARTERMAIN, and A.D. DENTON.	

Lt. Col.,
Commanding 11th Bn. "THE QUEEN'S OWN"
Royal West Kent Regt. (Lewisham.).

NOT TO BE TAKEN FORWARD OF BRIGADE HEADQUARTERS.

SECRET.   OPERATION ORDER NO. 78,   Copy No. 4
                   by Lieut. Col. A.C. Corfe, D.S.O.,
                   Commanding 11th Bn. "THE QUEEN'S OWN"
Ref :- Map 28 S.W.2.   (Royal West Kent) Regt. (Lewisham).
Edition 5A 1/10,000.

                                             19th July, 1917.

INTENTION.   An attack will be carried out by 41st Division in conjunction with the 19th Division on the Right, and 24th Division on the Left.

                 The Objectives of the 41st Division are shown on the attached Map "B".

                 <u>1st Objective.</u>   RED LINE, i.e.   The enemy's Front Line.

                 <u>2nd Objective.</u>   BLUE LINE, i.e. FORRET FARM - HOLLEBEKE
                                            cross roads and new
                                            German Trench.

                 <u>3rd Objective.</u>   GREEN LINE, i.e. Final Objective.

                 Should the opportunity offer, it may be decided to exploit a further advance on ZANVOORDE. One Brigade of the 47th Division will be held in readiness for this.

                 122nd Infantry Brigade will attack on that part of Divisional Front which is South of the Canal.
                 123rd Infantry Brigade will be on the Left, and a Brigade of the 19th Division on the Right of 122nd Infantry Brigade.

                 1 Section 228th Field Company R.E. will be attached to 122nd Infantry Brigade for the attack.

OBJECTIVE.   The Objectives of the 122nd Infantry Brigade will be :-

                 <u>1st Objective.</u>   RED LINE within Brigade Boundary.

                 <u>2nd Objective.</u>   (BLUE and GREEN) LINES within Brigade
                                                  boundary.

                 The Objectives, and Brigade Boundaries are shown on Map "A".

ATTACK.   The attack will be carried out by 2 Battalions.-

                 18th K.R.R.C.   on the Right.
                 11th Bn. Royal West Kent Regt. on the Left.

FORMATION.   The Battalion will attack in 2 waves on a two Company Front with each Company on a 4 platoon front.

                 <u>1st Wave.</u>   "A" Coy. on the Right.
                                "B" "   on the Left.

                 <u>2nd Wave.</u>   "C" Coy. on the Right.
                                "D" "   on the Left.

                 The leap-frog method will be employed.

               The 1st Wave will capture RED LINE, Mop it up, construct and garrison the strong points already detailed. Special parties will be told off by "A" Company for mopping up OBLIQUE TRENCH, and Dug-outs in Wood at O.5.d.8.4.

              The 2nd Wave will pass through the 1st Wave and take BLUE and GREEN LINES, mop up area between RED and GREEN LINES, make Strong Points about GREEN LINE as already detailed, consolidate about this LINE, and push out Posts to limit of barrage.

                                                         P.T.O.

-2-

FORMATION.
(Contd.).

O.C. "C" Company will detail special mopping up parties for OPTIC SUPPORT, VERBRANDEN - HOLLEBEKE Road, between RED and GREEN LINES, C.T. between WOOD at O.5.d.8.4½, and GREEN LINE.

ASSEMBLY.

Approximate positions of Assembling for Battalions are shown in attached Map "A". Units will assemble on Y/Z night under orders to be issued later, and will be in position by Zero minus one hour.

Positions of Headquarters, Communication Trenches Tracks, Tramways, Dumps, R.A.P.s are shown in attached Map "A".

CONSOLIDATION.

Strong Points will be made on capture of RED LINE at -

(1) O.5.d.6.6. by "A" Company.
(2) O.6.a.05.00. by "B" Company.
On capture of BLUE and GREEN LINES at
(3) O.12.a.5.8. "C" Company

Strong Points will be garrisoned by 1 Platoon with Lewis Gun which will be told off in advance as follows.-

No.1. "A" Company.
2. "B" "
3. "C" "

A Vickers Gun will be attached to each Strong Point.

The GREEN LINE will eventually form our Front Line, and Strong Points in the neighbourhood of this Line will serve as a basis for its consolidation.

The Line will be sited by the Officer on the spot with due regard to observation over the ground in the immediate front. Posts will be pushed forward as far as the Artillery barrage permits, to cover the consolidation of the GREEN LINE. These Posts will be withdrawn under orders of Battalion Commander when no longer required.

ARTILLERY.

There will be a preliminary bombardment lasting several days.

CREEPING BARRAGE.

The Time Table of attack and Artillery barrage will follow. The rate of the Creeping Barrage will be 100 yards in 4 minutes. The barrage will advance to a final position 400 yards beyond the GREEN LINE.

MACHINE GUN BARRAGE.

The attack will be covered by a Machine Gun barrage. One section of the 122nd Machine Gun Company will accompany each Battalion to follow the Second Wave.

TRENCH MORTAR.

One Mortar and carriers with 40 rounds will accompany the Battalion.

KIT AND EQUIPMENT.

As carried on June 7th, 1917.

(sgd) A. J. JIMENEZ, Captain & Adjutant,
11th Bn. "THE QUEEN'S OWN" Royal West Kent Regt. (Lewisham).

Copy No.1. C.O. No.2. Sec. in Command. No.3. Adjutant. No.4. Asst. Adjt. No.5. War Diary. No.6. Office Copy. No.7. O.C. "A" Coy. No.8. O.C. "B" Coy. No.9. O.C. "C" Coy. No.10. O.C. "D" Coy. No.11. L.G.O. No.12. I.O. No.13. S.O. No.14. B.B.O. No.15. M.O. No.16. T.O. No.17. Q.M. No.18. R.S.M.

SECRET.

BARRAGE TIME TABLE for PRACTICE ONLY.

Ref:- O.O. 72 of 19.7.17.

Zero Hour.	Creeping Barrage commences 150 yards in front of OPTIC TRENCH and on OBLIQUE TRENCH.
Zero plus 4 minutes.	Barrage advances.
Zero plus 16 minutes.	Barrage halts on BLUE LINE.
Zero plus 26 minutes.	Barrage creeps forward from BLUE LINE.
Zero plus 46 minutes.	Barrage halts and remains 400 yards beyond GREEN LINE.

1. The above Time Table will be followed in Practice Attack on July 20th, but it will not correspond with Time Table for coming operations.

2. Watches will be synchronised at Rendezvous by an Officer of Brigade Staff.

S E C R E T.　　　　　　　　　　　　　　　　　　　　Copy No.

ADMINISTRATIVE ARRANGEMENTS
for
Forthcoming Operations, ref:-Operation Order No.78
dated 19th July, 1917.

Ref:- Map 28 S.W.2.
HOLLEBEKE 52. 1/10,000.

---

1. **RATIONS and WATER.**

    In order to reduce wheeled traffic on roads and tracks on "Y" day, barrage rations as under will be dumped near forward limit of horse transport.
    One day's complete rations for consumption on "Z" day.
    Sites selected for these dumps are as follows:-
    11th Bn.Royal West Kent Regt.　　　WHITE CHATEAU.
    Battalion's strength has been calculated at 575.
    One third gallons of water per man per diem in petrol tins will be dumped with these rations.
    The method of drawing these rations and petrol tins will be issued later.
    Rations for consumption on "Z" plus 1 and subsequent days will be delivered as normally by pack or wheeled transport under Battalion arrangements.

2. **WATER.**

    Details of water supply in Forward Area are as shewn in Appendix "A".
    A reserve of water carts is being placed at the disposal of the Division. In the event of the pipe line being broken, these carts will be put forward to a convenient central point (probably near Bridge I.33.d.3.6.) where water carrying parties can exchange empty for full petrol tins.
    Battalions will be issued with 100 Petrol Tins each, with which to form mobile dumps of water as far forward in the trench system as possible.
    Dumps of Petrol Tins, filled by reserve water carts, will be established at NORFOLK LODGE BRIDGE I.33.d.3.6.

3. **S.A.A., GRENADES and LIGHT TRENCH MORTAR AMMUNITION.**

    Divisional Dump will be at N.4.c.5.2.
    Brigade Dump will be at   O.3.b.8.9.
    Dumps for the two Assaulting Battalions are being established in recesses in OPAL RESERVE.
    These are being prepared and partially filled by 47th Division.
    Appendix "B" shows amounts allotted for Operations.

    Battalion ammunition dumps to hold:-

S.A.A.	100,000
Mills Grenades, No.5.	2,000
Rifle Grenades	1,000
Stokes Shells	500
Ring Charges.	500
Green cartridges	500
Very lights I"	500
" " I½"	250

    are being constructed and partially filled by 47th Division at the following places-
    Left Battalion.　　) Neighbourhood of junction of OPAL RESERVE
    11th R.W.Kent Regt.) and OAK AVENUE.

    Left Battalion. Dumps at O.5.c.5.5. and O.5.c.5.3. are nearly completed. Dump at O.5.c.45.80 is under construction.
    Flares and S.O.S. Rockets.- The Battalion has been allotted 1,000 flares, and 25 S.O.S. Rockets.

P.T.O.

4. **R.E. STORES.**

   Divisional R.E. Dump will be at BRASSERIE N.6.a.1.1.. An Advanced R.E. Dump is being formed at OAK DUMP O.3.b.9.7.

5. **MEDICAL.**

   Regimental Aid Posts.-
   18th Bn. King's Royal Rifle Corps. - O.3.d.6.8.
   11th Bn. Royal West Kent Regt. - O.4.a.6.2.
   Collecting Post.- SHELLEY LANE I.32.d.3.3.
   Advanced Dressing Station.- VOORMEZEELE I.31.c.4.6.
   Collecting Station for Walking Wounded.- BRASSERIE N.6.a.2.2.
   Main Dressing Station for seriously wounded. LA CLYTTE ROAD M.6.a.8.8.
   Main Dressing Station for Walking Wounded - LA CLYTTE N.7.c.2.5.

6. **PRISONERS OF WAR.**

   Escorts to Prisoners of War being sent back should not exceed 5% of the number of prisoners.
   A Relay Post will be formed at the Headquarters of the Battalion in Reserve (15th Bn. Hampshire Regiment) at O.3.b.9.7½, where escorts will be organised from the Battalion in Reserve, and the original escorts returned to their unit.
   The Officer in charge of the Cage will give a receipt to the escort for all prisoners handed over to him, and return escorts to their units.
   Prisoners Cage will be at N.3.a. Central where all prisoners will be sent.

7. **PACKS AND SURPLUS KIT.**

   Packs and surplus kit will be stored at RENINGHELST in the barn at G.34.d.65.80. In order to admit of great-coats being rapidly issued should opportunity occur, these will be rolled in bundles separate from the packs.
   Men should be warned to leave no private property in their great-coat pockets.

8. **MACHINE GUNS and LIGHT TRENCH MORTARS.**

   The attack will be supported by a Machine Gun Barrage.-

1 Machine Gun Company.		23rd Division.
1	do do	41st Division. (124th M.G. Coy.).
1	do do	47th Division.

9. The three Barrage Companies will be organised in six Machine Gun Batteries each consisting of 8 guns, A,B,C,D,E and F Batteries. The approximate positions of these batteries are shown on the attached map.

10. The barrage will come down 400 yards beyond the BLUE LINE and remain till Zero plus 20 minutes.
    At Zero plus 20 minutes M.G. barrage lifts to a line 800 yards beyond the GREEN LINE and remains till Zero plus 70 minutes.
    After this, the Batteries will be ready to answer any S.O.S. Call.
    Arrangements will be made whereby all Barrage Batteries can concentrate on to any particular Map square on the Divisional Front.

Contd.

MACHINE GUNS and LIGHT TRENCH MORTARS. (Contd.).

10. Rate of Fire Zero to Zero plus 20 - 1 belt per gun per 4 minutes.
    Rate of Fore Zero plus 20 to Zero plus 70 - 1 belt per gun per 8 minutes.

11. 122nd Machine Gun Company will support the Attack of 122nd Infantry Brigade.

12. Position of O.C. 122nd Machine Gun Company will be with Section of Guns in vicinity of OPTIC TRENCH.

13. Position of O.C. 122nd Light Trench Mortar Battery will be at Light Trench Mortar Battery Headquarters in the Line.

        (sgd) A. J. JIMENEZ, Captain & Adjutant,
               11th Bn. "THE QUEEN'S OWN" Royal West
                    Kent Regt. (Lewisham).

S E C R E T.

EXERCISE - ATTACK - 20th July, 1917.

Ref:- Pudding Map issued 18th instant,
and Sheets 27 S.E.2 & 28 S.W.1.

----

1. Reference Operation Order No.78, practices for this attack will take place on the IXth Corps Training Area on 20th and 22nd instant.

2. The Battalion will parade at 6 a.m. at Cross Roads at X.2.d.9½.4 and march to the Training Area.
   Order of March - Signallers, Snipers, Band, "A", "B", "C", and "D", Lewis Gun Limbers.
   DRESS.- Drill order.
   Signallers and Snipers will parade with their Companies, except those permanently in Headquarters.

3. Breakfast 5 a.m.

4. Dinner at Training Area, after operations, about 11 a.m. The T.O. will arrange for the cookers to be at M.13.d.9.4. Sheet 26.

5. Lewis Guns will be taken on Lewis Gun Limbers. These must be loaded to-night. Lewis Gun Limbers will march in rear of the Battalion tomorrow.

6. The Battalion will rendezvous at 8.30 a.m. between tracks labelled OAK AVENUE and OBLIQUE ROW.

7. Zero Hour will be at 9.30 a.m.
   The forming up in this case will take place in daylight to be able to better supervise the manœuvre, and to enable all ranks to get a view of the ground, and have explained to them what portion of our front the features on the ground are intended to represent.

8. The Canal, Trenches, etc., on our front are represented by roads and tracks on the ground which are signboarded and flagged. HOLLEBEKE is represented by a Farm.

9. The near end of Creeping Barrage will be represented by men with white flags under 2nd. Lieut TAMBLYN, 12th East Surrey Regt.

10. Barrage Time Table attached.

11. Probable hour of return to Camp - 1 p.m.

(sgd) A. J. JIMENEZ, Captain & Adjutant,
11th Bn. "THE QUEEN'S OWN" Royal West Kent) Regt. (Lewisham).

SECRET.

Ref: Hazebrouck 5a
    Sheet 28 1/40,000.
    Sheet 27 S.E.
    Sheet 26 S.W.

OPERATION ORDER NO. 79,   Copy No. 5.
by Lieut. Col. A.C.Corfe, D.S.O.,
Commanding 11th Bn. "THE QUEEN'S OWN"
(Royal West Kent) Regt. (Lewisham).

22nd July, 1917.

1. The 122nd Infantry Brigade will march to the WESTOUTRE area tomorrow.

2. The Battalion will parade in column of 3's at 6.50 a.m. at cross roads at X.2.d.9.4., and march to DE ZON Camp M.12.c.6.3.
   Order of march - Headquarters, Band, "B", "C", "D", "A", and Transport.
   <u>Dress</u> - Fighting Order.

3. The Battalion will march with an interval of 200 yards between half Battalions.
   The nromal clock hour halts will be observed.

4. There will be one motor lorry allotted to the Battalion to transport packs. All packs must be stacked outside their respective Company Headquarters by <u>8 a.m.</u> to be loaded on the lorries.
   O.C. Companies will each detail 2 men to proceed with the lorries. These men must have passes.
   O.C. "D" Coy. will detail an Officer to report at Battalion Headquarters at 8 a.m. to proceed with the lorry and supervise the loading.

5. Officers kits must be stacked outside their respective Company Headquarters by <u>7 a.m.</u>, the G.S. wagons calling for same.
   The Quartermaster will detail a representative to supervise the packing, and he must report to the T.O. by 7 a.m.

6. Lewis Guns and Tool Carts must be loaded up to-night.

7. Mess Cart will call at each Company H.Q. at <u>7.30 a.m.</u> to pick up the one mess box allowed per Company on the mess cart.

8. G.S. wagons and mess cart must <u>not</u> be delayed at Company H.Q.

9. Dinners will be had on the arrival in new camp.

10. Sick Parade - 7 a.m.

11. Particular attention to be paid to march discipline. No man will be allowed to ride on any wagon. Company Commanders will be responsible for taking the name of any man who falls out.

12. All waterbottles will be filled before moving off.

                  (sgd). A. J. JIMENEZ, Captain & Adjutant,
                    11th Bn. "THE QUEEN'S OWN" Royal West Kent Regt.
                                          (Lewisham).

Copy No. 1. C.O.   6. O.C."A" Coy.   11. S.O.   16. M.O.
       2. Sec. in Com. 7. O.C."B" Coy.   12. I.C.   17. R.S.M.
       3. Adjt.   8. O.C."C" Coy.   13. B.B.O.
       4. War Diary.   9. O.C."D" Coy.   14. T.O.
       5. Office Copy. 10. L.G.O.   15. Q.M.

SECRET.

Ref:- WYTSCHAETE 5A,
HOLLEBEKE,
and Sheet 28.

OPERATION ORDER No.60   Copy No.......
by Lieut. Col. A.C.Corfe, D.S.O,
Commanding 11th Bn. "THE QUEEN'S OWN"
(Royal West Kent) Regt. (Lewisham).

24th July, 1917.

1. The 122nd Infantry Brigade will relieve the 140th Infantry Brigade South of the YPRES - COMINES CANAL to-night. Relief to be complete by 5 a.m., 25th instant.

2. The Battalion will take over from the 6th Londons' in the left Sub-Sector, with the 18th K.R.R.C. on its right.

3. Companies will take over from their opposite numbers and will relieve in the following order,-
    "A", "B", "C", and "D" Coys., Headquarters.

4. The leading platoon of "A" Coy. will not pass Old German Front Line before 10 p.m.

5. One guide per platoon from the 6th Londons' to be at Junction of Tramway and O.b.1., near NORFOLK ROAD at 10 p.m.

6. One guide from each Lewis Gun will be at Junction of Tramway and O.b.1., near NORFOLK ROAD, at 8.30 p.m.
    Lewis Gun teams will parade at 5.30 p.m. to-day under Lewis Gun Officer, and march off independently. The Transport Officer will arrange for the Lewis Gun limber to proceed with the Lewis Gun teams.

7. INTERVAL. Companies will march off in order named at 10 minutes interval.
    "A" Company will lead off at 7.30 p.m. Platoons must keep a distance of at least 100 yards.

8. Trench Stores, Maps, Aeroplane Photographs, etc., will be taken over and receipt for same sent to Battalion Headquarters on relief.

9. Completion of relief will be notified by new B A B Code to Battalion Headquarters.

10. Surplus Officers kits, mess boxes, packs etc., must be stacked by Companies at the Quartermaster's Stores by 6 p.m. to be stored while the Battalion is in the line.

11. O.C. Companies will detail their C.S.M. to proceed to the trenches at 4 p.m. to take over the Trench Stores.

12. Rations for tomorrow will be carried on the man.

13. Sergt. Alderton and 1 cook per Company will proceed to LOCK HOUSE with 1 limber.
    They will take sugar and tea and necessary number of dixies. Parade with the Lewis Gunners at 5.30 p.m.

14. Officers trench bundles and mess boxes will be stacked by 5 p.m.
    The Transport Officer will arrange for 1 limber to carry same to junction of Track and O.g.1., near NORFOLK ROAD.
    Representatives from each Company will accompany this limber.
    This party will parade with Lewis Gunners at 5.30 p.m.

15. The following Signallers will report to Signalling Officer at 5.25 p.m. and proceed to the line with Lewis Gunners.-
    "A" Coy.   1.
    "B" "   1.
    "C" "   2.
    "D" "   1.

16. All waterbottles must be filled before moving off.

(sgd) A. J. JIMINEZ, Captain & Adjutant,
11th Bn. "THE QUEEN'S OWN" Royal West Kent Regt. (Lewisham).
P.T.O.

REPORT ON ATTACK DATED
31st July, 1917.

BEFORE ASSEMBLY.   Heavy hostile shelling in vicinity of WHITE CHATEAU woods and support lines at 12 midnight. Continued until Zero Hour.

ASSEMBLY.   The Battalion arrived in position of Assembly by 3.20 a.m.
The enemy spotted our left Company during Assembly and started shelling this Company putting down a barrage 100 yards in rear of same.
Only few casualties during Assembly.

ZERO.   At 3.50 a.m. barrage opened on enemy lines.
Hostile barrage at once came down on WHITE CHATEAU WOODS AND SUPPORT LINE.

ATTACK.   The waves pushed forward satisfactorily.

RED LINE captured after some delay. This line was pushed 150 yards beyond OBLIQUE TRENCH and consolidation started.

The second wave pushed forward towards BLUE LINE.
This wave started consolidating this side of HOLLEBEKE.
One Platoon, (about 12 men) under 2/Lt. L.G. Preston pushed forward passing outskirts of HOLLEBEKE and started digging in at 0.12.a.3.4.
My Battalion was not in touch with LOYALTY.
A Runner returning from 2/Lt. Preston's platoon reported having passed LOYALTY digging in about 0.11.b.4.8. to 0.11.b.1.6.
The forward platoon under 2/Lt. L.G. Preston had to withdraw back to our new front line as they were gradually being surrounded by enemy.

COMMUNICATION.   Very difficult owing to heavy barrage between CHATEAU WOODS and FRONT LINE which has continued intermittently since Zero hour.

MACHINE GUN FIRE.   Much sniping and machine gun fire from HOLLEBEKE and other side of Canal in vicinity of Lock.

REINFORCEMENTS.   At 5.15 a.m. I ordered my right Company in RED LINE to send up 25 men to RIGHT FORWARD Company.
At 7.49 the position was still unsatisfactory, so that I ordered Captain ROONEY to take 20 men from my left Company in RED LINE to reinforce Captain LINDSAY on the right of the BLUE LINE, and to push forward and work through HOLLEBEKE.
At 11 a.m. Capt. ROONEY reported that he had mopped up HOLLEBEKE and our present front line was about 100 yards from the GREEN LINE.

PRISONERS.   About 60 taken and sent down.

Army Form C. 2118

WAR DIARY
or
INTELLIGENCE SUMMARY
(Erase heading not required.)

XI R.W.Kent Rgt
Oct 16

Place	Date	Hour	Summary of Events and Information	Remarks and references to Appendices
HOLLEBEKE.	1.8.17.		Strength of Battalion. Officers 21. Other Ranks 756.	
	1-4.8.17.		Battalion holding HOLLEBEKE and line captured 31.7.17. Weather conditions very bad, heavy rain and heavy shelling	
			2/Lieut. C.C. BERGER wounded 31.7.17. Evacuated to Eng. 3.8.17.	
			2/Lieut. B.W. ASHWORTH died of wounds 4.8.17. 2/Lt.D.G.GODDEN.Wded.31.7.17.	
	4.8.17.		Battalion relieved in front line by 15th Hants and moved into tunnels in Reserve.	
			Lieut. J.B. NUTT (U.S.R.) joined for duty as Medical Officer vice	
			Lieut. D.I. CONNOLLY to England.(contract expired).	
			Strength of Battalion. Officers 22. Other Ranks. 781.	
			2/Lt. DENTON,A.D. & 2/Lt.A.ROYLE wounded 24th & 31st July,1917 respectively. Evacuated to Eng. 4.8.17.	
RENINGHELST.	5.8.17.		Battalion relieved in Reserve by 18th K.R.R.C., proceeding by Route March to WOOD CAMP, RENINGHELST.	
	6-7.8.17.		Rest and Re-organisation.	
			2/Lt.D.J.DEAN, wounded to England 7.3.17, rejoined for duty. 2/Lts. J.H.TURNER, and C.W.LOUDOUN joined for duty.	
	8-9.8.17.		Rest and Re-organisation.	
			2/Lts. H.A.QUARTERMAIN wounded 3.8.17., and G.H.ARDILL wounded 31.7.17. Evacuated to England 8.8.17.	
HOLLEBEKE.	10.8.17.		Battalion plus 1 Company of 12th E. Surrey Regt. relieved 15th Hants. in front line at HOLLEBEKE, vide O.O.81 (attached).	
	11.8.17.		Battalion in line. Strength of Battalion.offrs.24. Other Ranks 754.	
	12-13.8.17.		In the Line.	
	13.8.17.		Battalion relieved by 14th Hants, and 12th R.Sussex, and proceeded to Camp at ELZENWALLE, vide O.O-82 (attached).	
ELZENWALLE	14.8.17.		Battalion proceeded by lorry to rest billets at the ROUKLOSHILLE.	
ROUKLOSHILLE	15.8.17.		LIEUT. A.V.D.MORLEY, wounded 7.10.16, rejoined for duty.	
	16.8.17.		In rest; bathing.	
	17.8.17.		Inspection by G.O.C. 122nd Infantry Brigade.	
	18.8.17.		Inspection by G.O.C. 41st Division.	
			Inspection by 2nd Army Commander.	
			Strength of Battalion officers 25. Other Ranks 608.	

Army Form C. 2118

WAR DIARY
or
INTELLIGENCE SUMMARY
(Erase heading not required.)

Instructions regarding War Diaries and Intelligence Summaries are contained in F. S. Regs., Part II. and the Staff Manual respectively. Title Pages will be prepared in manuscript.

Place	Date	Hour	Summary of Events and Information	Remarks and references to Appendices
ROUKLOSHILLE	18.8.17.		Captain L.V. STONE and 2/Lt.H.D.P. HALL rejoined the Battalion for duty to-day. 2/Lts. F.H. STOCK, L.C. SHANNON, S.C. HARRIS, and C.J. TUCK joined the Battalion for duty.	
	19.8.17.		Rest.	
	20.8.17.		Battalion proceeded to the STAPLES Area by route march en route for Training Area. O.O.83 attached.	
STAPLE.	21.8.17.		The Battalion marched to LE NIEPPE and embussed. vide O.O.84 attached, arriving at billets at BOISDINGHEM at 12.30 p.m.	
	22.8.17.		Kit etc inspections. 2/Lts. F.W.RUSHTON, G.A.HUTCHINSON, and J.DALTREY joined for duty with the Battalion.	
	23.8.17.		Company organisation and Specialist Training.	
	24.8.17.		The Division was inspected by the Commander-in-Chief (Sir Douglas Haig).	
	25.8.17.		Battalion firing on open rifle range. Strength of Battalion, Officers 33. Other Ranks 606. Temp. 2/Lt. G.RADCLYFFE relinquishes commission on account of ill-health and is struck off strength of Battalion.	
	26.8.17.		Baths and Church Parade. Inter-Company football. 2/Lts. G.F.C.MACASKIE, W.DENT, and W.G.LEISHMAN joined the Battalion for duty.	
	27.8.17.		Battalion in Rest. Training.	
	28.7.17.		Training. 2/Lts. H.C.CAME, T.E.DADD, S.THOMSON, and J.C.PARMINTER joined the Battalion for duty.	
	29.8.17.		Training.	
	30.8.17.		Training.	
	31.8.17.		Training and Baths. "B" Company inspected by Brigade Commander at Training Area. Strength of Battalion Officers 41. Other Ranks. 642.	

1.9.17.

A.J. Jimmy Cape
for Lt.Col.
Commanding 11th Bn. "THE QUEEN'S OWN" Royal
West Kent Regt.(Lewisham).

S E C R E T.

OPERATION ORDER NO.81,   Copy No...6..
by Lieut. Col. A.S.Corfe,D.S.O.,
Commanding 11th Bn. "THE QUEEN'S OWN"
Royal West Kent Regt.(Lewisham).

Ref. Hazebrouck 59

10th August, 1917.

1.   The Battalion with one Company DAGGER Regt. will relieve the HAMLET Regt. in the line to-night.

2.   Companies will take over in the following order:-
"C" & "D" Coys. from "B" & "C" Coys. HAMLET.
"A" & "B" Coys. from "A" Coy. HAMLET, and
Company of DAGGER from "D" Coy. HAMLET.

3.   The 50 men at present under Captain POWLYS in the line will rejoin the Battalion to-night, and will be accommodated in WHITE CHATEAU.

4.   Maps, aeroplane photographs, and all trench stores will be taken over by relieving Companies, and copy of receipts forwarded to Battalion Headquarters.

5.   Relief will be reported to Battalion Headquarters by runner.

6.   Marching out States and nominal roll of men remaining behind will be handed into the Orderly Room by 2 p.m. to-day.

7.   The Battalion with Company from DAGGER will parade ready to march off at 5.30 p.m. and will be conveyed up by lorries.

8.   Ten Lewis Guns, very pistols will be taken over from HAMLET on relief and receipts given, copies to be handed to Battalion Headquarters.

9.   Four cooks under Sgt. Alderton will parade at 5 p.m. and will proceed to LOCK HOUSE with dixies. The Transport Officer will provide a limber for same.

10.   Each man will wear fighting order and will carry two Mills grenades and rations for tomorrow.
Waterbottles must be filled.

11.   Packs will be stacked under Company arrangements by 4.30 O.; and will be handed over to the C.Q.M.S.s. Officers valises will be stacked at Orderly Room by 4.30 p.m.
Mess boxes, Officers trench bundles will be carried on the lorries.

12.   Rations for Platoon at WHITE CHATEAU under Captain Powlys will be sent up as usual.

       (sgd) A. J. JIMENEZ, Captain & Adjutant,
11th Bn. "THE QUEEN'S OWN" Royal West Kent Regt.(Lewisham).

Copy No. 1. C.O.
2. Sec.in Com.
3. Maj. Murdoch, 2.
4. Adjutant.
5. Asst. Adjutant.
6. Office Copy.
7. War Diary.
8. I.O.
9. O.C. "A" Coy.
10. O.C. "B" "
11. O.C. "C" "
12. O.C. "D" "
13. L.G.Sgt.
14. Sig. Sgt.
15. M.O.
16. R.S.M.
17. C.O. Hamlet.
18. 2. Hamlet.

SECRET. OPERATION ORDER No. 82
by Lieut. Col. A.C.Corfe, D.S.O.,
Commanding BOW Battalion.

Ref Hazebrouck 5a   12th August, 1917.

1. BOW and DAGGER will be relieved in the Front Line on the night of August 13/14th, by two Companies of the Hampshire and two Companies of the 12th Royal Sussex Regt respectively. -14th Hants will take over "BOW" Battalion Headquarters.

2. DAGGER will be relieved by "C" Company Royal Sussex Regt. in FORRET FARM. and by "B" Company in posts on right of HOLLEBEKE. "BOW" will be relieved in posts 1, 2, and 3 on the right by "B" Company 12th Royal Sussex and by 2 Companies 14th Hants as follows- Post 4,5,and 6 of right front Company. and posts 1,2, and 3 of left front Company by "D" Coy. 14th Hants Regt.
   Posts 4,5,and 6 of left front company and frontage to Canal by "C" Coy. 14th Hants.

3. For the purpose of relief the posts in HOLLEBEKE occupied by DAGGER will come under O.C. Right Front Company BOW.

4. The garrison in OBLIQUE ROQ will be relieved by a supporting Company of the 14th Hants under arrangements to be made by Battalion H.Q. This party on relief will march off independently of its Company.

5. One guide from each day post at present held by "BOW" and "DAGGER" will report to the Adjutant, "BOW" at 7.30 p.m. on the 13th instant. They will bring a slip bearing the number of their post and Company and will act as guides for the incoming Battalion. O.C. Companies will be responsible that these men are thoroughly and picked men.

6. Lewis Gun teams will be relieved with their Companies and will march off with their Companies on relief. On the way out the guns will be left at OAK DUMP in charge of 1 man per team. Officers trench bundles and mess boxes will also be left there under 1 man per company. These men so left will stay with the guard in charge of Company Property.

7. Before leaving the line Lewis Gun Magazines will be emptied, all ammunition and bombs carried on the man, except 20 rounds per man collected under Company arrangements and handed over as a reserve to relieving Company.

8. The Transport Officer will detail 3 limbers for Lewis Guns and 2 for bundles and boxes to be at OAK DUMP by 5 a.m. 14th August, 1917. The guard left there and 2 men per Company as above will load limbers and accompany them back to Camp in charge of the other Company property.

9. O.C. Companies will report relief as they pass Battalion Headquaters on the way out. O.C. Right Front Company, BOW, will report relief of DAGGER party in HOLLEBEKE.

10. Maps, aeroplane photographs, Ammunition and Trench Stores will be handed over and receipts taken, the latter to be handed to the Adjutant in due course. O.C.Companies will assist O.C. relieving Companies in taking over the posts to the fullest extent.

11. On relief Companies will march off independently to Camp at ELZENWALLE. O.C. DAGGER Company will proceed to Camp as notified by his Battalion Headquarters.

12. BOW Garrison in WHITE CHATEAU will march off on relief independently. The Officer in charge will hand over the contents of the Battalion Dump there to O.C. relieving party 14th Hants and forward a list to this Office.

13. The remaining Companies of 14th Hants and 12th Royal Sussex Regt. will relieve under arrangements to be made by DAGGER.

                    (sd) R.KERR, Lieut.,
12.8.17. 5 p.m.   A/Adj. BOW.

    3 copies BELL.
    Copy to Lt. Rogers.
      "   2/Lt. Preston.
      "   Capt. Walker, DAGGER.
      "   Sergt. Mayston, DAGGER.
      "   2/Lt. TURNOW, BOW.
      "   T.O.
      "   Major Beadle.
      "   DAGGER.
      "   2 copies War Diary.

SECRET.   OPERATION ORDER NO. 83   Copy No. 5
by Lieut. Col. A.C. Corfe, D.S.O.,
Commanding 11th Bn. "THE QUEEN'S OWN"
Royal West Kent Regt. (Lewisham).

Ref. Hazebrouck
S.a. 1/100000

19th August, 1917.

1. The Battalion will march tomorrow to EBBLINGHAM area.

2. Distance of march is 12 miles, apart from the usual clock hour halts, there will be no long halt.

3. The Battalion will parade in column of 3s at 5.45 a.m. on road outside "A" and "B" Companies billet facing North.
   Order of march - Band, "D" Company, "C" Company, "B" and "A" Companies, Headquarters, Transport.
   DRESS. Fighting Order.

4. O.C. Companies will see that the leading and rear platoons of the Battalion will have magazines charged in case of attack by hostile aircraft.

5. Immediately on arrival in billets, O.C. Companies must send one runner per Company to Battalion Headquarters to report exact position of their Headquarters.

6. Packs will be stacked outside the respective Headquarters by 5.30 a.m. to be loaded on motor lorries. One lorry will collect packs from Headquarters, "A" and "B" Coys., one from "C" and "D" Coys., and another will report to the Quartermaster. The two lorries for packs will proceed to Quartermaster's Stores when loaded.

7. O.C. Companies will detail 4 men each to report to the Quartermaster at 5.30 a.m. to accompany lorries to billets. Men unable to march should be detailed; they must be provided with a pass signed by an Officer to ride in the lorries.

8. Officers kits will be stacked outside their Company Headquarters by 4.30 a.m. and the G.S. wagons will call for same. The Quartermaster will detail a man to supervise the packing. He will report to the Transport Officer at 4.30 a.m.

9. Mess cart will call at Battalion Headquarters about 5 a.m. Company mess boxes will be put on the motor lorries.

10. G.S. wagons must on no account be delayed at Coy. Headquarters.

11. Breakfasts will be at 4.30 a.m. Dinners will be had on arrival at new billets.

12. Sick Parade will be at 4.30 a.m. The Medical Officer's cart will be packed as far as possible to-night.

13. Lewis Guns will be loaded on limbers to-night under the supervision of the Lewis Gun Officer.
    The Lewis Gun Officer will arrange for the Lewis Guns on anti-aircraft guard to be loaded as late as possible in the morning. These guards must not be dismounted to-night.

14. Transport will march in rear of the Battalion.

(sgd) A. J. JIMENEZ, Captain & Adjutant,
11th Bn. "THE QUEEN'S OWN" Royal West Kent Regt. (Lewisham).

Copy No. 1. C.O.
2. Major C. Murdoch.
3. Adjutant.
4. Asst. Adjt.
5. War Diary.
6. Office Copy.
7. L.G.O.
8. I.O.
9. Sig. Sgt.
10. R.S.M.
11. M.O.
12. T.O.
13. Q.M.
14. O.C. "A" Coy.
15. O.C. "B" "
16. O.C. "C" "
17. O.C. "D" "

SECRET.   OPERATION ORDER No.84.
          by Lieut. Col. A.C. Corfe, D.S.O.,
          Commanding 11th Bn. "THE QUEEN'S OWN"
          Royal West Kent Regt. (Lewisham).

Ref Hazebrouck 5a   20th August, 1917.

1. The 122nd Infantry Brigade will move tomorrow to BOISDINGHEM area.

2. The Battalion (less Transport) will parade at Cross Roads, "Blanche Maison" at 7.15 a.m. in fighting order, and will proceed to Cross Roads, LE NIEPPE to embus.
   Companies and Headquarters will be told off into parties of 25 all ranks, not more than 25 other ranks will be carried in one bus, and no kits will be carried.

3. Companies will report position of their Coy. Headquarters on arrival in the new area.

4. Company handcarts may proceed with the Transport in which case O.C. Companies must detail necessary personnel to pull them. They must report to the Transport Officer by 7.30 a.m.

5. The Quartermaster will arrange for one lorry to proceed to "A" and "B" Coys. Headquarters at 7 a.m. to load up kits and Officers kits.
   O.C. Companies will each detail one responsible man to accompany the lorries with the packs.

6. Sick parade will be held at Battalion Headquarters at 6 a.m.

           (sgd) A.J. JIMENEZ, Captain & Adjt.,
      11th Bn. Royal West Kent Regt.

INSTRUCTION No. II. (Continued).

NO. II. PRISONERS OF WAR. (Continued).

Method of evacuation will be as follows:-

Prisoners captured will be escorted by Troops from Front Line to back of OLD FRENCH TRENCH at I.32.d.1.3. where Tramway Track crosses it.

At this point a provost Sergeant and 2 men to be detailed by O.C. 15th Hampshire Regt., will be stationed. Their duties will be to organise prisoners and escort parties so that the minimum escort, namely 10%, is employed to take prisoners from this point to the Divisional Cage. Surplus escorts will be returned to their units in the line The Provost Sergeant detailed, will report at Brigade Headquarters at 6 p.m. 5th June, when a book will be given him in which he will enter numbers of all prisoners passing through this point.

INSTRUCTION No. II. (Continued).

NO. II. PRISONERS OF WAR. (Continued).

Method of evacuation will be as follows:-

Prisoners captured will be escorted by Troops from Front Line to back of OLD FRENCH TRENCH at I.32.d.1.3. where Tramway Track crosses it.

At this point a provost Sergeant and 2 men to be detailed by O.C. 15th Hampshire Regt., will be stationed. Their duties will be to organise prisoners and escort parties so that the minimum escort, namely 10%, is employed to take prisoners from this point to the Divisional Cage. Surplus escorts will be returned to their units in the line. The Provost Sergeant detailed, will report at Brigade Headquarters at 6 p.m. 5th June, when a book will be given him in which he will enter numbers of all prisoners passing through this point.

XXXII   TANKS

1. Two sections of Tanks N° 2 and N° 3 respectively (Section = 4 Tanks), will co-operate in the Advance of the 41st Division.
    N° 2 Section will assist 124th Infantry Brigade
    N° 3 Section will assist 122nd Infantry Brigade

2. The Tanks will assemble on "X/Y" night at I 31 b 5.2., and will move forward to be at SHELLEY DUMP I 32 d 3.3½ half an hour after ZERO

3. N° 3 Section will cross the DAMMSTRASSE and move on OBOE TRENCH and OBSCURE TRENCH, subsequently moving on OBSCURE SUPPORT

TABLE SHEWING DISTRIBUTION OF BARRAGE IN DEPTH

Nature of Barrage	Depth from leading portion	Distance in advance of Infantry and Objective
18 pdr shrapnel Barrage	30 yards	Creeping barrage about 75 yards in advance of Infantry and composed exclusively of Shrapnel shell
18 pdr shrapnel and H.E.	80 yards	On definite trenches in advance of Infantry attack, and to remain on such trenches until creeping barrage reaches the line of the trench. Composed partly of H.E. and partly of Shrapnel — the latter when Infantry advance close to the trench
4.5" Hows	60 yards	On definite trenches not less than 200 yards in advance of the attacking Infantry. To "walk up" consecutive trenches in advance of the Infantry within above safety limit
Medium How (6")	110 yards	On definite trenches not less than 300 yards in advance of the attacking Infantry
60 pdr & 8" how	250 yards	On definite trenches and strong points not less than 400 yards in advance of the attacking Infantry

N.B. The above system should never allow sufficient depth to the barrage, and allow necessary elasticity to admit of local circumstances being decided according to their requirements

2. On the assumption that 106 fuzes are not used

In connection with barrage it is to be noted that the effect of the 106 fuze is dangerous to our own troops as follows:
- With 4.5" Hows — laterally within 60 yards
- front to rear within 300 yards
- With 6" Hows — laterally within 750 yards
- front to rear within 350 yards
- With 8" Hows — laterally within 100 yards
- front to rear within 500 yards

Army Form C. 2118.

WAR DIARY
or
INTELLIGENCE SUMMARY.
(Erase heading not required.)

Instructions regarding War Diaries and Intelligence Summaries are contained in F. S. Regs., Part II. and the Staff Manual respectively. Title pages will be prepared in manuscript.

Place	Date	Hour	Summary of Events and Information	Remarks and references to Appendices
BOIDINGHEM.	1.9.17.		Battalion in Rest. Training. Strength of Battalion 41 Offrs. 644 O.R.	
	2.9.17.		do	
	3.9.17.		do	
	4.9.17.		Practice attack near MORINGHEM. Vide O.O.85 attached.	
	5.9.17.		Training for attack.	
	6.9.17.		do	
	7.9.17.		Battalion held Sports in field at ZUTOVE, but rain cut them short after about half the programme had been completed.	
	8.9.17.		Gas demonstration at MORINGHEM. Strength of Battalion. 40 Offrs. 701 O.R. Captain G.D.HENDERSON, M.C. rejoined the Battalion for duty from 20th Durham Light Infantry.	
	9.9.17.		Sunday. Parade service and bathing. Sports were finished off in the afternoon. Lieut. G.W. HILL joined the Battalion for duty.	
	10.9.17.		Battalion practised the Divisional attack near TATINGHEM. Vide O.O.86 attached. 2/Lieut. R. BARTHOLOMEW joined the Battalion for duty.	
	11.9.17.		Battalion practised the attack (vide O.O.86 attached) on ground near TATINGHEM.	
	12.9.17.		Training.	
	13.9.17.		G.O.C. Brigade lectured the Battalion on "The War".	
	14.9.17.		Practice attack. Vide O.O.86 attached. Draft of 30 O.R. joined for duty.	
	15.9.17.		Training on Battalion area. Battalion proceeded by route march to WALLEN CAPPELL area vide O.O.88 attached. Strength of Battalion 42 Offrs. 716 O.R.	
WALLEN CAPPELL.				
LE ROUKLOUSHILLE.	16.9.17.		Battalion marched to LE ROUKLOUSHILLE Area vide O.O.88 attached. Battalion proceeded to CHIPPEWA CAMP, RENINGHELST, by route march. Vide O.O.88a. attached. 2/Lieut. H.G. HARDING rejoined the Battalion for duty from England. Draft of 38 O.R. arrived, including C.S.M.J.C.HAYLEY.	
RIDGE WOOD.	17.9.17.		Battalion proceeded to RIDGE WOOD CAMP by route march vide O.O.89 attd.	

Army Form C. 2118.

WAR DIARY
or
INTELLIGENCE SUMMARY.

(Erase heading not required.)

Instructions regarding War Diaries and Intelligence Summaries are contained in F. S. Regs., Part II. and the Staff Manual respectively. Title pages will be prepared in manuscript.

Place	Date	Hour	Summary of Events and Information	Remarks and references to Appendices
	17.9.17.		2/Lieut. R.G.G.CARTMELL rejoined the Battalion for duty from the Base. Details under Major J.C. BEADLE, M.C., proceeded to CARNARVON CAMP, RENINGHELST.	
CAESTRE.	19-22.9.17.		See attached report on attack on TOWER HAMLETS. Strength 38 Off. 823 O.R.	
	23.9.17.		Battalion moved from RIDGE WOOD to camp near CAESTRE entraining at OUDERDOM and detraining at CAESTRE. Lieut. C.F. HALL rejoined the Battalion for duty from 23rd Labour Group.	
	24.9.17.		Rest and reorganisation. 2/Lieut. W.C. RHODES joined the Battalion for duty, also draft of 21 O.R.	
	25.9.17.		Baths. Congratulatory speech by G.O.C. 122nd Infantry Brigade.	
	26.9.17.		Rest and reorganisation.	
TETEGHEM.	27.9.17.		Battalion moved by lorry to TETEGHEM arriving about 12.30 p.m. Billeted for the night.	
LA PANNE.	28.9.17.		Battalion proceeded to LA PANNE by route march and occupied billets.	
	29.9.17.		Baths and reorganisation. Conference re method of training for winter season. Bombers under Company arrangements, Machine Gunners and Snipers under their respective Officers.	
	30.9.17.		Strength of Battalion 34 Officers, 709 O.R. 2/Lt.G.SKARDON joined for duty Rest and Church Parade.	

1.10.17.

[Signature]
Major,
Commanding 11th Bn. "THE QUEEN'S OWN"
Royal West Kent Regt. (Lewisham).

REPORT ON OPERATIONS SEPT. 20th - SEPT. 23rd, 1917.-
ATTACK ON TOWER HAMLETS.

At 6.45 p.m. Sept. 17th Battalion moved from CHIPPEWA CAMP, RENINGHELST, to bivouacs in RIDGE WOOD. STRENGTH.- 17 OFFICERS, and 360 OTHER RANKS.

About 12 midnight Sept. 18th it proceeded by march, route, to trenches at LARCH WOOD (N. of YPRES-COMINES CANAL) and remained there till 10 p.m. 19th instant.

During this time 3 officers, Capt. L.V. STONE, 2/Lieuts. H.D.P. HALL and W. DENT and 40 other ranks became casualties from hostile gas and shelling.

At 10 p.m. Sept. 19th Battalion marched by Companies to tapes already laid, through BODMIN COPSE, and lined up for attack. The Battalion was in position on tapes by 1 a.m. 20.9.17 and the men lay disposed in shell-holes till ZERO hour at 5.40 a.m.

There was intermittent hostile shelling all night, but no casualties were incurred.

At 5.40 a.m. our barrage opened up, and the Battalion led by Col. CORFE advanced slowly behind the 15th Hampshire Regt. and in touch on both flanks.
The barrage was magnificent, the little hostile barrage that was put down was too far back to be troublesome. After going forward about 4/500 yards with few casualties, the Battalion in front was hung up in front of JAVA AVENUE by a small but determined body of Germans. Col. CORFE, Capts.G.D.Henderson and KERR went forward to reconnoitre the situation and found many casualties being inflicted on the 15th Hants. and the advance at a standstill. As no Officers appeared to be on the spot, Col.CORFE went up and down the line of attackers, who were in a ditch in front of a small wood, trying to get them to rush the strong point which could be seen to be but lightly held. He was eventually shot through the right shoulder, standing on top of the far side of the ditch waving the men on. Captain G.D. HENDERSON took command of the Battalion and, on our two leading Companies arriving ordered them to rush the strong point, which they did, led by Col CORFE who rallied himself sufficiently to stagger forward 40 yards.
By this time, the barrage was 400 yards ahead, so men of both Battalions went forward together to the RED LINE, under the remaining Officers.
The RED LINE was captured up to time by 6.15 a.m. with few additional casualties.
All our remaining Officers and men with the 15th Hants. Regt. lined up under the barrage at 7.8. a.m.and going forward behind it, captured the BLUE LINE with few casualties by 7.40 a.m;the 15th Hants reached this line slightly in rear of our men and commenced to dig in.
LIEUT. A.V.D. MORLEY, now in command of our front line here reorganised his line for the final advance to the GREEN LINE. He had under him 2/Lieuts. J.B.FREEMAN, C.J.TUCK, C.W.LOUDOUN, F.W. RUSHTON and A. DRUMGOLD with about 70 other ranks.
Touch was maintained with 23rd Division on left, but there was no-one on right as the 15th King's Royal Rifle Corps and 15th East Surrey Regt. had not yet come forward.
Machine gun fire so far only had been troublesome,particularly from the exposed right flank, and the casualties we had were mainly from this. There was no enemy shelling to speak of forward of BODMIN COPSE.
At 9.53 a.m. the Battalion moved forward under the barrage to capture the GREEN LINE.

-2-

Little enemy opposition was met, but enfilade machine gun and rifle fire from right was troublesome. This line was gained, and 40 to 50 prisoners, including 3 Officers, were sent back, and 3 machine guns and 1 Trench Mortar captured. As there was nobody on our right, a defensive flank was pushed out but this was annihilated from the right by machine gun fire before it could dig in.

2/Lieut. J.B.FREEMAN and some 40 men were made casualties in this way so LIEUT. A.V.D. MORLEY decided to dig in on a line 150 yards in front of BLUE LINE in order to maintain touch with the 12th East Surrey Regt. on the right.

At 2 p.m. the enemy was seen massing for a counter-attack about 1,000 yards in front, but this was smashed by our artillery and rifle fire.

On visiting the line at night Captain G.D.HENDERSON found the Battalion well dug in, with the YORK and LANCS. on left and 20th Durham Light Infantry on right.

No news of 2/Lieut. A. DRUMGOLD could be got, so he was presumed killed.

The night was quiet till 4.30 a.m., 21.9.17 when we put down a barrage to which the enemy retaliated heavily, for 1 hour.

There was desultory shelling all day on the 21st and enemy machine guns and snipers from right flank were very troublesome along line of BASSEVILLEBEKE.

About 3.10 p.m. a message was received from 2/Lieut. DRUMGOLD to say he was established with 12 men on left of GREEN LINE, where he had been since 10.5 a.m. of the 20th. Direct communication could not immediately be established, as no runner coming down from line was able to find his way back.

About 6.30 p.m. 2/Lieut. S. THOMSON and 25 other ranks reinforcements arrived and went up to BLUE LINE. Shelling, which had been free all the afternoon developed into a barrage of our lines about 6.30 p.m.

This shelling had broken up the Headquarters of the 12th EAST SURREY REGT., wounding the Colonel, and these moved over and shared our position. About 7.15 p.m. it was reported to Captain G.D. HENDERSON that men were retiring.

Leaving Captain WALKER (O.C.12th EAST SURREY REGT.) to stop further retirement across the BASSEVILLEBEKE, Captains HENDERSON and KERR went after the retiring party for a distance of 600 yards and finally came up with the rear 50 men who were made to return.

The remainder, to the number of 10 /200 could not be rounded up without going too far away.

These 50 men were marched back, and finally handed over to an officer of the 15th Hants. Regt., and ordered to dig in 60 yards West of the BASSEVILLEBEKE in line with position held by his party and left under his command.

By this time, about 8.30 p.m. the enemy barrage had slackened, so Captain HENDERSON collected further stragglers stopped by Capt. WALKER and posted them in a trench parallel to and 150 yards behind front line.

He then visited our front line, and found everything in order, except that the line was badly smashed and many casualties had been sustained from the enemy barrage.

The remainder of the night 21/22nd was quiet until 4.45 a.m. when our artillery put up a practice barrage evoking retaliation on our lines. During the night 2/Lieut. F.W.RUSHTON succeeded in locating 2/Lieut. DRUMGOLD and party, whom he rationed and reinforced with a party of 15 men from BLUE LINE.

This party was in touch with 23rd Division on left, but was entirely unprotected on right, and had had a most gruelling time both from our own and enemy barrage and hostile sniping.

The morning of the 22nd was quiet. About 3 p.m. hostile artillery became very active and consistently searched trenches and communications, until the Battalion was relieved about 11.30 p.m by the 14th Hampshire Regt.

The relief was successful notwithstanding and only 2 casualties were sustained in process.

The Battalion marched out, and reached RIDGE/ WOOD with 6 Officers and 120 Other Ranks about 5 a.m. 23.9.17.

Total casualties during period 19.9.17 - 23.9.17.-

Officers.	Killed.	2.
"	Wounded.	9.
Other Ranks.	Killed	26
"	Wounded	170
	Missing & believed killed, or wounded.	53

The following Officers went into action for the attack.-

Lieut. Col.	A.C. CORFE.	Wounded.
Captain	G.D. Henderson.	
"	R. Kerr.	
Lieut.	A.V.D. Morley.	
"	G.W. Hill.	Wounded.
2/Lieut.	A. Drumgold.	
"	C.W. Loudoun.	
"	F.W. Rushton.	
"	L.C. Shannon.	Wounded.
"	H.C. Came.	Killed
"	J.B. Freeman.	Killed.
"	D.J. Dean.	Wounded.
"	C.J. Tuck.	
"	J. Daltrey.	Wounded.
"	W.G. Leishman.	

G.D. Henderson

Captain,
11th Battn. "THE QUEEN'S OWN" Royal
West Kent Regt. (Lewisham).

Army Form C. 2118

11th (S...) Bn ...
ROYAL WEST KENT REGT.
NOV 2 1917
Ref: 4938

WAR DIARY
or
INTELLIGENCE SUMMARY
(Erase heading not required.)

Instructions regarding War Diaries and Intelligence Summaries are contained in F.S. Regs., Part II. and the Staff Manual respectively. Title Pages will be prepared in manuscript.

Place	Date	Hour	Summary of Events and Information	Remarks and references to Appendices
LA PANNE.	1.10.17.		Reorganised Battalion commences systematic training under Company Commanders and Specialist Officers, as per attached programme of work. LIEUT. C.E.MALPASS and 2/Lieut. C.F.C. MACASKIE rejoined Battalion from Hospital, and Lewis Gun Course respectively.	
	2.10.17.		Inspection and congratulatory speech by G.O.C. Division, (Major General S. LAWFORD). Battalion bathing.	
	3.10.17.		The following extracts from London Gazette dated 2.10.17. The undermentioned to be Temp. Captains.- 14th June, 1917. Temp. Lieut. R.G. ROGERS. Temp. 2/Lieut. R. MALTBY. The undermentioned to be Temp. Lieutenants.- Temp.2/Lieut.J.H. GREENWOOD. 20th December,1916. Temp.2/Lieut. T. ROONEY,M.C. 24th December,1916. (A/Captain). Temp.2/Lieut.C.E. MALPASS. 6th March,1917. Temp.2/Lieut.L.G. PRESTON. 14th June,1917. (A/Captain). 2/Lieut. L.E. HALE.(Sco.Rif.T.F.) 24th June,1917. Training under Company arrangements. "A" and "B" Coys. firing on Dune Range. Programme of work for period 3.10.17 to 10.10.17. Lecture on training, etc. by G.O.C., 122nd Infantry Brigade.	
	4.10.17.		Company training as per programme of work.	
	5.10.17.		Battalion Inspection by G.O.C., 41st Division ordered, but cancelled owing to rain. The following officers joined for duty.-2/Lt. K.H. DANIEL, 2/Lt.E.W. BATES, and 2/Lt. W.S. CLARIDGE.	
	6.10.17.		Training under Company arrangements. Strength of Battalion. Officers 38, Other Ranks 674.	
	7.10.17.		Battalion ordered to move to ST.IDESBALD AREA Camp, vide O.O.No. 90. This move was cancelled and Battalion remained in same billets.	

Army Form C. 2118

WAR DIARY
or
INTELLIGENCE SUMMARY
(Erase heading not required.)

Instructions regarding War Diaries and Intelligence Summaries are contained in F.S. Regs., Part II. and the Staff Manual respectively. Title Pages will be prepared in manuscript.

Place	Date	Hour	Summary of Events and Information	Remarks and references to Appendices
LA PANNE.	7.10.17.		2/Lieut. J.P. COTTRELL joined the Battalion for duty.	
	8.10.17.		2/Lieut. S.C. HARRIS rejoined from Corps Reinforcement Camp.	
	9.10.17.		Training under Company arrangements.	
			Training under Company arrangements.	
			The following awards were granted to N.C.O.s and men of the Battalion for gallantry in the Field.—	
			BAR TO MILITARY MEDAL.	
			11243. Sgt. J.W.J. BARNHAM. "D". 20-22.9.17.	
			17411. Cpl. J.B. TWEED. "A". do	
			THE MILITARY MEDAL.	
			18491. Pte. A. RICKWOOD. "C". 20-23.9.17.	
			735. " P. PANKHURST. "B". do	
			18829. L/C. T.P. HARRIS. "A". 22.9.17.	
			12292. Pte. E. HOMEWOOD. "A". 20-21.9.17.	
			18441. Cpl. F. HOLLANDS. "A". 21.9.17.	
			12175. Pte. H. SCRACE. "A". 22.9.17.	
			25355. " G. WOOLGAR. "A". 20-23.9.17.	
			18487. " C.G. PARREN. "B". do	
			7081. Sgt. J. SIDGWICK. "C". do	
	10.10.17.		Training under Company arrangements.	
			The following extracts from London Gazette dated 6th and 8th October, 1917, respectively.—	
			"Temp. 2/Lieutenants. to be Temp. Lieutenants.	
			R. BARTHOLOMEW.	
			T.G. PLATT.	
			H.D.P. HALL.	
			G.H. ARDILL. (July 8th)."	
	11.10.17.		Training under Company arrangements, with range practice for "C" and "D" Companies.	
	12.10.17.		Training under Company arrangements.	
			Awards.— DISTINGUISHED CONDUCT MEDAL awarded to 2432 Pte. E. SMART, "A" Company.	
	13.10.17.		Training under Company arrangements.	
			Strength of Battalion, Officers 38, Other Ranks 701.	

Army Form C. 2118

WAR DIARY
INTELLIGENCE SUMMARY
(Erase heading not required.)

Place	Date	Hour	Summary of Events and Information	Remarks and references to Appendices

LA PANNE.	14.10.17.		Divine Service, and hut and lines inspection by O.C. Companies. Awards.- The following awards were granted to Officers of the Battalion for gallantry in the Field on the dates stated:-
			 THE DISTINGUISHED SERVICE ORDER.
			     Temp. Captain G.D. HENDERSON, M.C. 20.9.17.
			     Temp. 2/Lieut. A. DRUMGOLD. 20-23.9.17.
			     THE MILITARY CROSS.
			     Temp. Lieut. A.V.D. MORLEY 20-23.9.17.
			     Temp. 2/Lt. F.W. RUSHTON. 22.9.17.
			     Temp. Lieut. (A/Capt.) R. KERR. 20-23.9.17.
			     Temp. 2/Lt. C.W. LOUDOUN. do	

COXYDE BAINS	15.10.17.		The Battalion moved to COXYDE BAINS to form part of the Brigade on Coast Defence. Vide O.O. No.91.	
	16-19.10.17.		2/Lieuts. F.H. STOCK and F.W. RUSHTON transferred to R.F.C. Battalion on Coast Defence, "A" and "B" Coys. in front line, "C" and "D" Coys. in reserve.	

	19.10.17.		The following officers joined Battalion for duty.—
			     2/Lieut. J.O. MOODY.
			     2/Lieut. R.J. DICKINSON.
			     2/Lieut. F. DARK.	

	20.10.17.		2/Lieut. E.O.E. AYLETT, wounded 24.3.17, rejoined the Battalion. Lieut. Colonel A.C. CORFE, D.S.O., was awarded Second Bar to DISTINGUISHED SERVICE ORDER, and 9441 Corpl. W.H. HOOKER the DISTINGUISHED CONDUCT MEDAL for gallantry in the Field 20.9.17. No.18534 L/C. H.J. WRIGHT was awarded the MILITARY MEDAL for gallantry in the Field while attached to 228th R.E. on 20.9.17. Strength of Battalion, Officers 42, Other Ranks 712.	
	19-23.10.17. 23.10.17.		Battalion on Coast Defence. "C" and "D" Coys. relieved "A" and "B" Coys. respectively in front line. 2/Lieut. A.A. PERRY joined the Battalion for duty.	
	24-28.10.17.		Battalion on Coast Defence.	

Army Form C. 2118

WAR DIARY
or
INTELLIGENCE SUMMARY
(Erase heading not required.)

Instructions regarding War Diaries and Intelligence Summaries are contained in F. S. Regs, Part II. and the Staff Manual respectively. Title Pages will be prepared in manuscript.

Place	Date	Hour	Summary of Events and Information	Remarks and references to Appendices
COXYDE BAINS.	25.10.17.		Warning order received re relief in line of 10th Queen's Regt.	
	27.10.17.		2/Lieuts. H.G. HARDING and G.A. HUTCHINSON transferred to Machine Gun Corps and were struck off strength. Strength of Battalion Officers 41, Other Ranks 725.	
	28.10.17.		Warning order received re relief of Battalion by South African Infantry Brigade and move to SYNTHE, near DUNKIRK.	
PETITE SYNTHE.	29.10.17.		Battalion relieved by 2nd Regiment South African Infantry Brigade and moved by lorries to billets in PETITE SYNTHE, vide O.O.91ª attached. Previous orders re moving into the line cancelled. 2/Lieut. R.H.W.F. BERNARD, wounded 7.6.17, rejoined Battalion for duty.	
	30-31.10.17.		Checking and making up kits of men, and preparations being made to move out of area. Route Marching. Strength of Battalion Officers 42, Other Ranks 777.	
	1.11.17.			

John Beadle
Lieut. Col.,
Commanding 11th Bn. "THE QUEEN'S OWN" Royal
West Kent Regt.(Lewisham).

S E C R E T.   OPERATION ORDERS No.91,   Copy No. 4
                by Lt. Col. J.C. Beadle, M.C.,
                Commanding 11th Bn. "THE QUEEN'S OWN"
                Royal West Kent Regt. (Lewisham).

                                    14th October, 1917.

1. Battalion will move to COXYDE BAINS area tomorrow, 15th inst., and will there form part of Brigade on coast defence.

2. Parade 11 a.m. under orders to be issued later.

3. Blankets, packed in bundles of 10, and clearly labelled will be stacked at Quartermaster's Stores by 9 a.m.
   O.C. "A" Coy. will provide a fatigue party of 1 N.C.O. and 6 men to report to Quartermaster at 9 a.m. to load these on a lorry which is being supplied.
   This party will be under orders of Quartermaster for the day till all stores have been removed, when they will rejoin their Coy.

4. Lewis Guns will be loaded on limbers to-night, excepting the Anti-aircraft gun, which will be placed on limber and guard dismounted by 10 a.m. tomorrow. Transport Officer will arrange to collect Lewis Guns by 6 p.m. to-night from Camp.

5. Transport Officer will send one limber at 6 p.m. to-night to collect all Coy. mess boxes, except one per Coy. and surplus Orderly Room boxes.

6. He will also arrange for the G.S. waggons to be at Headquarters Mess at 9.30 a.m. tomorrow to collect Officers valises and remainder of Orderly Room boxes. Quartermaster will detail party to see that these are properly loaded.
   Mess cart will be at Headquarters Mess 9.30 a.m. to collect Headquarters and Coy. mess boxes.

7. M.O.'s cart will so far as possible be packed to-night; remainder will be loaded by 9.30 a.m. tomorrow.

8. Baggage waggons will report this afternoon.

9. Quartermaster will strictly supervise all packing of waggons and lorry to ensure that the minimum number of journeys only be made by the latter.

10. Transport will march with Battalion.

            (sgd) R. KERR, Captain & A/Adjutant,
    11th Bn. "THE QUEEN'S OWN" Royal West Kent Regt. (Lewisham).

        Copy No. 1. C.O.   9. I.O. & B.B.O.
                 2. Adjt.   10. L.G.O.
                 3. Off. Cy.   11. M.O.
                 4. War Dy.   12. T.O.
                 5. O.C. "A".   13. Q.M.
                 6. O.C. "B".   14. Sig. Sgt.
                 7. O.C. "C".   15. R.S.M.
                 8. O.C. "D".

S E C R E T.   OPERATION ORDERS NO. 91a   Copy No. 32
                by Lieut. Col. J.C. Beadle, M.C.
Ref: Sheets 11 & 19. Commanding 11th Bn. "THE QUEEN'S OWN"
                Royal West Kent Regt. (Lewisham).

                                    29th October, 1917.

1. The Battalion is about to proceed to a new portion of the front.

    In future it will not be possible to provide extra transport for anything except blankets.

    Officers and men's kits must be cut down to recognised winter scale.

    Officers must despatch surplus kits over and above 35 lbs. by 12 noon, 30th instant to England.

    A certificate to this effect will be rendered by O.C. Coys. by 12 noon 30th instant.

2. At the same time, Officers and men must be possessed of full winter kit, and Battalion in possession of every item of mobilisation equipment. Probably, no deficiencies will be made up for some time.

    Only one blanket per man will accompany Battalion. O.C. Coys. will be prepared to hand in the second blanket to Quartermaster at shortest notice after noon 29th instant.

    Indents for any clothing or equipment required to complete will be rendered to Quartermaster for transmission to D.A.D.O.S. by O.C. Coys. forthwith.

    A report will be rendered by Quartermaster to Battalion Headquarters by 12 noon to-day and daily of any articles required to complete establishment.

3. Reference instructions already detailed to O.C. Coys., the Battalion will be relieved by a Battalion, South African Brigade to-day; on relief Battalion will move to SYNTHE Area.

4. One N.C.O. per Coy. and Headquarters will report to 2/Lieut. Macaskie at Battalion H.Q. 7.45 a.m. to-day as billeting party. They will report on bicycles, fully equipped to Captain REAH at 8 a.m. at Cross Roads, COXYDE BAINS; they will carry two day's rations.

5. On relief Coys. will march to Battalion H.Q.; Battalion will proceed to Cross Roads, COXYDE BAINS and embus.

6. Battalion will proceed to and be billetted in PETIT SYNTHE, billeting party will meet buses at Cross Roads, G.18.b.4.9 and conduct Coys. to billets.

7. Lorries will be available for extra blankets and small proportion of surplus stores of Quartermaster and Coys.

    These will be stacked on site of COXYDE BAINS - ST. IDESBALD ROAD, W.6.a.9.6. by 8.30 a.m.

    Loading party, as already detailed, under an Officer of "B" Coy. will be left in charge. This Officer will be responsible for the loading of all kits of Brigade units, which will be dumped near same spot in lorries to be detailed by the embusing Staff Officer.

8. SUPPLIES. Battalion will draw rations from ST. IDESBALD for last time on 29th instant for consumption on 30th instant, and for first time on 30th instant at LEFFRINCKHOUKE for consumption 31st instant onwards. To-day, unexpired portion of day's rations will be carried on men.

                                            P.T.O.

-2-

9. On arrival in billeting area R.S.M. will detail guide to go to Brigade H.Q. to bring ration limbers to Battalion.

10. Transport will proceed to PETIT SYNTHE area by road in accordance with attached March Table:-
   (a) Starting Point.   Cross Roads, COXYDE BAINS.

   (b) Time.   12 noon.

   (c) Route.   COXYDE BAINS, - COXYDE - KERME PANNE - LA PANNE - ADINKERKE - DUNKERKE.

Usual distances between units (200 yards) will be kept; horses should be watered before starting.

Reference above, Transport Officer and Quartermaster under orders previously issued will arrange to collect Officers valises, cookers, Orderly Room and mess boxes by 10 a.m.

11. O.C. Coys. and R.S.M. will send one guide per Coy. and Headquarters to Brigade Headquarters by 10 a.m. to conduct advanced party of relieving unit to Coy. and Battalion H.Q. respectively.

12. Completion of relief of Coys. and H.Q. will be reported to Adjutant by Code Word "ITALY" in present sector.

Arrival at destination will be notified with Map Reference of Coy. H.Q. by Code Word "Ireland".

13. Personnel of H.Q. and Coys. will embus under Battalion arrangements for new area, dress - Full marching order, with blankets; L.G. sections will carry Lewis Guns and magazines not already loaded.

14. All Trench and Area Stores will be handed over to relieving units, a receipt taken, and the latter handed to Adjutant.

15. Maps, Defence Schemes, etc. will be handed over on relief; huts and billets will be left clean. O.C. Coys. will give O.C. relieving Coys. all details of Coast Defence, and every assistance in handing over.

                (sgd) R. KERR, Captain & A/Adjutant,
    11th Bn. "THE QUEEN'S OWN" Royal West Kent Regt. (Lewisham).

        Copy No. 1. C.O.   9. S.O.
               2. Adjt.   10. L.G.O.
               3. War Dy.   11. I.O.
               4. Off. Cy.   12. T.O.
               5. O.C. "A". 13. Q.M.
               6. O.C. "B". 14. M.O.
               7. O.C. "C". 15. R.S.M.
               8. O.C. "D".

11th BN."THE QUEEN'S OWN" ROYAL WEST KENT REGT.(LEWISHAM).

STANDING ORDERS I.

1. When Coys. are on the march wearing pouches, 120 rounds S.A.A. per ma will be carried. The leading 12 and the rear 12 men will have magazines, charged with 5 rounds to deal with the possibility of hostile aircraft.

2. When Coys. are on the march in fatigue dress, to bathing and similar parades a Lewis Gun and 6 charged magazines will be carried per Coy. for the same eventuality as above.

3. One Lewis Gun will accompany each Coy. when range firing is being done.

4. The above orders must be strictly adhered to.

(sgd) R. KERR, Captain & A/Adjutant,
11th Bn. "THE QUEEN'S OWN" Royal West Kent Regt.(Lewisham).

APPENDIX "A".

1. Water Cart refilling point. —   I.31.d.2.4.
2. Water Tanks and Stand Pipes.—   N.6.a.10.10
                                                     N.5.a.90.95.
                                                     N.5.b.30.80
                                                     I.31.d.20.40
                                                     I.31.d.80.85.
                                                     O.1.d.35.75.
                                                     O.8.a.65.90.
                                                     C.9.a.70.20.
                                                     I.33.a.50.10.   ø
                                                     I.33.c.80.70.   ø
                                                     I.33.c.50.45.   ø
                                                     I.33.d.30.50.   ø
                                                     O.4.a.75.60.   ø

Tanks marked ø mean supply unreliable.

3. Stand pipes only —   N.6.a.2.9.
                            N.6.b.4.9.

4. Wells.   I.31.c.40.60)
              I.31.c.60.40)
              O.2.a.60.70.) Notice board
              O.3.c.95.10.) erected showing
              I.33.c.80.85.) amount of
              I.32.d.85.20.) chlorination
              O.10.b.10.40.) required.
              O.9.d.35.25.)

-:-:-:-:-:-:-:-:-:-:-:-:-:-:-:-

APPENDIX "B".

	BRIGADE DUMP.	TOTAL of FORWARD DUMPS.
S.A.A.	150,000	100,000
No. 5 Mills Bombs.	3,000	2,000
Rifle Grenades and blanks.	1,000	1,000
Very Lights 1"	500	500
Very Lights 1½"	250	250
Webley Pistol S.A.A.	250	250
"P" Grenades.	250	250
S.O.S. Flares. Rockets. Coloured Very Lights. Smoke Candles.	50% of allotment from Division.	50% of allotment from Division.

This does not include the equipment of Bombers, Grenadiers, or any establishment on wheels.

-:-:-:-:-:-:-:-:-:-:-:-:-:-:-:-

To:- Headquarters,
        122nd Infantry Brigade.

      War Diary and Appendices for the month of September, 1917, are forwarded, please.

                                                                               John C Beadle
                                                                                 Major,
                                       Commanding 11th Bn. "THE QUEEN'S OWN"
1.10.17.   Royal West Kent Regt. (Lewisham).

MUSKETRY COURSE.

No.	Range.	Description.	No. of rounds.	Time al'd	Target.	Remarks.
FIRST PRACTICE.						
1.	100	Grouping.	5.	-	Bullseye.	Lying.
2.	200	Application.	5.	-	2nd Class figure.	Lying.
3.	200	Rapid.	10.	One min.	-do-	Lying, Firing over cover. Rifle empty loading by 5 rds. from pouch.
4.	200	Snap-shooting.	5.	5 secs exp. ea. shot.	Figure 3 silhouette.	Firing over cover. Firer to be under cover till target appears.
SECOND PRACTICE.						
1.	200	Grouping.	5.	-	Bullseye.	Lying.
2.	200	Application.	5.	-	2nd Class figure.	Lying. Firing round cover.
3.	200	Rapid.	15.	One min.	-do-	Lying. Firing over cover. Rifles to be loaded with 5 rds. from pouch afterwards.
4.	200	Snap-shooting.	5.	4 secs exp. ea. shot.	Figure 3 Silhouette.	Lying.

PROGRAMME OF FIRING.

FIRST PRACTICE. "A" Coy. 7.30 - 11.30 a.m.   3.10.17.
                 "B" " 12.30 - 4.30 p.m.   do.
                 Snipers. 4.30 - 5.30 p.m.   do.
                 "D" Coy. 7.30 - 11.30 a.m.   5.10.17.
                 "C" " 12.30 - 4.30 p.m.   do.
                 Snipers. 4.30 - 5.30 p.m.   do.

SEC. PRACTICE. "B" Coy. 7.30 - 11.30 a.m.   8.10.17.
                 "A" " 12.30 - 4.30 p.m.   do.
                 Snipers. 4.30 - 5.30 p.m.   do.
                 "C" Coy. 7.30 - 11.30 a.m.   10.10.17.
                 "D" " 12.30 - 4.30 p.m.   do
                 Snipers. 4.30 - 5.30 p.m.   do.

    The conditions in the Remarks Column above should be strictly observed.

    If it is possible on any of the ranges here, some practices should be fired from a trench or from behind a breastwork, firing over the parapet.

    Where this is possible, practices Nos. 2, 3, & 4, (2nd Practice) should be so fired.

    All Practises except No. 1 should be fired with Bayonets fixed.

                         (Sgd) R. KERR. Capt. & A/Adjt.
                         11th Bn. "The Queen's Own"
                         Royal West Kent Regiment (Lewisham).

2.10.17.

11th BATTALION "THE QUEEN'S OWN" ROYAL WEST KENT REGIMENT. LEWISHAM.

PROGRAMME OF TRAINING
Wed. Oct. 3rd to Wed. Oct. 10th
inclusive.

Oct. 3rd.

7.30 - 11.30 a.m.	"A" Coy.	Range practices (See attached table).
2.30 - 3 p.m.		Kit Inspection.
7. - 7.45 a.m.	"B" "	Physical Training & Squad Drill.
9. - 9.30 a.m.		Kit Inspection.
12.30 - 4.30 p.m.		Range practices.
7. - 7.45 a.m.	H.Q. "C" & "D" Coys.	Physical Training & Squad Drill.
9. - 10 a.m.	"C"	Bombing.
	"D"	Physical Training.
10 - 11 a.m.	"C"	do.
	"D"	Musketry.
11-12 noon	"C"	Musketry.
	"D"	Bayonet Fighting.
12 - 1 p.m.	"C"	Squad and Arm Drill.
	"D"	Bombing.
2.30 - 3.30 p.m.	"C" & "D"	Platoon Drill.
		N.C.O's Class under the R.S.M.

For Range Firing every Officer and man will fire the practices, including all employed men in the Battalion Transport, Quartermaster's Stores, etc.
Snipers, Orderly Room personnel and Police only excluded.
Lewis Gunners of "C" & "D" Coys., will parade under Lieut. Morley, from 9. - 11 a.m., when they will rejoin Companies.
Signallers of "C" & "D" Coys., and all Snipers will parade under arrangements made by their own Officers.
Remainder of Headquarters will parade under Corpl. Hooker 10 - 11.30 a.m. for Drill etc.
Snipers will use range each day it is in use from 4.30 - 5.30 p.m.

Oct. 4th.

9 - 1 p.m. Route Marches under Company arrangements. Dress - Drill Order. Every available man will parade exclusive of Transport, Quartermaster's Stores personnel, Signallers & Snipers, who will be under their own Officers for work. O.C. Companies will submit proposed route by 4 p.m. the day before.

2.30 - 3.30 p.m. N.C.O's Class.
Foot Inspection for all Companies.

Oct. 5th.

Range Firing for "C" & "D" Coys.
Orders the same as for October 3rd, in each case substituting "A" Coy for "D" Coy., and "B" Coy., for "C" Coy.

OCT. 6th. Work will be carried out on same lines as laid down for October 2nd. Parades for Companies are amended as under.

7. - 7.45 a.m. Physical Training and Squad Drill.

9. - 10 a.m.	"A" Coy.	Bayonet Fighting.
	"B" "	Bombing.
	"C" "	Musketry.
	"D" "	Squad and Arm Drill.

P.T.O.

- 2 -

Oct. 6th contd:-

10 - 11 a.m.	"A" Coy.		Bombing.
	"B" "		Musketry.
	"C" "		Squad and Arm Drill.
	"D" "		Bayonet Fighting.
11 - 12 noon.	"A" "		Musketry.
	"B" "		Squad and Arm Drill.
	"C" "		Bayonet Fighting.
	"D" "		Bombing.
12 - 1 p.m.	"A" "		Squad and Arm Drill.
	"B" "		Bayonet Fighting.
	"C" "		Bombing.
	"D" "		Musketry.

2.30 - 3.30 p.m. For all Companies - Platoon and Company Drill.

Oct. 7th.

SUNDAY. Rest Day.
The Commanding Officer will inspect kits and Camp at 12 noon under orders to be issued later.

Oct. 8th.

Same as on October 3rd. (as varied by attached table of practices to be fired.
Parades for "C" & "D" Coys., exclusive of early morning parade will be varied as under:-

9 - 10 a.m.	"C" Coy.		Musketry.
	"D" "		Squad and Arm Drill.
10 - 11 a.m.	"C" "		Squad and Arm Drill.
	"D" "		Musketry.
11 - 12	"C" "		Bayonet Fighting.
	"D" "		Extended Order Drill.
12 - 1 p.m.	"C" "		do. do
	"D" "		Bayonet Fighting.
2.30 - 3.30	"C" & "D" Coys.		- Platoon and Company Drill.

N.C.O's Class under the R.S.M.

Oct. 9th.

7.30 - 1 p.m. Company Route Marches. Dress - Drill Order. Same arrangements will hold good as detailed for Oct.4th.
2.30 - 3.30 Vide October 4th.

Oct. 10th. Same as for October 8th, in each case substituting "A" Coy for "D" Coy., and "B" Coy for "C" Coy.

(Sgd) R. KERR. Capt. & A/Adjutant.
11th Bn. "The Queen's Own"
Royal West Kent Regiment. (Lewisham).

2/10/17.

www.ingramcontent.com/pod-product-compliance
Lightning Source LLC
Chambersburg PA
CBHW080914230426
43667CB00015B/2678